What Dawid Knew

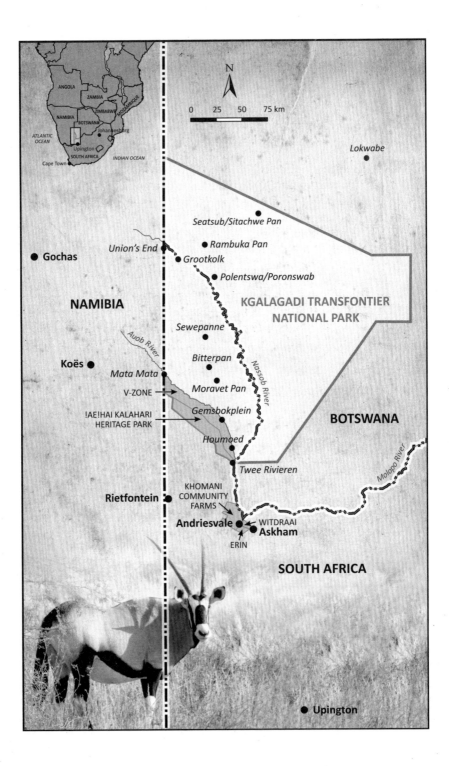

PATRICIA GLYN

What Dawid Knew

A Journey with the Kruipers

PICADOR AFRICA

First published in 2013 by Picador Africa
an imprint of Pan Macmillan South Africa
Private Bag X19, Northlands
Johannesburg, 2116

www.panmacmillan.co.za

ISBN 978-1-77010-304-7
eISBN 978-177010-305-4

Editing by Sally Hines
Proofreading by Sean Fraser
Design and typesetting by Triple M Design, Johannesburg
Map by MDesign
Cover design by K4
Printed and bound by Ultra Litho (Pty) Ltd

For the Kruipers, past, present and future,
and for the people who are helping them to heal.

'Three may keep a secret if two of them are dead.'
BENJAMIN FRANKLIN (1706–90)

Contents

AUTHOR'S NOTE ix

PRONUNCIATION GUIDE xii

Introduction 1

CHAPTER 1: This Land is Blood Land 3

CHAPTER 2: A Stop-Start Beginning 14

CHAPTER 3: A Baboon Sitting on a Rock 21

CHAPTER 4: The Truth, Only the Truth 37

CHAPTER 5: Patronage and Prejudice 55

CHAPTER 6: The String is Broken 71

CHAPTER 7: Standing Up Straight 86

CHAPTER 8: Scientific Studies and 'Cultural Curiosities' 103

CHAPTER 9: Like a Little Bird 121

CHAPTER 10: Santa Claus at the Human Rights Commission 139

CHAPTER 11: Released from a Secret 152

CHAPTER 12: You Can Never Wash It Away 170

CHAPTER 13: We Are With You, You Are With Us 181

CHAPTER 14: Dawid's Treasure Hunt 197

CHAPTER 15: Lion of the Kalahari 215

CHAPTER 16: Our Place and Purpose 222

SELECT BIBLIOGRAPHY 229
ACKNOWLEDGEMENTS 234
ABBREVIATIONS 236

Author's Note

'I was dead, but now that you have come I am alive again' is the way Bushmen of old greeted their visitors. One day, when Dawid Kruiper and I were chatting about this book, he tweaked the old adage and said to me: 'All I can say is that I was dead and now that the truth is coming out, I am alive again.'

Dawid looked upon this book as his, not mine. He saw it as a means of redressing the way he, his family and their history have been portrayed in books, articles and theses. 'It must be the truth, only the truth,' he often said. And, to his credit, he was anxious that the stories of his life and the account of our journey together should be written up in as candid and balanced a manner as I could manage.

Whether I have achieved this is for the reader to judge, and no doubt there will be some people who regard what I have written as brutally frank at times. The Kruipers and I had many problems in the early stages of this odyssey and I witnessed some distressing behaviour within the family. They have given me full permission to describe our *hobbeltjies* (trials) and I am humbled by their courage in throwing open their lives and conduct to such scrutiny. Through their honesty, perhaps we can help to liberate the Bushmen from what anthropologist John Marshall described as 'death by myth'. For centuries the Bushmen have worn a romantic, patronising straightjacket as one-dimensional cultural treasures who are 'gentle', 'harmless' and 'noble'. Certainly they are all of these things, and they have gifts and knowledge that we non-Bushmen have lost, but they also have the foibles and failings that bedevil us all.

The Kruipers want to be known as 'Bushmen', which is why I have chosen to refer to them this way. They speak Khoekhoegowab – one of the Nama languages – and in that tongue 'San' is a pejorative word for impoverished, thieving bush dwellers who do not own cattle or other material possessions. I am cognisant of the fact that the majority of people in the family's Khomani community wish to be known as 'San', as do many other 'First People' in South Africa. Indeed, the Working Group of Indigenous Minorities in Southern Africa and the South African San Institute recommend that 'San' is used when referring to our country's aboriginal people. Nonetheless, this book is about the Kruipers, so I have acceded to their choice of nomenclature, and, in order to avoid confusion, I have decided to refer to all Bushmen as such throughout this book. I mean no offence by doing so and am mindful of the fact that the term can be deemed sexist.

I have used the word 'coloured' when referring to people of a mixed group because it is in common usage in the Northern Cape. Again, I apologise to readers who might think it inappropriate or offensive.

Because the Kruipers' history rests largely in an oral tradition, it has been extremely challenging to check and cross-reference some of the information I received. Regrettably I was not given access to the interviews that were conducted with the community's elders at the time of the land claim. They would have been helpful in confirming – or otherwise – my findings. Many of these men and women have since died, so I have not been able to include their memories and comments in this book. The transcripts of these conversations were lodged with the South African San Institute but were, tragically, stolen and destroyed.

Getting to grips with the Khomani's complex social issues and community dynamics is difficult to say the least and 'if I have seen a little further it is by standing on the shoulders of giants', as Isaac Newton once said. These giants in compassion, service and philanthropy have worked with, and for, the Khomani for many years and have seen them go through some of the traumatic events described in the following pages. Without their input and advice, *What Dawid Knew* would quite definitely not have seen the light of day. At the end of this book I have listed the kind people who helped me before, during and after our expedition but would like to make special mention of, and extend my heartfelt thanks to: Phillipa Holden, David Grossman, Nanette Flemming, Richard Gordon, Claire Barry, Nigel Crawhall and Roger Chennells.

My sincere thanks also go to my friend, assistant and expedition back-up, Sue Oxborrow, who was critical to the success of this journey. Once again she shared and enhanced a remarkable experience in the great African outdoors and showed herself to be loyal, extremely hard working and, above all, humorous. Thank you to Richard Wicksteed and Karl Symons, who joined us at very short notice to film the trip and who worked long and hard hours in difficult conditions. To Karin Slater goes my huge appreciation for two years' worth of hard work, and great regret that she could not join us. We received great moral and practical support from the staff and rangers of the Kgalagadi Transfrontier Park for which I am most grateful. Dr Wendy Anneke was especially enthusiastic about our expedition's goals and has been of great help with my research.

What a treat it has been to work with the 'gals' at Pan Macmillan. Terry Morris said, 'Yes please, we'll take it!', which was such a thrill, and my editors, Andrea Nattrass and Sally Hines helped me up my game as a writer – and then some. To the rest of the team from designers to marketers – thank you!

To my three, patient and long-suffering dogs who lay next to my desk for months on end while I sighed and muttered to myself through these pagers, thank you for sharing the agony!

Above all, my deepest thanks go to the Kruipers, for their trust, affection and open-heartedness.

Pronunciation Guide

| = dental click, rather like the sound used to express disapproval or pity, as in *tsk tsk*.

‡ = palatal click, a sound made when the tongue makes broad contact with the roof of the mouth and is pulled back, rather like the 'giddy-up' sound one would make to urge on a horse.

! = post alveolar click, a much more hollow and more resonant sound than the palatal click because the tongue is concave and pulled down rather than back.

Introduction

It was windy the day we found the graves. Lemon grasses arched their feathered heads to the Kalahari sand, leaving haphazard trails through the dry Nossob riverbed that resembled those of a million foraging ants. The old Bushman shuffled through the tufts, stabbing the air with crooked fingers and lifting his milky eyes from the ground only to give terse directions.

'Look carefully. They're somewhere here, I know they're here. My grandfather told me so. And I myself saw the graves 50 years ago when I was out collecting wild honey with my uncle. They were long mounds, all facing roughly the same direction. After all this time they're probably not big mounds any more but they *must* be here.'

The youngsters of the clan spread out across the low riverbank, using their bows and digging sticks to part the bushes and grass. Nothing.

This is like looking for a marble in a granary, I thought. Graves on a windy plain over 100 years since they were dug? Fat chance. But I suppose with their amazing veld skills, if anyone is going to find them, a Bushman will.

More shuffling, probing, muttering. '*Kyk mooi*, look carefully,' the old man repeated. 'It's been a very long time.' The sun rose in the white sky and he rested in the shade of a shepherd's tree.

'Okay, let's try over there,' he grunted after he had finished his smoke, then struggled up from his haunches and hobbled away.

The search party changed its locale and swept slowly across a new section of the veld, moving through the terrain with the kind of patience and meticulous attention to detail for which Bushman trackers are renowned.

Then a triumphant cry from the old man. His face, lined with all the sun and suffering of 76 years in this arid place, glowed with glee: 'Come, Mama! Look! Here is a grave!' And a grave it certainly appeared to be. A long, low mound of sand, covered with a thin layer of black, crusty silt. How fitting that the first find should be his.

A second shout, this time from his son a few metres away. It was a similar mound, again topped with a black crust. Another shout, another find. And yet another. We seemed to be at the site of a battle and, to my knowledge, an unrecorded one.

'You see, Mama, I told the truth. And so did my grandpa. It's the last time before I die that I can show my descendants the truth about what happened here. Now I can rest.'

The old Bushman's secret was out, but the full horror of what his ancestor witnessed at this place we had yet to learn.

CHAPTER 1

This Land is Blood Land

D awid Kruiper was mildly the worse for wear the day we first met. He was sitting on the sand, legs folded under him, his body shrouded in an outsized coat that was splayed out around him. Wheezy chuckles rocked his tiny torso, making the coat crumple and flex like an old paper bag. On his feet were towelling slippers, child-sized and fit for padding around an urban bathroom. They looked incongruous in this harsh place and on a man with such an ancient face.

It was a face that was much in demand throughout his life. Textbook Bushman: light tan skin with deep folds and creases, high cheekbones and full lips. His eyes were opaque and watery after 76 years of searing sun, sand and smoke and his mouth was nearly toothless. But he knew the market value of his face, and wore it with a mixture of pride and nonchalance. That day, like all others, Dawid was as you found him: a tired old man in great pain from injuries, arthritis and a lifetime of traumatic experiences. But also a wise and shrewd man with a ready sense of self-deprecating humour.

He welcomed my translator and me with a wry smile.

'See, Mama,' he said, pointing to his surroundings with two knobbly fingers hooked around a roll-up of cheap tobacco in newspaper, 'here are the only things I own in the world: my little grass hut, my dog and my rooster. He sleeps in the rafters and shits on my head during the night.'

I laughed. We both knew this was not entirely true, but it was a genial game we would play often in the months to come as Dawid tested my credulity and sense of the ridiculous. Desperately poor though he might have been, Dawid had more to his name than a hut, a dog and a sure-fire pooping cockerel. For a start, the farm on which he lived is one of six that he and his community were awarded in a land claim designed to compensate them for being forcibly evicted, during South Africa's apartheid years, from the land that was their ancestral homeland – the area that is now the Kgalagadi Transfrontier Park (KTP), 70 kilometres to the north of his hut. And it was not so much that Dawid never had any money, but rather that it had slipped through his fingers like the sand on which he sat. Besides, money has little value to those who treasure what it cannot buy: rain, wild food and freedom. And family, of course. Dawid had plenty of family, both immediate and extended and, true to Bushman tradition, they shared everything. Cash earned by one today is enjoyed by the whole family tomorrow. No doubt the coat, donated by some well-meaning foreigner, would be a child's blanket that night, and on someone else's back the next day, should their need for warmth be greater than his.

Dawid was used to strangers coming to visit him, but the never-ending retinue of academics, movie-makers, do-gooders, no-hopers and government flunkies made him wary of outsiders. Many had ripped him off or let him down and at times he had answered them in kind. By the time we met, the only thing he had come to like about the fix-it folk was the colour of their money. When the cameras rolled, he would perform for a fee. And when the researchers questioned him, he would answer, but again only for a fee. '*Praat is werk,*' Dawid often said, 'talking is our profession. They come here for information and stories. I don't know what they write but I never see most of them again. And if I don't like them I tell them rubbish,' he quipped, in his colourful, old-fashioned Afrikaans.

Initially it did not matter if Dawid told me rubbish because I was on a mission that would need his blessing but not necessarily his

involvement. I have a passion for the journeys of migration and ex-
ploration that abound in southern Africa's history. In 2005 I walked
the 2 000-kilometre route of one of these travellers, my ancestor,
Sir Richard George Glyn. Piecing together his route from the sea
to the continent's interior was an investigative thrill and being able
to compare the landscape, lifestyle and politics he described in his
journal with our current environment and world view was fascinating. Above all, on that trip I came to love the contemplation that
walking evokes, and the observations and encounters that are inspired by an unhurried approach to far-distant horizons.

Now I wanted a 'footing' challenge with the first inhabitants –
and later, migrants – of our land and was recruiting Bushmen from
Dawid's community, who had the knowledge and fitness to accom-
pany me on a walk through the Kalahari semi-desert of South Africa and Botswana. I sought a kind of master class in which I could
learn some of the bush skills and attitudes that made their ancestors such masters of environmental adaptation and intelligence.
And, once again, I would have the chance to compare what was
known with what is lost, this time in Bushman culture.

After I had visited Dawid several times in the course of finding
Bushman walkers, he and his advisers suggested that I might like
to get involved in a different quest.

'I'm old now, Mama,' Dawid confided, 'and I don't know how
much time I have left. Because we were thrown off our land, there
are places in the Park [the KTP] where I grew up that I haven't seen
in 50 years and which my children and grandchildren don't know
about. They are the places where we roamed and hunted when we
were free, our heritage sites and birthplaces. I need my family to
see them, and I also need to have my father's and grandfather's
stories recorded so that the children will never forget them. Please
can you help us go back there?'

Frankly, I wondered what could be left to learn about the Kruipers, quasi-royal family of the southern Bushmen. They have been
called, with good reason, the most over-researched indigenous family in South Africa and Dawid was easily our most famous – and for

some, infamous – Bushman. He was the elected traditional leader of the Khomani, the last surviving – albeit fractured – group of South Africa's Bushmen. While most of the community want to be known as San, he dismissed the term as a pejorative Nama word with overtones of backwardness and thieving. Dawid proudly claimed the name Bushman because it conveys his and his ancestors' deep knowledge of the veld and their even deeper connection with wilderness – even though some of their culture and traditions were lost forever during their post-eviction years as destitute vagrants.

But if I was to undertake this precious heritage exercise with him it was vital that he did not tell me rubbish. And what were the chances of that? Good, I was told, because of the great trust he had in the people who had introduced me to him.

Phillipa Holden and David Grossman – 'Grossie' as he is called by the Kruipers – are ecologists who have worked in the community for fifteen years – largely pro bono – trying to help bring the kind of social justice and economic prosperity that should have come with the land claim, but which remain elusive. Over the years, Phillipa and Grossie have broadened their involvement in Khomani issues and dynamics to the point where they are now not only the community's technical advisers but the local agony aunt and uncle, too. They have been joined by several people with experience in law, education, social services, arts and crafts, housing development and other fields, all of whom have spent years in the service of this marginalised group of people. Grossie has coined the term 'FOKS' for these folks – Friends of Khomani San – and their motto is 'Justice Will Prevail!' Having seen Dawid duped and exploited so often by outsiders, Phillipa and Grossie promised that whoever they introduced to him would be assessed beforehand and found to be reliable and honest.

'And I've looked deep into you, Mama,' Dawid said, 'and I can see who you are.'

I felt unnerved by this apparent ability to read my heart and mind, but wondered why he was so often scammed if he had this fail-safe internal lie detector.

'He's a very sweet, trusting man,' Phillipa said. 'And the Krui-pers' desperate need for an income sometimes leads them into alliances that are very damaging.'

I felt intimidated by the importance of the work ahead as I am neither an anthropologist nor a historian. But if it was me he want-ed, it was me he would get, and I was moved by the urgency of his request.

During the ensuing months I drove the eleven-hour journey from Johannesburg to Dawid's farm several times with my friend and colleague, Sue Oxborrow, who has worked with me on two previous expeditions and who would be doing the driving, cater-ing, moral supporting and Afrikaans translating on this trip. We sat under the tree next to Dawid's hut for many hours, moving to follow its shade, while we worked on the logistics of the trip.

Who would Dawid take along? 'My brother, Buks, who is a very good veld doctor, and three generations of my children, grand-children and cousins.' How much time would he need? 'About two months.' Would they need payment? 'Just a little. We need lots of tobacco. To be a Bushman is to smoke, Mama!' We agreed on sliding-scale stipends appropriate to their age and knowledge. Where would we go? 'We'll start in the south of the Park in the section that we were given in the land claim along with the farms. I have some things I want to tell you about there. Then we'll move northwards. The big work is in the north so we'll spend most of our time near the Nossob River. And we will need permission to walk into Botswana. Please could you organise that?'

How would we get to the sites he wanted to show us, given that driving off-road is forbidden in the Park? 'We'll drive as close as we can, park the car and then walk to these places.' I looked down at his frail legs and had grave doubts that he could walk more than a few paces. Dawid's body was a mass of injuries from a bad car ac-cident the family had in 1994. His legs were full of pins and screws and he had a plate in his head. I made a mental note to pack a light hammock in case we had to carry him.

What would we eat? 'Some things from the veld and some from

the shop – things like flour, sugar, coffee. You'll have to take those in your truck. We'll hunt if we get a chance but please take some meat in your freezer in case we're not lucky.' And where will we sleep? 'In tents. Definitely not on the ground. The lions in the Park are dangerous these days because they've got used to people. They see tourists all the time and the scientists who work there are often darting them. In the old days the lions still feared us. It's different now.'

Once we had covered everything else, I tentatively brought up the subject of alcohol. While I did not want to seem rude or patronising, I knew that some of the Kruiers were slaves to booze and that it was the one thing that had the power to derail the project. Were they going to take any? 'We are going to work, Mama, and *dopping* (drinking) will make us lazy. So let's just take a couple of bottles of brandy, which you can keep in your vehicle for a little celebration at the end of successful days.' That seemed reasonable, and I felt relieved that Dawid had so readily agreed to a dry camp. Just before we left, one of his sons asked if we wanted them to wear their traditional skin clothing. 'No,' I replied, 'not unless you want to. This is not a movie. We're not trying to pretend you're something that you're not. You must wear what you find warm and comfortable.' He seemed relieved by my answer.

We drew up a legal agreement so that Dawid, Phillipa and Grossie were satisfied that the Kruipers' knowledge and interests were protected. I insisted that anything they did not want the outside world to know they would discuss in Khoekhoegowab, their first language and one that we did not understand. I would teach them to use my camcorder so that they could disappear over the dunes by themselves and record private or secret information for posterity. The rest would be filmed and recorded by my team to be archived in an academic institution and a planned community heritage centre.

Yet more hours were spent talking to the management of the KTP, through which we would be travelling and working, and whose support we would need. Not only were they very keen to assist us, but they were excited by the heritage knowledge that they, too, would get about life in the Park prior to its declaration and shortly thereafter. They allocated us campsites far from tourist activity where we could go about our work undisturbed, but had concerns about our safety on foot among the Park's predators so insisted that we have an armed game ranger with us at all times. This was the source of some resentment to the Kruipers, given that most of them have more bush savvy than any modern ranger could hope to acquire in ten lifetimes.

Slowly the expedition began to take shape, and with every trek down to the Kalahari from Johannesburg I learned more about this family's extraordinary psychological and historical narrative. From the first time I visited their settlement I knew I was hooked. No – more than that – I was beguiled, even entranced, by the Khomani people's gentleness, tolerance, patience, ready humour and eccentricity. Their lives were unhurried and unmaterialistic, and their needs were simple.

It took a while, though, to realise that I would be severely tested by my involvement in their troubled existence. Their settlement is a surreal, topsy-turvy place where nothing is as it seems, where outsiders' ideas of normalcy must be abandoned and criticism suspended. This is the nexus of the oldest despair in our sad country, where centuries of hatred and persecution often play out in bitter self-loathing among the victims. Some rise above their pitiful circumstances on the faintest of hopes, only to be crushed by their ignorance and innocence of external realities and by the jealousy of friends. The Kruipers live at a heart-rending cultural turnpike where the Bushmen try to find a space that honours their past without compromising their future. Throughout history they have been regarded as either despicable vermin or noble human prototype, depending on whom they encountered, so their view of themselves see-saws between these extremes and is echoed in their behaviour. In those early encounters I found them to be amusing then horrifying, fascinating then drunk-dull, genuine then masters of manipulation.

Witdraai is the farm on which most of the Kruipers live – a 3 500-hectare piece of Kalahari dune veld in the Northern Cape province of South Africa, not far from where the country borders Namibia and Botswana. The farm lies at the crossroads of two tarred roads: one between the Namibian border and the largest town in the province, Upington; and the other that leads to the KTP. It is well placed for catching lifts and taxis to town, or capitalising on curio sales to passing tourists. But Witdraai is a bleak place, undeveloped and unyielding. Low dunes covered with sparse vegetation constitute the repetitive landscape of the Kruipers' existence. Like all farms in the area, it is extensive because of its water scarcity and low carrying capacity for game and domestic animals. A few tin shacks and grass huts are dotted across the dunes, linked by haphazard sand paths. The family lives in small units, well separated from one another, as they did in the old days.

At one corner of the farm is the police station, home to a legendary breed of pure white camels that were used to patrol parts of the territory not accessible by vehicle. Witdraai police station has been witness to decades of petty prosecution, internment and torture of the Khomani by the local cops. Caves, excavated from the riverbank and used to imprison Bushmen until the mid-1900s, are still there today, as is the tree – and bullet holes – against which one of their Nama informers was summarily executed. A Bushman youngster took us to see these awful places. He seemed so matter-of-fact. Is it healing, I wondered, to guide tourists through your forebears' anxious ends? Or does repeating the story cause the trauma to leach into the synaptic furrows of the brain, like arsenic into an old clay mug?

Across the road from Witdraai is the settlement of Andriesvale, a ghetto where most of the other Khomani people live in abandoned buses and miserable dwellings. The ugly twins born of poverty, Hunger and Despair, stalk this outpost by day and their doppelgängers, Alcoholism and Domestic Violence, haunt it by night. HIV/AIDS is rife, as are car accidents, theft and damage to property. Donkey carts whip through the township, driven with derring-do by the community's whooping youngsters who deliver household water in drums from the only borehole in the area. The water is brackish and so high in fluoride that it stains and rots the children's teeth. Cooking and communing are done over open fires, and, as a result, anyone over twenty invariably has a deep, hawking cough.

Many of the Khomani are on government pensions or poverty alleviation payouts, and few can afford more than the staples that are for sale at high prices in Andriesvale's general store. Besides, why bother with food when the dodgy alcohol on sale at the Molopo Lodge Bottle Store next door is cheaper? The fourth-grade wine might taste like nail varnish remover, but it swiftly brings the bliss of forgetfulness. Old men fondle young girls and bob and shuffle through the sand in pathetic mimicry of the sacred dances they once knew. Brothers knife each other at night and hug the next morning. People speak harshly, laugh raucously, and are quick to anger and take offence. But in the kind of perverse togetherness that destitution often fosters, they are also forgiving and open-hearted.

The junior school in nearby Askham offers a substandard education and Bushman children are often taunted by their coloured classmates, who regard them as backward and ignorant. Those who endure the treatment might make it into an equally substandard high school 100 kilometres away in the town of Rietfontein. Daily transport there is beyond their parents' means, so many of the children board in the school's hostel. Until recently both boys and girls were sold as prostitutes by their so-called carers.

At Andriesvale's Molopo Lodge, tourists to the game park spend the night before roaring off in their state-of-the-art camping vehicles to enjoy Park sights and sounds that were once exclusively the experience of the Khomani. Some stop to buy trinkets from Bushmen at the side of the road, dressed in their traditional skins and selling artefacts that were indispensable long ago – bows and arrows, skin bags, bone pipes. But the bushwackers see little of the pain in those dunes, and little do they care. They, we, are all in transit in this cruel and beautiful place because few have the courage to endure it.

The Northern Cape originally became home to the Bushmen because its parched land and taxing climate offered them protection from the waves of newcomers who came from Europe and elsewhere in Africa, occupied the more temperate parts of the country and killed, subdued or squeezed the Bushmen out. The Kalahari is famous for its scorching hot summer days and brutally cold winter nights. In August, Harmattan-like winds arrive that scour the land and sap the life force of all its creatures. When the rains come in December and January, they are heralded by sky-splitting lightning and thunder fit to summon the ancestors. He-rains, the Bushmen call the rains that are hard and torrential. Those that are soft and nurturing are named she-rains.

Critically, the Kalahari was originally impossible for the settlers to farm, either with livestock or crops. But, in the mid-nineteenth century, the Bushmen's hideout was breached by advances in engineering that enabled deep boreholes to be sunk into the ancient aquifers that lie far beneath the sand. Merino sheep were soon to follow, as they had been found to thrive in dry and scrubby conditions. The new farmers sank their roots as deep as their boreholes and since then the Northern Cape has been a kind of frontier country for all who occupy it – South Africa's Wild West, where men are ruthless and only resilience is rewarded. As the billboards on the side of the Upington road remind visitors: 'The Northern Cape is red meat country.' It is a province built on flesh, blood and manly pursuits.

Cross-border smugglers and cattle rustlers, poachers and body snatchers have all relished trading here, so far from the reach of the law and polite society. The area has been witness to war, land grabs, drought and famine. Rapes and murders often go unpunished to this day and threats, bribes and ransoms whisper on the wind. 'This land is blood land,' say the Bushmen.

The province is also a land of secrets – secrets that cure, secrets that poison and, above all, secrets of allegiance and tradition. For the Bushmen, a people so tyrannised and exploited over the centuries, secrets have become a valuable source of pride, bonding and strength, a way of preserving their uniqueness in the face of cultural assimilation and annihilation. The Kruipers, like other Khomani families, have many secrets, passed down through the generations from mother to daughter and from father to son. Most concern the ways of the wild and the magical powers of the creatures that inhabit it. Others are cultural and ritualistic and may have lost their usefulness and died. Still others are eternal, and 'what make us Bushmen', Dawid told me. 'You wouldn't understand even if I tried to explain them.'

But some secrets are kept out of fear and they can make a man very lonely. All his adult life, Dawid Kruiper had been the custodian of one such secret, the same secret his father kept before him and his grandfather before that. It was told to him when he was a young man and repeated often, word for word, so that he would remember all its nuances and details. He guarded it through all the drunkenness and despair, the nosy probes of the inquisitive and the scrutiny of well-intentioned researchers. But now he was tired.

'It's time for me to show my sons that place and hand on the secret,' he whispered to me. 'Please can you take us soon?'

CHAPTER 2

A Stop-Start Beginning

And so my envisaged long walk through the Kalahari was hijacked by a charming old man and turned into a heritage expedition, but I became increasingly excited by its prospects. We would be travelling through a place of seductive natural beauty and I would have the opportunity of spending two months with a Bushman's memories of a life that has all but disappeared. Unlike many people who have researched the Khomani, I would have the privilege of actually taking them to the places they wanted to tell me about, and, most importantly, the information would be passed on to younger generations, not simply written up in a thesis or book that they would never read. We would be far from the crime and chaos of Witdraai and its environs, and I would be able to do something for Dawid that I had never been able to do for my own father.

Dad died when I was 25 and at a stage in my life when he was still more hero than human. He took tales to his grave that, in his old-fashioned way, he did not deem appropriate for my young, female ears. They were tales of his work as a medical doctor with the headhunters of Sarawak, with the Bemba of northern Zambia and with the ravaged inmates of the Bergen-Belsen concentration camp when he accompanied the Allied forces that liberated them at the end of the Second World War.

There is hardly a month that goes by when I do not ache to know the details of his experiences. Now I had the opportunity to ensure that Dawid's children would never suffer the same frustration.

We decided to leave in late autumn when the days were not too hot and the nights not too cold, which gave me little time to provision for the trip. At least on this expedition I would have my tried-and-tested team from the outset and would not have to endure the exhausting business of interviewing young bucks who dream of being in the outdoors but have no idea what relentless work such trips entail.

Sue Oxborrow was, of course, already on board, and it was clear that the Kruipers were taken by her gentle ways and ready laughter. Sue is a remarkable 60-year-old. Very little daunts her: she is game for anything I throw her way; she is physically strong; and she is hugely long-suffering. A soft exterior masks a no-nonsense core that she will use if pushed too far, and I have learned that I can rely on Sue to watch my back 'out there'. She maintains the high standards I expect in my camp, is a cleanliness and tidiness fiend, a qualified field guide and a great cook of vegan food. We have complementary strengths and personalities and I would not consider doing an expedition without her.

Karin Slater, the internationally acclaimed film-maker who had documented my walk to the Victoria Falls, had been working with me for the previous two years, trying to get funding for the movie about my Kalahari trek. When I phoned her with the change of plan, she jumped at the chance of being with the Bushmen again, albeit on a different kind of quest. Karin had filmed Bushmen in northern Botswana a few years beforehand, and her unobtrusive style of shooting had been rewarded with some unique and dramatic footage. Not only is she a brilliant documentary-maker but she is an asset in any camp – completely at home in the bush, permanently unfussed, professional and empathetic. Her husband, Steve, and their two daughters would come to the KTP and enjoy a holiday in its commercial camps while she worked. On days off she could catch up with them. Karin's involvement was sorted out and I was delighted.

By my standards, the expedition planning was going far too smoothly, with the exception of getting sponsorship, and eventually I decided to give up trying. It is a disheartening, begging-bowl process that has always failed me, so I re-mortgaged my house to pay for the project, hoping to get back in the black with this book and talks about the trip. With the assistance of the Peace Parks Foundation, Phillipa and Grossie had applied successfully to South Africa's National Lotteries Board (Lotto) for funding for heritage mapping and information capture, so that relieved me of having to pay Karin's salary and equipment hire, but I would meet all the other expenses. They had also managed to get a Toyota Land Cruiser from Lotto that the Khomani used to visit the Park. The Kruipers would travel in that, Karin had her own 4x4 and Sue and I would drive in 'Priscilla, Queen of the Desert', my fully kitted-out Toyota Hilux that is equipped with everything a girl might need out there, barring a hair dryer and a SodaStream. She is no beauty, my Priscilla, but working in the field is very different from a camping holiday, so she has everything that heats and freezes, charges and powers, and opens and shuts. When she is reversed up to my custom-made gazebo, Priscilla makes for a very comfortable home-from-home and my dogs and I spend many weeks of the year visiting beautiful places in her functional, if not gracious, accommodation.

Sue and I made reams of lists and bought enough dry stores, meat and vegetables to fill a country shop. We trundled down to the Kalahari and left one load in a safe place, drove back, did our final packing for the journey and left Johannesburg again on Sunday, 17 April 2011.

And that is when the trouble started. One day out of town we heard a noise from the front chassis that sounded life-threatening. It turned out we had popped a wheel bearing – no doubt because of the huge weight on Priscilla's frame. Repairing it took two days, so that put paid to the intended departure day. Then Karin was delayed leaving Cape Town and decided that her family could join her once we had found our stride. She would drive through the night and meet us for the grand departure from Witdraai.

D-Day arrived. Our meeting time of 6.00 a.m. passed, as did 7, then 8. No Karin. So unlike her, both of us agreed. Then a call from Steve: 'Kari's been in a bad accident about half an hour from you. The Land Rover's a write-off and she's been rushed to hospital.' The notorious Upington-to-Andriesvale road had claimed another victim. Every year, dozens of people and hundreds of animals, particularly nocturnal ones, are injured or killed on this road. It is as long, straight and glistening grey as a shotgun barrel and drivers become mesmerised as they rise and dip over the area's dunes. Georg Wandrag, the implementation officer for one of the Khomani projects, rushed to the scene to collect all Karin's belongings before they were stolen. Sue and I got there shortly afterwards. At the bottom of a steep embankment lay the Landy, bashed and dented on both sides and both ends after rolling over and over down the shoulder. The driver's door was folded like a tortilla. How the hell had she survived? A deep gouge in the road told the story – a tyre blow-out that had caused the car to careen across the tar before pitch-poling down to her landing spot. No doubt the barrels of water I had asked her to bring had worsened the tumble as they swished from side to side in the vehicle.

It was a devastating start to our trip and the beginning of a painful road to recovery for Karin. When we found her in Upington hospital, though, she was grinning. 'Nice stuff, morphine, huh?' I quipped. But her right arm was a mosaic of cuts, scratches and bruises. She had hit her head badly and given her back its third terrible tumble: the first having been in a helicopter crash, the second in an aeroplane, and now in a car. 'Perhaps she should stick to bicycles!' I said to Sue on our way back to Andriesvale that night. Karin gamely maintained that she would soon be fine and would call and let us know when she was ready to rejoin the expedition.

'Everything happens for a reason' is not one of my maxims. It is a phrase that is invariably offered as a kind of condescending pat on the head when bad things happen to good people like Karin. I was gutted that she could not make it for at least the next fortnight and set about trying to find a stand-in until she was feeling better.

The film-makers I called and who came barrelling up to the Kalahari from Cape Town at a week's notice had a different approach to their art and camera techniques to Karin, but they turned out to be welcome additions to our team. Richard Wicksteed is a social activist who uses his camera to document the many tragic circumstances that face the disempowered of the subcontinent. He has long had an interest in Bushman issues and has made several documentaries that highlight their plight. I had met Richard in a campsite in western Botswana when he was shooting the cultural genocide against the Bushmen that is taking place in that country. When I flipped through my mental contacts file in the aftermath of Karin's misfortune, his name immediately jumped out at me as someone who would have the skills that this project needed. Added to that, Richard is used to roughing it, he has good knowledge about the Khomani, having worked with them before, and he understands Afrikaans.

Richard speaks quietly, walks lightly and has the kind of laidback mannerisms that surfers like him get from hours in a buoyant universe with nothing but sea, sky and a board. His working partner is Karl Symons, who does the camera work and supplies his gear and 4x4 for their joint projects. Karl is a big-time celebrity in Belgium, having presented many television series, news shows and documentaries. One look at him tells you why. He is charming, articulate, tall and handsome, with blond hair, blue eyes – the full shebang. Nowadays, Karl works behind the camera as much as in front of it and he has a passion for Africa and its indigenous people. He has a great eye for natural beauty and his shots are slow and exquisitely crafted.

Karl and Richard's work schedule was such that they could not join us until we were already in the Park, so we arranged another departure date with the Kruipers and arrived at Witdraai in the morning of the following Friday – Good Friday – ready and eager to leave. Then an even bigger blow. Oupa Dawid was crouched at the fire with his head in his hands. 'Pain, Mama. Pain in my legs, my back, everywhere. I'm sorry but I can't come with you. It's too sore.'

I felt numb. 'This trip is jinxed,' I said to Sue. 'Maybe we've left it too late and he'll never get back into the Park. So much for Good Bloody Friday!'

I gave Oupa some of the strong painkillers from my first-aid kit and we sat next to him in silence, wondering what the next step might be.

'You go on with Buks,' he rasped. 'He knows a lot of our history and will look after you until I can come.'

It did not seem right. This was Dawid's dream trip, probably the last journey of his life and I was reluctant to leave without him. But how to tell the family that once again we could not leave? They had felt the previous delay so keenly; one of the women had thrown herself into my arms, wailing, 'I want to go to the Park! The Park, the Paaaark!'

I turned to one of Dawid's sons. 'What should we do, Toppie?'

'Let's go,' he said. 'This often happens to my dad. He'll be all right and can come later.'

'Go, Mama, just go. I'll rest and see you soon,' echoed Dawid.

Behind him the Kruiper youngsters were already packing their vehicle, so clearly the consensus was to go.

'Okay, Oupa. I'll phone you on my satellite phone in a few days and see when we can come and collect you.'

Three-legged black pots, wood, barrels of water and tents were being shoved into the space underneath the game-viewing seats of the Land Cruiser, along with more blankets and duvets than I had ever seen outside a shop display. 'Crikey, Sue,' I muttered, 'just how cold is it going to be out there?' I had been told on one of my previous trips that Bushmen do not use sleeping bags because 'that way, if a lion comes to take you in the night, he only runs off with the blanket and not you as well'. The Kruipers' bedding seemed to confirm this. Suitcases held together with twine and small, battered bags contained their clothing and the traditional skins they would wear if and when they felt like it.

The tailgate of the Cruiser began to bounce and droop as eleven

Kruipers, aged from three to 70, clambered onto their seats and yelled their goodbyes to the glum relatives whom Dawid had not chosen to come on the trip. I pitied them the drive into the Park with no windscreen or windows to protect them from the wind and sand. Off we trundled, Johnny Bok driving their swaying khaki ship, Sue and I behind in Priscilla, watching their bobbing heads and waving hands as the canvases flapped and billowed above them.

CHAPTER 3

A Baboon Sitting on a Rock

By the time we got to our first camp, the Kalahari sun was high and the temperature in the upper thirties.

'Sure am glad we're not doing this trip in summer,' said Sue, as we stepped out of Priscilla's air-conditioned cab.

The Kruipers had stopped in a shallow bowl encircled by sand dunes. I climbed to the top of one of them and scanned the area. Long, parallel dunes extended for many kilometres in an east-west direction, like red ribs on a cow's carcass. In between them were valleys, or 'streets' as they are known here, and the entire landscape was covered in ash-blond grass, small shrubs and the odd wizened tree. The air was dry and still and I felt as if our little band of travellers could have been the only people on Earth, surrounded by this endless, undulating vista.

The southern Kalahari is the driest part of the sandy wilderness dubbed the 'Great Thirst', which covers some 2.5 million square kilometres of southern Africa. But it is classified as an arid area rather than a desert because it has sufficient rainfall to support sparse vegetation and some hardy species of animals. The belt of dunes we were in is roughly 800 kilometres long and about 200 kilometres wide and it is not characterised by great floral variety. But that is precisely what makes it so restful for outsiders. The eye is not constantly teased by a new leaf shape or bright flower, and the gentle repetition of the dunes' plants and curves allows the mind to quieten and the left brain to retire. The Bushmen, though, know each bush and tree as intimately as we do our back gardens and for them the effect of the landscape is as much stimulant as relaxant.

Oupa Dawid named this place Bobbejaanskop (Baboon's Head), but I could find no physical feature to suggest why. 'No, Mama,' Buks told me, 'my brother called it that because he sometimes feels like a baboon sitting on a rock with all the tourists staring at him!'

'That's our Dawid,' I chortled to myself.

At one end of the sand bowl was Dawid's veld school – an area the size of three tennis courts, enclosed by a thick fence of thorny branches. When the Khomani won their land claim in 1999 they were allotted 25 000 hectares in this section of the Park and are entitled to stay here for short periods, providing they build traditional, non-permanent structures. They are allowed to hunt and gather, with certain conditions; they can conduct their old rituals, dance their old dances and sing their old songs. It is a place of retreat and reflection where the Bushmen can enjoy some of the harmony that once characterised their lives.

But many of the community's youngsters were born and raised during the years when the Khomani were landless, so Dawid built this humble school in order to teach them about their natural heritage. There is a long-drop toilet at the lower end of the enclosure – so that the children do not have to leave the protection of the fence after dark – a large, domed hut of sticks and grass built around a shepherd's tree, and the tiniest of dens for Dawid, where he slept curled up on the sand like a mouse in its burrow. It seemed strange to be here without him.

The Kalahari had had excellent rains that summer and the school was thick with grass and weeds. We set about the backbreaking task of clearing the area before putting up our tents. I dreaded living cheek-by-jowl in the enclosure but the school is directly on the lions' route to the Nossob River, and Albert Bojane, a relative of the Kruipers and our first ranger of the trip, would not hear of us sleeping outside it. Sue and I erected our field kitchen in

Priscilla's gazebo, outside the stockade, and she prepared a light veggie meal for us while the Kruipers cooked sheep stew on a small fire near their tents.

'Please hurry up,' Albert called to us. 'It's not safe and we need to close up the gap in the fence.' I did not envy him the responsibility of looking after us in the camps to come where there would be no fence to protect us.

By dusk the dunes had turned deep amber and a light breeze came up. The low sun turned the grasses into a pond of shimmering mercury. I started to feel the tension of the past few weeks falling away. The sweet smell of *Boesman's twak* (dagga) swirled around camp, and its after-effects made the Kruipers calm and congenial. 'Dagga makes you cautious,' Dawid always told me. 'It makes you think.'

The Khomani have been smoking dope for hundreds of years, but they have always been punished for doing so. To this day, the Witdraai police seem to be more concerned with the dagga 'problem' in the community than they are with the alcoholism and violent crimes that plague it. But on this trip I was quite happy for the Kruipers to indulge in one of their favourite stress-relievers and hoped it would take the edge off their withdrawal from alcohol. By nightfall the family was in bed and their chatter gradually cross-faded with the mysterious night calls of the Kalahari's creatures. I settled down for the first night of this great adventure.

Similar sounds woke me pre-dawn – muted chortling from around the fire that the Bushmen had rekindled from the previous night's embers. Their conversation was punctuated by sputum-soaked coughing. We had had our first introduction to the rhythm and acoustics of the journey – early to bed and extremely early to rise, to the accompaniment of vigorous lung-clearing. Both would take some getting used to.

By first light the men were up on the surrounding dunes, reading the tracks of who had come a-calling while we slept. Oom Buks pointed at the intricate messages left in the sand by the night visitors and reconstructed the stories that lay at his feet. Two big lions had sauntered past our sleeping heads, their tracks straight and unhurried.

Like the work of the art world's grand masters, tracking combines both acute observation and a refined imagination – observation of what is there, and the imagination to interpret it. The great difference between the canvas and sand artists, of course, is that the tracker's work is impermanent and unrecorded. It survives only in detailed – and constantly repeated – fireside accounts of the day's decipherings. Becoming a great tracker involves knowledge of animal behaviour as much as it does recognition of the prints and signs themselves. One of the reasons why Bushmen were – in some cases, are – so talented is because of the hours and hours they spend watching animals and piecing together their inner world. It is one thing to recognise an animal's spoor, but altogether more useful to know its intent after a slow and detailed process of deduction, reconstruction and projection.

I have no doubt that many people would regard the Bushmen's views on animals' thoughts as sentimental fantasies – and scientists would dismiss them as anthropomorphic – but hundreds of years' worth of successful hunts and evading danger must surely testify to their ability to project themselves into the animal mind. And there is nothing that hones a tracker's skills better than hunger. This is why the older members of the Kruiper clan are so much more adept than the youngsters we had on board. The elders tracked well because in the past they would have starved if they did not. For the teenagers, catching a porcupine at Witdraai is necessary only when they do not have the money to buy meat at the Andriesvale store.

For the next few days I was a child again, learning the ABCs of a completely foreign language from these patient teachers, so eager to give me insights into the interpretative skills on which their lives once depended: how wind alters the spoor and how colours in the sand indicate its age; how to assess an animal's gender, speed and injuries. I was deeply moved by the vulnerability of the animals, so unaware of what their spoor revealed about them and how the information could be used against them. I had read that the Kalahari is regarded as having ideal conditions for tracking, but wondered why as I gazed at one cratered pug mark after another in the soft, collapsing sand. They all looked identical and I felt blind, deaf and, above all, intuitively disabled. It was as if a vital, ancient part of my brain had been asleep during decades in the rowdy city of Johannesburg and that its fast and furious life had stunted the intuition that is the tracker's greatest asset. In the Bushmen's company, even the smallest insect duel became an exciting tale of death in the dunes and I sat cross-legged on the sand with all the wonder of a little girl while they re-enacted the dramas of the previous night.

It was a dimension of the natural world that I had never fully appreciated, this ability to know about events long after they had happened and to 'see' animals when they were no longer there. What does it matter if a kill is over and you missed it? With the Bushmen you have full action replay as long as the evidence survives. The tracks made the Bushmen inquisitive, made them scrutinise things, and enhanced a deep connectedness to all the life that surrounded them. I envied that. And I collapsed with laughter when they described how useful their skill is in keeping their partners faithful. 'We know our lovers' footprints as well as we know their feet, so we can follow them to whatever bush they may be hiding behind, doing nonsense with their *skelms* [rascals].'

Buks, Dawid's younger brother by six years, is a bushcraft master and my impression was that of all the Kruipers he had the deepest yearning to be back in the wild. In his day, Buks was the most renowned tracker of the southern Kalahari – fast, meticulous and tenacious. At the back of his neck is the long scar of a cut made when he was a toddler in which his parents placed a lion's whisker so as to enhance his intuition in the field, particularly towards predators. I am told that Buks has an uncanny ability to know when there is a lion in the vicinity, long before it is in sight. And, like anyone who has had to face down lions without a firearm, Buks has a healthy respect, even fear, for them. His skills as a veld doctor bring him clients from far afield and from many other cultures.

He makes beautiful Bushman artefacts for sale to tourists and has all the charm and skill of a born hustler, able to wheedle money out of people within the first two sentences of a conversation. And Buks' hands are never still. Unless he is fast asleep, he is busy and often sat at the edge of the fireside group working on his bows and arrows and contributing very little to the conversation.

Buks' features put you in no doubt that he is Dawid's brother but he is small, even by Bushman standards. His birth name is Hendrik but he is always called Buks, an Afrikaans nickname meaning 'little guy'. Tiniest of all the Kruipers he may be, but he is still the fittest. For a man of 70 with bad knees, he walked fast and confidently across the dunes, stick at the ready and a woman's handbag of faux black leather slung over his shoulder. Its shiny silver studs looked out of place here, but inside the bag were what its skin equivalent would have held a hundred years ago: pieces of bone, some roots, sinew, a knife, tobacco, newspaper and matches. When he found what he was looking for – and sometimes the plant's presence was betrayed by a mere twig above the ground – he put his handbag aside and dug like a man possessed. Sweat ran down his face as the mound of sand grew at his side and slowly the subterranean jewels he was after were teased from the soil. He broke off a root, only one, so as to leave enough to sustain the plant, before placing a lock of hair or a coin in its midst in appreciation for what it had provided. Carefully he pushed back the sand and turned to me in triumph.

'This is leeuhout [lion wood], mama, we use it when we're out hunting and lose our way home. You feel a bit drunk for a few minutes after you've chewed it but then you have a very clear head and you know where to go.'

GPS-by-mouth. Sounded good to me. The genuine concern of his next statement was touching: 'Let me make some medicine for you, Mama, so you can become pregnant. *Ja*, trust me, even at your age, I can give you a baby!'

It thought it might be something of a shock for him to learn that a woman could be child-free by choice and decided to spare him that insight. Plus, I did not believe he could manage it, until

I worked out after the expedition that his wife, !Nat, had fallen pregnant in her mid-fifties.

We continued to forage in the dunes for the treasures that looked so prosaic to my untrained eye – plants for making beer, necklaces and skin creams, others for curing psoriasis, diarrhoea and eye infections. It struck me how hard the Bushmen had to work for everything that they wrested from the soil. Hours and hours to dig up plants in the morning, even longer to slice, dry and powder them in camp during the midday heat. Who could blame them for taking what they need from modern mechanics and medicine, as they have done increasingly since the days when they got regular access to Western inventions?

When not with Buks I spent time with two of Dawid's sons, Toppie and John, both intimately au fait with this terrain because they, too, had grown up in the veld, albeit at a time when it only supplemented their food and medicine. They are a great foil for each other. John is serious and reflective, always observing, often disengaged. 'I'm a porcupine,' he joked. 'Don't get on the wrong side of me!' To me, though, he was always calm and polite, but at times his face became overcast and he sat alone on the dunes, holding his head in his hands. What haunts him, I wondered? Was he battling without booze, or did he have regrets that this contemplative landscape would not allow him to evade? Several times I went up to him and asked in my very broken Afrikaans if he was okay.

'Yes, thank you, Patrish, I'm just thinking. A man must think, you know?' Long before our journey Dawid had elected John to be the head of the Kruiper family after his death and left the deep Bushman cultural secrets in his care. It was a good decision because John is wise and cool-headed, he reads people well and has great respect within the community for his sane, unemotional input at meetings.

If John is happy to be in the stalls, however, his elder brother was born for the stage and John is content to let him steal the limelight. Andries' nickname is Toppie, meaning 'old man', on account of the shuffling gait he had as a child. The nickname is still fitting today because a huge curve in his spine makes him slightly stooped. He broke his back in the same 1994 car accident that so afflicted Dawid. His Bushman name is Tokar, meaning the lead ox in a span. Toppie is affable, enthusiastic and impish. His face is wide, and his many missing teeth give him a permanently comical air. But he uses his humour as a protective shield for his sensitive and loving nature. He has a subtle and perspicacious intelligence, like so many of the Kruipers, and his self-knowledge is well developed.

Toppie adores his partner, Tina, and at night they sat by the fire, arms and legs entwined, whispering and giggling. He can neither read nor write but his bush literacy is beyond question. 'Nature is my book and pen,' he told me, as he pushed his knuckles into the sand, then added nails and a heel to provide what looked like a perfect replica of a black-backed jackal's spoor. I have no doubt that his keen eye and great interpretive ability were developed because of his lack of a formal education, where talents like these are so often neglected or drummed out of us.

Toppie was born in the Kalahari Gemsbok National Park in 1971, but when he was four years old the family was evicted from the Park and condemned to an uncertain future as itinerant farm labourers. Dawid's father bought three donkeys and a cart, packed up his family, their pots, pans and blankets and set off to look for work. He found it nearby, herding sheep for a coloured farmer but the family was not allowed to stay on the farm, so they set up grass-and-stick shelters in the *gorrel* (no-man's land), between the fences that run parallel to the road into the Park. It was a dangerous place to live, especially for their children and animals. Next the Kruipers tried settling in nearby Botswana but the police moved them on, so the bulk of the family built shacks on the outskirts of a coloured township called Welkom, about 15 kilometres from the Twee Rivieren gate into the Park, where they were anything but welcome in the early days.

Dawid, his wife and children trekked hundreds of kilometres away to Namibia, where he had extended family. He went herding for a white farmer and, because it looked like the job might last, he enrolled Toppie in the local junior school where he did well in his first year. One week into his second year, Dawid had a fight with his boss and the family moved on. That was the last of Toppie's formal education. For the following decade, the Kruiper family lived as rootless vagabonds with no human rights or labour laws to protect them from the whims of employers, who beat them routinely, paid virtually nothing, provided little food and no job security. Without notice and in any weather they were bundled onto their cart and sent into the diaspora, strangers in their own land, looking for a place to settle. Maybe the next farm would have work, or the next. In a hostile world even the youngsters learned to live by their wits and perfected survival techniques that serve them to this day. They supplemented their meagre meals by hunting small game or digging for nutritious tubers on the sheep farms, and this is how Toppie learned what his ancestors' land could provide. While his father worked, Toppie was in the veld with his mother, Gais.

Eventually Dawid returned to South Africa and got work in Riet-fontein, a coloured settlement north-west of Andriesvale. Toppie was now thirteen and was expected to help support his younger siblings. So, like his father, he got a job herding sheep and goats. And, like Dawid, he got used to the sting of his boss' sjambok and had the added pain of being separated from his mother.

'I was just a little boy and I got so tired looking after 50 sheep or more, keeping them safe from the jackals. When the sheep were sleeping, I would sleep, too, lying under a tree and donating blood to the tampans and ticks. And the farmer would catch me and he would make me run ahead of his horse like a jackal while he whipped me.'

It is surprising that such an abusive childhood did not whip Toppie's sense of humour out of him, too, but far from it. He is the Kruiper family joker, and that night he gave us the first taste of his panache as a storyteller. We settled down around the fire after supper and by the light of the flickering flames he began. I expected an old-world Bushman tale from him, something along the lines of 'how the moon married the sun' or 'how the jackal outwitted the lion'. But out of his mouth came his rendition of a popular Khomani standard: a contemporary, fantastical and hilarious story about a dog conference. The dogs had to pin their poops on the noticeboard before entering the hall for their meeting. When the bell went at the end of the day they rushed out, and, in all the confusion, some dogs picked up the wrong poo ... No, it does not bear repeating, because its effect is so dependent on Toppie's inimitable narrative style and inflection, along with the belly laughter to which he strutted his stuff on that starry Kalahari night.

Historically, Bushman stories have 'floated from afar'. They drift from community to community, like seeds on the wind, to be nurtured and developed wherever they land. Because of this cross-pollination, it is seldom that a narrator can claim to be the inventor of a tale, and his art – this is invariably a male domain – is in the telling, the characterisation and the gauging of his audience's tastes and responses. The storyteller is not averse to exaggeration in order to keep his listeners' attention and uses gesture, imitation and tonal variety to keep them hooked. Tangential forays into minor details are common, so much so that the story's thread is sometimes completely lost, but usually the plot is well known and its demise is incidental to the enjoyment of the whole experience. This is an actor's art using a personalised script and Toppie is a humble master of the genre.

Throughout our trip, water would be our most precious resource because, with one exception, we would be camping in areas with no surface water whatsoever and it would be several hours by road to replenish our stocks. I had worked out that we would need to average between 6 and 10 litres per person per day for everything – cooking, drinking and washing – and I had already become a dab hand at bathing in six cups of water. I watched with growing concern as one 25-litre barrel after another was lifted off the vehicle until there was only one left. We had only been in the Park for two days and I had expected our water to last for at least six.

A rainstorm the next day was exactly what we needed, and Sue and I rushed out for an impromptu shower in our undies, crouched behind the kitchen and tittering like schoolgirls. The Bushmen huddled in their tents until it passed. Heavy pools of water had collected on the canvases of the Cruiser and my gazebo, which the menfolk carefully funnelled into a barrel. But we were still desperately short and eventually there was no option but for Johnny, the driver, and one of the Kruipers to head home for more.

We had become used to constant petitions from the family to return to Andriesvale: 'I've forgotten my skins; I owe so-and-so money; I need to collect my pension.' I found it curious, given how much money I had paid them upfront to settle their debts and obligations. Then it hit me: that old devil, liquor, was tugging at their sleeves, and knowing that he was only an hour-and-a-half's drive away was becoming too much to resist.

I knew the kind of mayhem that booze would cause in camp, and chose someone who I thought was the most dependable to go with Johnny to replenish our water and wood. Had I written about this incident at the time, I would have had no hesitation in outing the culprit who sneaked booze into camp that night, but such is the affection I have come to feel for the Kruipers, their broken hearts and heavy addiction that I am not going to now. Besides, he was put up to it by the others, so all were guilty. Our peaceful camp in the dunes turned into a madhouse within an hour of his return. Sue and I slunk to the far side of our tents and listened as the sound of brawling took over the veld school. An elder cowered as a bow and arrow were aimed at him, youngsters were challenged to a punch-up and women cowered in their tents, screaming at their men to stop fighting.

It did not last long, but the after-effects did. I felt now as if I was on tour with complete strangers, not the people I had met in Andriesvale. The trust and cooperation we had so carefully built up in order to do this important work were gone, and I questioned my ability to manage this mercurial group. All the gains of a few days off alcohol were lost, and the Kruiper men would now have to endure a repeat of the early days of withdrawal.

At a meeting the next morning to discuss what had happened, they were contrite and small-voiced. 'I think, Mama,' Buks said, 'no one must go out of the Park except you and Soos [as they had named Sue]. We need alcohol and will always find it, so it's better if we stay away from there.'

We packed up and moved to another site in the Khomani's section of the Park, further away from the outside world and temptation. Rolletjies it is called, because the dunes roll into the distance like waves. Now there was no thorn fence and I was delighted not to be cooped up. The Kruipers laagered their tents around the fire, but I faced mine east so as to be woken by the dawn and have an uninterrupted view of the long, wide valley that our camp overlooked.

At the far end of the valley was a windmill but the blades were still and looked as though they had not moved in a long time. The borehole brought to mind the poor farmers who had once tried to make a living in this harsh place. Aside from the sandscape, the two outstanding geological features of the KTP are rivers – the Auob and the Nossob – which join just north of Twee Rivieren camp (hence its name, 'Two Rivers'). They flow only once or twice a century, but the V-shaped land between them has always been rich in wildlife and vegetation and therefore attractive to settlers. Before the arrival of whites here, in the mid- to late 1800s, coloured and black pastoralists shared the area in peaceful coexistence with the Khomani's ancestors and other nomadic Bushmen.

But European expansionist ideals in Africa gradually infiltrated this quiet corner and eventually it became the border between two of the world's most powerful nations at the time. Germany occupied South-West Africa in the 1880s and South Africa was under British sovereignty for almost a century before it became an independent state in 1910. The dead-straight border between them ran along the western boundary of the KTP and it was not long before growing tensions in Europe, on the eve of the First World War, spread to this region and made it an important area to defend – and attack.

A Baboon Sitting on a Rock

The government of the Union of South Africa decided to drill boreholes along both the Auob and Nossob rivers in 1913–14, to provide water for its troops, should an invasion of German territory be called for. In the end, those battles happened elsewhere, but coloured farmers were settled at the boreholes along the Auob to guard them in exchange for the rights to graze their herds. The idea was that they would also help to tame the area between the two rivers that had already become notorious for illegal activities.

After the First World War, the drive to settle more farmers on this land intensified and the area was surveyed by a Scot who divided it into farms that he named after places in his home country, although a greater contrast in terrain can hardly be imagined. Roger 'Malkop' Duke Jackson was his name, and while I do not know why he was called 'Malkop' (madman) I like to think it was because of the absurdity of his and the government's plans to populate this toughest of places. The Union of South Africa encouraged so-called poor whites to inhabit the land abutting the Nossob River by selling it off at bargain rates. Even though many were living on the breadline after the war, few came and even fewer lasted.

All but one of their cottages is long gone, and it has been preserved as a museum called Auchterlonie, on the bank of the Auob River. It was built by hand out of calcrete stone and is a dark and cramped place, redolent with suffering and hardship. On the walls are photographs of the Human family who farmed sheep and goats here. Their faces look resolute but pitifully careworn.

When the white settlers left – and some sources claim they were evicted for overshooting the game of the area – the coloureds continued to eke out a life, if not a living, until the declaration of the Park in 1931, when they, too, were moved off. And, of course, all this activity in the game-rich area between the two rivers prevented the Khomani's ancestors from accessing their traditional hunting grounds. Their boundless world began to shrink and they spread out to drier, more inhospitable land where their expertise in finding food and water was tested even further.

Richard and Karl arrived the next day and we met them at the

33

KTP's main camp, Twee Rivieren, to guide them to our little camp tucked away in the dunes. Richard was greeted effusively by the Kruipers, particularly Buks, and they were soon nattering away by the fire as Buks worked on his trinkets and arsenal. Knowing from experience what the Bushmen enjoy, Richard had brought along a guitar. Toppie grabbed it and began strumming and humming as the sun set. I felt relieved to have my team complete and to have Richard's friendship with the Kruipers to fall back on in the months to come. Karl put up his bright blue rooftop tent, Richard his tiny dome and we all collapsed into our sleeping bags under the bright moon. Jackals sang their canticles on the dunes around us as I finished my audio diary for the day. The group was at peace, at least for now.

In the morning Buks and the lads said they were going to check out the spoor of a lion that had been roaring at the windmill during the night. I had not heard it, nor had I heard Albert calling me to wake up. Richard, Karl, Sue and I bounded after them, eager to see the pad prints of our nocturnal visitor. We huffed and puffed up a dune after the guys and, when we caught up, Buks called Richard aside. 'Ag, please man, the lion was nowhere near here, we just want some quiet time for a poo in the bush!' We scrambled down the dune in peals of laughter.

Later in the day we travelled by car to Sebobogas salt pan so that Buks could show us the famous hoodia plant, traditionally used by the Bushmen to suppress their hunger when they are out hunting and the subject of an international pharmaceutical furore a decade ago. The hoodia's properties became the source of great interest to the massive international market in diet supplements and in 1986 South Africa's Council for Scientific and Industrial Research began investigating the plant's biochemical make-up. After nine years of research, they patented their findings and sold the licence on to a United Kingdom-based pharmaceutical company, Phytopharm, which then re-licensed the patent to Pfizer, which in turn sold the licence to Unilever. But no benefit-sharing agreement was initially negotiated with the Bushman communities in southern

Africa whose knowledge was being exploited. It was only when human rights activists and lawyers got involved in the case in 2001 that any financial benefits accrued to the Bushmen – and those have been modest to date. Currently, there is some debate as to hoodia's efficacy in pill form and the Mayo Clinic is of the opinion that 'there is no solid evidence that hoodia is effective'. There have also been claims of the plant having some harmful side-effects.

The precious hoodia was old and very wrinkled and I gazed down at the ugly, cactus-like plant that had caused all the trouble. A couple of new growths were emerging on one side but Buks said they needed time to grow, so he would wait until they were taller before harvesting them. His is a conservation ethic that we have lost: take what you need, not what you want. He should be on the speaker circuit sharing a platform with Al Gore, I thought as we walked away.

On the way home we climbed a high dune and sat on its summit, kings and queens of all we surveyed. One of the Kruiper youngsters carried a massive *gifbol*, or tumbleweed bulb, up to us, presenting it like a trophy with a huge grin on his face. Buks explained that it has anti-inflammatory properties and his nephews peeled off the papery sheaths and showed us how to wrap them on arthritic joints and sprains. The sheaths were then bandaged onto the body with the long, fanned leaves of the plant. Nothing goes to waste in Oom Buks' pharmacy in the sun. While he worked Toppie and John teased and shredded the *gifbol*'s leftover wrappers and kneaded them into tight little balls. 'We use these as firelighters in the rainy season when the wood is wet,' they said, 'like those white blocks you use to light your braais.'

We spread out in the valley below to look for things that might be edible or medicinal, the Bushmen calling to each other when they had found something to be excavated, and nibbling on plants as they walked through this untamed garden. My view of the Kalahari began to change, from forbidding terra incognito to bountiful provider – at least for those who know what to look for. And I began to understand the difference between them and me. I was observing the landscape, they were in it, of it. The Kalahari would look after them if they looked after it as in an unspoken contract between lovers who had known each others' secret places for millennia. Foraging with the Kruipers was one of the most satisfying experiences of my life. I wandered through the veld, pulling *tsamma* melons off the vines, cutting them open, sucking the clear juice from their mint-green flesh and spitting the pips into the grass. It was like the Easter-egg hunts of my childhood and I felt again the triumphant joy of finding a sweet treat hidden in the foliage. The family's three-year-olds bobbed through the tall grasses, eating what their mothers popped into their mouths and being warned constantly to look out for snakes and scorpions.

Life felt timeless and uncomplicated out there, and I look back on those days with both fondness and regret – regret that so-called progress prevents not only the Bushmen from enjoying these elemental activities, but people like me, too. And even deeper regret that our views of land ownership have changed so much. The Bushmen believe that the land does not belong to them so much as they belong to it. By reversing that simple philosophy we have brought war, environmental destruction, envy and greed into what was once a paradise just like the one through which we were travelling.

CHAPTER 4

The Truth, Only the Truth

Old Dawid arrived at dusk and eased himself out of Grossie's car with difficulty. He hobbled to the fire and slumped into a camping chair while his family touched and greeted him lovingly. Grossie's welcome was only marginally less effusive and showed how much affection and respect the Khomani have for him. He and Phillipa make great foils for each other and over the years have managed the tricky situations they face in the Kalahari with what seemed to me to be a good cop, bad cop technique.

Grossie is a born diplomat with a sharp mind, a big heart and a walrus moustache that twitches when he laughs – which is often. Phillipa is more feisty and straight talking but equally devoted to the Khomani people and their issues. She is a beautiful woman with the kind of supple and strong figure that only yoga and jogging can produce and she is not averse to training in the Kalahari, regardless of the heat.

Grossie had brought *twak* (tobacco), sugar, flour and water – the same things that visitors have been bringing to the Bushmen for hundreds of years. It struck me how welcome the gifts must have been when they were living in the middle of nowhere and had none of the goodies that tumbled daily out of Priscilla's ample rear end.

Tina took Grossie's hand. 'You're only here for one night. Would you like your favourite?'

'Ooo, yes please, Tina. *As brood* [ash bread]– nyum!'

What the Kruiper women could achieve with flour, yeast and water was nothing short of an art form, and we sampled three different types of their bread on the expedition, as well as Sue's scrummy 'ODB', or Our Daily Bread, a multi-seed and grain loaf that she cooks in a heavy loaf tin on the coals. *As brood* is a large, flat loaf that is buried in a hole in the ground and baked under layers of sand and coals. The women know when it is ready by tapping the sand with their knuckles and listening for a hollow sound. I was not looking forward to eating gritty bread, but when the loaf came out, it was brushed off and left completely clean. We tucked in, slathering peanut butter and jam onto hot chunks.

After only a few days with the Kruipers it was already clear that division of labour in the family was unequal to say the least. In the old days this was not so, as both genders had roles to fulfil that kept them busy. The men hunted, collected wood and made their implements, while the women gathered, cooked and looked after the children. Now that the necessity to hunt is not as pressing and collecting wood is not allowed in the Park, the menfolk largely sit around tending the fire, chatting and working on their tourist artefacts, while the women perform all the traditional tasks their grandmothers had – and then some.

Toppie's partner, Tina, is slight and dainty with neat mannerisms and a quiet charm. She is extremely knowledgeable about veld food and is South Africa's first registered female tracker. Not that I knew this until the very end of the trip, mind you, because Tina hides her light under a bushel. She and the other two women, Galai and Brenda, laughed and *skindered* (gossiped) over never-ending peeling, chopping, stirring and washing up, and seemed to accept their fate as the help-maidens in camp, always the last to eat.

Galai is Dawid's youngest daughter and is so desperately shy that it took all of six weeks for her to speak a word to Sue or me. She looks at the world through lowered eyes and has the demeanour of a woman who has been traumatised by something or someone. Her son, Kabe, is the apple of his grandfather's eye and played all day with one of his mother's shoes, pushing it around camp and making *vroom vroom* sounds.

His playmate was Brenda's daughter, Mefi – also three – a cute and pretty little girl with great inquisitiveness and self-confidence. Both children had an endless capacity to entertain themselves without toys or adult supervision and their presence in camp was often a welcome tension diffuser. There is great security growing up in an extended family, as I know from my own childhood. Being bundled from Aunt's hip to Dad's shoulder and then to Grandfather's knee gives a child a feeling of great comfort and sense of belonging. Kabe would go to sleep in Dawid's arms in front of the fire with adult laughter lulling him to sleep; Mefi would help her mother fetch and carry to much praise and encouragement. The two children were remarkably undemanding on long days in the field or in the vehicle, and I found them to be a welcome change from city toddlers who are the constant object of suffocating adult attention.

Brenda is Dawid's niece on his mother's side of the family. She is a smart and capable young woman who was given the name 'Bantam' by her mother's white boss because she was born in the back of his Bantam bakkie on the way to hospital. Not surprisingly she changed this insulting name when she reached adulthood. Brenda is very beautiful, despite having only one eye since she was little. The other was accidentally burned with battery acid when she was crawling around the farm on which her mother worked. Brenda has a matric qualification, and of all the Kruipers she most embodies the two different worlds that modern Bushmen try to inhabit. But the schism I saw in her life was certainly not apparent to her.

'Mefi can go to a formal school, but I would like her to know about the veld as well,' she told us, confident that it was possible for her daughter to enjoy high fashion and cellphones at the same time as tracking and foraging. If this is so, then the Park land that the Khomani were awarded is a wonderful cultural resource, there to be used in the same way that an IT geek in Kathmandu uses a

Buddhist monastery in the mountains – as a place to reconnect with the past, with tradition and with spirituality.

After the greetings were over, Grossie took me to one side.

'Oupa Dawid said he was ready to come so I brought him straight away before he changed his mind.'

'Why would he change his mind?'

'Troublemakers at home, telling him that a "whitey" is leading him by the nose again. He's pulled this way and that so much by those people that sometimes he doesn't know which way is up.'

I went over to Oupa to say how pleased we were to have him with us and that we would not start work until he was feeling up to it.

'Don't worry, Mama, I'll be okay now that I'm away from those chatter-bags. One whispers in this ear, another in that one and it makes me sick. See how sick I am? Anyway, how do you like our dummy?'

'Your what?' I asked.

'We call this area that we were given in the land claim our dummy because we never got the breast. It's far from the river and is so dry that there are very few animals around here.'

What little land the Khomani were awarded inside the Park was hard fought for by the 50 or so people who had been born and raised within its boundaries. While the farms provided the community with homes and the opportunity to start herding, tracking and commercial hunting businesses, the so-called Kruiper extended family consistently asserted during the land claim negotiations that it was the Park that they most wanted. This was the heartland of their ancestors' wanderings and the site of their graves.

'I know this land like I know my wife's body,' said one old man. But how to prove that? There was almost no evidence of their historical occupation of the area because the Bushmen had lived so lightly on the land, used local resources and built impermanent structures. Sure, they remembered the trees under which major events in their lives happened – births, deaths and unions – but how to substantiate them, given that their historical curatorship was oral and not written?

The claim process was initiated in 1994 when South Africa's newly elected democratic government put land restitution for the historically dispossessed at the top of its reform agenda. The Khomani's claim was managed by human rights lawyer Roger Chennells, who appointed researchers who could analyse the community's past. Anthropologist Hugh Brody and sociolinguist Nigel Crawhall spent months in the area interviewing the Khomani elders in great depth and recording their stories of life in the KTP.

Several times their knowledge of the terrain was astounding. One elder looked at an aerial photograph of that vast expanse of dune veld and pinpointed his old kraal, which the researchers then marked by GPS. When they went to the site with the old man, there were the trees he had described and the bare, compacted sand that showed that the Bushmen had cleared the area of grass year after year. His margin of error was only 3 metres.

The kind of physical evidence that the investigators were after eventually came from an old lady. Ouma |Una Rooi – who died while I was writing this book – told them that if they went to a particular tree they would find a plate that was given to her in 1936 and broken by her sister. |Una had so loved the plate and was so upset by the mishap that she buried the fragments under the tree. Sure enough, the pieces were still there over half a century later.

Because the Khomani traditionally used roughly 400 000 hectares of the South African section of the KTP, that is what they were legally entitled to claim. Botswana, with whom the KTP is co-managed, was not part of the negotiations and its government has shown itself to be vehemently resistant to honouring Bushman land rights. It soon became clear that a claim of this size would be challenged by the Park's authorities and other organs of state, so models of redress from abroad were investigated.

The international standard for compensating aboriginal communities who utilise large tracts of land for subsistence hunting and gathering is a one-in-four rule, meaning that the claimants get a quarter of the land over which they once roamed. Using this formula, the Khomani were entitled to roughly 100 000 hectares of land within the Park, an idea that was also vigorously opposed by the Park's management. Instead, a valuation of the land was done. According to some, it was grossly inflated so that the Bushmen landed up with a mere 25 000 hectares inside the Park. And their pleas for more, better land got subsumed by the wider land restitution process.

In terms of the proposed agreement, this so-called Contract – or Heritage – Park would be privately owned by the Khomani, and the South African National Parks (SANParks) would be responsible for its conservation management. The community would be awarded commercial development rights to a further section of the Park, as far north as the Auob River (referred to as the V-zone – see map on the frontispiece), and cultural and symbolic rights to the rest of the claimed area. This entitled them to visit their heritage sites, gather plants and hunt and live there traditionally, but not permanently, by agreement with management.

But resistance to this proposal from the old-guard Afrikaners and others within SANParks was huge. There were even alleged incidents of Park management cutting down trees that had been homes to the Khomani so as to destroy evidence of them having been there. Dries Englebrecht, head of the Park at the time, famously expressed the view that 'tourists come to the Park to see animals, not people'. The fight got ugly, with accusations flying that the families who had lived in the Park were a bunch of drunken poachers; that they had destroyed anything they were given; and, besides, they were not proper Bushmen anyway.

The task of ascertaining whether or not the Khomani were 'the real thing' fell to Nigel Crawhall. Shortly after starting his research, Nigel was told that there was an old woman living in Rietfontein who spoke 'Bushman'. He rushed to the bleak settlement and was introduced to 102-year-old Elsie Vaalbooi. Their meeting turned out to be life-changing for both of them. With a portable CD player, Nigel played Elsie some 1936 recordings of N|uu, one of the original Bushman languages of the territory that had been thought to be extinct since 1974. 'A veil lifted from Ouma's face,'

Nigel told me. 'Time evaporated, she was transported back across a lifetime. She … understood every word.'

With the help of Elsie's son, Petrus, Nigel found a further 26 speakers of N|uu, scattered across the farms and townships of the Northern Cape. 'Each discovery brought back this moment of becoming a human again, of a return of dignity, of being seen and heard,' Nigel wrote of these encounters.

N|uu was older than all the other Bushman languages of our subcontinent and the people who spoke it were the original occupants of the southern Kalahari and the Karoo. It was the only Bushman language from South Africa's past that had survived contact with its subsequent migrants and colonists, in part because its speakers lived in a climatically harsh area that was not attractive to the newcomers. Sadly, since the land claim, so many of the N|uu speakers have passed away that the language must now be regarded as all but dead, despite the fact that Nigel Crawhall and some community elders established a N|uu language school. The speed at which it reached its moribund state was extremely fast – it happened within one generation – not only because of the displacement of its speakers but because those who spoke the language were often beaten by their employers for using a *skinder taal* (gossip language). During apartheid many Bushman children became ashamed of their heritage and their grannies often hid their knowledge of the language from their descendants.

Finding living N|uu speakers put paid to SANParks' legal attempts to stop the land claim process but it did not result in improved relations between the two parties. Part of the problem was that key individuals from either side did not fully understand the provisions of the settlement proposal, a lengthy contract referred to as the 'Brown Book' – 55 chapters of rules and procedures, drafted by lawyers, that were complicated even for the educated, let alone for illiterate Bushmen.

Years passed without the Khomani visiting their land in the Park, even though its allocation had been agreed upon in 1999. Phillipa and Grossie increased their pressure on SANParks to find a solution to the impasse. Then the authorities saw the perfect opportunity for a well-timed transfer of the land. The World Summit on Sustainable Development was being held in South Africa in August 2002, and, with the global media in Johannesburg, it would be an ideal time to maximise the publicity potential of the handover. With fitting fanfare, but not nearly enough media coverage as far as the minister was concerned, the dummy was given to the Khomani.

But any hopes they had of seeing it soon were slowly crushed. For a start, the Contract Park is about 80 kilometres from Andriesvale. The community had no vehicles and walking there was completely beyond the old folk. A document called the 'Welkom Declaration' throws some light on the depth of the Bushmen's anguish and frustration during the long years of waiting. It was written in 2004, when they still had not visited their land, and was the result of a meeting attended by Khomani who were born in the Park and wanted to practise their cultural traditions there. The petition was sent to SANParks, the Department of Land Affairs and the Department of Environmental Affairs and it begins with touching gratitude for the Contract Park. Then it adopts an uncompromising tone: 'We are deeply heart-sore, and have carried this pain with us for the past five years, and we are bitterly dissatisfied over the manner in which our Kruiper clan has been treated, we are insulted, belittled and discriminated against ... we feel like strangers on our land of birth [and] are being completely brushed aside.'

The document ends: 'We are the last and original clan and insist on going back to ... living on the land of our forefathers, we insist on this.'

But still, going to the Park remained but a dream. Phillipa and Grossie kept banging on SANParks' doors and asking for the implementation of the agreement. Eventually SANParks' head office applied pressure on local Park management and in April 2006 – a full seven years after the land claim settlement in 1999 – Phillipa arranged for the clan elders to go to the Contract Park and they stood together on their land for the first time. They named it the

!Ae!Hai Kalahari Heritage Park, a N|uu name meaning 'oryx tail' because they had managed to catch the Park by its tail and hang on to the great beast. It is commonly referred to as the Contract Park by the community.

Phillipa and Grossie drew up a lengthy set of management protocols with Oupa Dawid and interested members of the community to protect the Park's resources and ensure that the community's rights were enjoyed, including mechanisms for the sustainable harvesting of animals and plants. In this memorandum the Khomani proposed a permit system to register how much hunting and gathering they did, and they undertook to hunt away from tourists' eyes, among other things.

Dawid had always described the Park authorities as lions, commanding but slow, and the Bushmen as jackals, quick, wily and always looking for a chance to outwit their more powerful adversaries. Now, he hoped, the old enemies would work together and the analogy of mutual interdependence that he used was contained in a story. Dawid told of the way in which rain collected in the fork of a shepherd's tree. Various creatures came to drink from the small pool, including bees that would then make honey that humans could enjoy. 'The jackal and the lion have drunk from the same water,' he said triumphantly.

And indeed they have. Since that time, South Africa has seen a fundamental change in its conservation philosophies, particularly as to the role that rural people can play in protecting natural assets. There is growing awareness of communities' rights to benefit from the resources and tourism on what was once their traditional land. Under the new head of the South African side of the KTP, Nico van der Walt, relationships between the Park and Khomani have improved with every passing year and continue to do so under his successor, Steve Smit. A division of SANParks, called 'People and Parks', is proactive in developing this relationship and contributed money towards that first, joy-filled visit to the Park by the Khomani elders, most of whom have subsequently died.

Since then, Phillipa and Grossie have applied successfully for funding from the Lotto and other donors and the Khomani bought their Land Cruiser – the one they were using for our expedition. The community has its own gate into its section of the Park as well as a camp called Mbewu, which, along with Dawid's veld school, is designed for the transfer of indigenous knowledge to the children of the community and for tourists who want to walk with the Bushmen.

Grossie left the next morning, having slept on the back of his bakkie during the first of many bitterly cold nights we would have on the journey. He looked none the worse for wear, but I felt ragged after an awful night and the realisation that I had not brought a sleeping bag rated to withstand temperatures below zero. Oupa Dawid battled to thaw out, too, and spent most of the day lying in a foetal position in the sun and complaining of being cold and sore. We said our goodbyes to Grossie and watched his bakkie disappear over the horizon, chased by a scud of red dust. Johnny Bok caught a lift back with him, saying he needed to get to a funeral. I suspected that he was battling without mod cons and hot showers and in time I was proved right. He never returned to the expedition, so Sue's duties now included driving the Kruipers' truck. As always, I was thankful for her can-do attitude to new challenges.

We left Dawid to rest and headed for the dunes. Earlier in the day, the young men had planned to go hunting but had been thwarted by a strong wind that would have made it difficult to conceal their scent from the animals they tracked. We found them practising target shooting with their bows and arrows. Their accuracy varied greatly and it was clear which of them had hunted regularly in their youth. The teenagers had a lot to learn, Toppie and John were good, but the best by far was Am Am as he is known to the family. Am Am means 'mouth' in Khoekhoegowab, and his nickname is a reference to his talkativeness as a child. Meeting him as an adult, one can hardly believe he was like this for Am Am is neither garrulous nor confident. But he is the kindest and most sensitive of men and when Sue and I were battling with lifting or packing, it was always Am Am who would leap to help us. 'Mumsie,' he called us and it soon caught on.

'Gawd,' I said to Sue, '"Mama" makes me feel old, but "Mumsie" is too frumpish for words!'

Am Am has had a hard life. He was born in Namibia when the Kruipers were trying to make a go of life there, and, like Toppie, he was trundled from farm to farm as a boy and missed out on an education as a result. His mother was a Kruiper and by the time Am Am had reached his teens both she and his father were dead, so Dawid took him under his wing. Am Am clearly loves being in the wild: he is a good tracker, an excellent hunter of small game and might even have potential as a shaman, I am told. But he has been deeply hurt in his life, and because he is obliging and easily led, he is often the fall guy when the youngsters get into trouble. His face and body carry many scars from the fights he has been in and they are at odds with the shy smile that is always on his lips. Am Am appeared to be the errand boy on our trip and was consistently the one ordered to fetch and carry by the group, despite the fact that there were younger guys with them. The Bushmen have always designed their own punishments for misdemeanours and these usually involve the guilty becoming what they call 'the dog' in camp. I wondered if Am Am had done something bad. No one would tell.

The shooting practice ended with Toppie giving us a demonstration on how to kill one of the smallest antelopes in the Kalahari – the steenbok – with a knobkerrie. Hunting in this manner requires great patience and stealth, but suppleness, too, I thought, as I watched Toppie creeping along the ground, moving his legs like an insect so as not to raise his back above the height of the grass.

'And what do you say to the steenbok, once you've killed it?' I asked him, hoping to hear about the Bushmen's respectful way of thanking the animal for giving its life for them.

'I say goodbye and go well. I'll see you soon because no doubt I will follow. Something or someone will finish me off.'

'Dear Toppie always has a unique take on an old idea,' I chuckled as we headed back to camp.

By late afternoon, Dawid said he was ready to start talking about the Kruiper history we had come to the Kalahari to capture. Richard and Karl positioned him on top of a dune with a backdrop of the land he had known and loved for all his life. His charisma seemed to fill not only the camera's viewfinder but the landscape, too. I sat nearby with my recorder for an audio back-up. The falling sun gave Dawid's skin a rich, copper patina as he sat smoking quietly while Karl set up the shot. When the camera rolled, he spoke before we had asked him a question, as if to state the intent of the work we were there to do.

'I'm not talking about things that I heard but things that I saw.'

His opening statement was like a stake driven into the ground by an old man with few chances left to tell his tale. Since we had started planning the expedition, Dawid had been adamant that this trip had to be about the truth. '*Die waarheid, net die waarheid*' (The truth, only the truth), he repeated over and over again. 'Everyone else has told their stories, now it's time to tell mine, because I've kept quiet while many lies were said.'

The story of the Kruipers begins with one man, lodestar of the family, hero of the community and, in the eyes of his descendants, the epitome of all that is truly Bushman – self-reliance, hardiness and deep spirituality. He was Dawid's grandfather and his name was Makai !Gam!Gaub.

The details of Makai's early years have been forgotten by the family, as has the date of his birth, but it was probably in the 1870s or 80s, unless we accept Dawid's belief that Makai died at the age of 120 in 1966, which would put his birth a couple of decades earlier. One account has it that Makai was orphaned as a child and brought up in the Rietfontein area of South Africa, to the southwest of the KTP, but the dialect of Khoekhoegowab that the Kruipers speak is that of the Gochas area in Namibia, which places his developmental years there.

What is certain is that as a young adult Makai roamed and hunted in an enormous area of the Kalahari, including Etosha and Grootfontein in northern Namibia, down to Swakopmund in the south, the whole of western Botswana and part of what became the KTP and its environs in South Africa. Those were the free years, when the Bushmen could still evade the colonists, farmers and conservationists who eventually stifled their lifestyle and robbed their land. Makai and his group followed the rains and herds, used a couple of donkeys to carry their few possessions, hunted with dogs and made their temporary grass shelters for a few months until it was time to move again. 'Their time was a nice time,' said Dawid, 'not so strict and full of laws like it is now.'

Makai's 'nice time' started coming to an end with the gradual occupation of the Kalahari by settlers from other parts of South Africa. The so-called Basters were one of these groups, immigrants from the Cape Colony who, under the leadership of Dirk Vilander, established themselves in the area around Rietfontein, which they later named Mier. The Basters were the products of liaisons between Dutch colonists and their Khoekhoe slaves, and in the 1860s, the Union government decided to solve the Baster 'problem' by giving them a 'reserve' in the southern Kalahari where they could live and farm, far from the so-called civilised men who begat them. Although the origin of their name is pejorative (literally 'bastards'), many of their descendants claim it proudly nowadays as testimony to their rebellious origins.

The newcomers' relationship with the Bushmen seems to have varied between cordiality and loathing. Indeed, Donald Bain, a champion of the Bushman cause, who was to enter the Khomani's lives roughly 50 years later, maintained that what transpired after the arrival of the Basters was a 'slaughter.' 'There are several old Bushmen living today who are able to give a very graphic description of the happenings of those days,' he said in a speech in 1937. The Basters' descendants deny that such violence was perpetrated. What is agreed is that the hunter-gatherers taught the herders about the edible and medicinal plants of their semi-desert home and were employed when and if they needed money for luxuries such as tobacco and coffee. Often they moved off when their wanderlust overtook them. Nonetheless, this was not a relationship between equals, and gradually the Basters took over the Bushmen's traditional water points for their cattle and goats.

In 1910, Makai was in Rietfontein and was employed as a shepherd and predator hunter by a Baster named Japie Jagers. The two families moved together to Botswana in the 1920s and then to the Nossob River valley a decade later. They were there when the Kalahari Gemsbok National Park (KGNP) was declared in 1931.

At that time the Kruipers' original Bushman tongue was still in use, Dawid told us. 'Makai spoke !Gabe, but I can only remember a few words, like salt, meat and water.' Quite what this language was remains a mystery. Nigel Crawhall says that !Gabe is a Khoekhoegowab generic word used to refer to Bushman languages. Makai did speak N|uu, but only as his second language, and it seems certain that his native tongue was Khoekhoegowab. This does not make him or his descendants any less 'Bushman'. For thousands of years Khoe-speaking peoples of the Kalahari could be found among all lifestyles, from hunter-gatherers to herders and all combinations in between. Makai never fully mastered Afrikaans but by the time Dawid was born, the family mostly spoke this language – the language of their employers and oppressors.

When Dawid was a child – in the 1940s – life had changed greatly for the Kruipers. Makai was now a late middle-aged man and Dawid's father, Regopstaan, was working for Park management. The children were left in the care of the family's womenfolk and elders, and because their grandfather's pace was slow and his patience infinite, it was Makai who taught Dawid and Buks all they knew about the veld, and particularly about tracking. For Makai was a master – able to tell the age of a spoor in the dark by placing his hand on it and feeling its temperature relative to the sand around it.

The boys would watch the old man leave home in the morning and follow his tracks over the dunes, hiding from sight until they knew they were too far to be sent home. 'Then my grandfather said, "You have to bear the hunger and thirst as well if you want to stay with me. It's a question of testing your limits, pushing through."' During those long, hot days, the boys learned the secrets of the sandy wilderness that was their home and legacy, what it could provide for body and soul and, above all, how to love and appreciate it.

At night, Makai taught them about the stars, and for Buks this was a particularly magical time. 'The best thing for me was if Makai lay on his bed and said to me, "Let me show you a letter", and he showed me a letter in the sky. He showed me Jupiter and [taught me] that if it shone red it would be cold.'

Makai was not only an extremely brave hunter, capable of killing a gemsbok with a flick knife, but a talented herbalist and '*snort doctor*' – this being the ability to 'smell' illness or poison in a patient and then draw it out with herbal medicine. He 'worked in the spirit', Dawid said. By means of trance and divining, Makai would identify both sicknesses and their cures, and could exorcise bad spirits. Above all, in a clan renowned for their gifts as rainmakers – as the Khomani were – Makai was one of their finest. 'Even the Park bosses would ask him to dance so that the rain would come,' Dawid told us.

Truly this sounded like a man among men and I could not help but wonder if Dawid and Buks were exaggerating Makai's gifts, as we all do about people we have loved and lost. So I checked with a couple of the Khomani elders who had known Makai. Yes, he was adored and admired both during his life and ever since for being gentle and helpful. 'He didn't have any bad manners and he never overlooked people,' one of them told me. A song about Makai's final, sad years when his land was being plundered is sung to this day by all age groups of the community:

> *Old Makai is old.*
> *Old Makai is very old.*
> *There come strange people,*
> *Strange people.*
> *Completely strange are the people that come.*

I had no idea what Makai looked like when we went on the expedition because the family has no photographs of him. With Nigel's direction, I scoured South Africa's museums and archives during the months following our trip and found a few shots taken by visitors to the Kalahari in the 1940s, 50s and 60s. Easily the best are by *Life* photographer, Nat Farbman, published in the 3 February 1947 edition of the magazine. I wept when I first saw the images of the man whose ghost we had followed for two months through the KTP. Not that his name was attached to the photos, mind you. To this day photographers of Bushmen are prone to labelling their shots after their subjects' occupations or features, as in 'an old hunter' or 'a wizened old lady' and the custom was particularly prevalent in racist times when the Bushmen were merely an academic curiosity and not deemed fully human.

But there was no mistaking who I was seeing because Makai was the image of Buks and was exactly as Dawid had described him – a proud but very short man, with erect posture and a wise, kind face. 'His skin looked like a porcupine's skin when you scratch off the quills – very wrinkly but the texture was velvety,' Dawid had told us. And there indeed was his grandfather, very wrinkled even by Bushman standards, the skin on his torso folded into long pleats, running from armpit to armpit, right down to his hips. There were the knobbly knees that slowed him down as an old man, and which both Dawid and Buks have inherited, and the small breasts that they, too, develop when food is plentiful and they gain weight.

Farbman's photographs comprise a beautiful tribute to Makai's skills and further corroborate what Dawid remembered of his grandfather. He is seated next to his medicine pots, grinding roots. The pots are made of horn and are beautifully decorated. Each has a little leather cap that fits perfectly. In another photo Makai is telling a story, surrounded by the peppercorned heads of rapt youngsters. His eyes are wide and his hands clawed, as if to pounce. Perhaps he is telling of a run-in with a lion during the day's hunt. There are photographs of the old man bringing meat back to his

Dawid Kruiper, old, wise and irreverent. © SO

Buks Kruiper, renowned tracker and veld master. © SO

John and Toppie Kruiper, Dawid's sons. © SO

Willem Swartz. © SO

Tina Swartz. © KS

Am Am Kruiper. © KS

Galai and Kabe Kruiper. © KS

Brenda Bladbeen-Kruiper. © KS

Mefi Kruiper. © SO

Klein Dawid Kruiper. © KS

Jeffrey Kruiper. © SO

Isak Kruiper. © KS

Klein Makai Kruiper. © SO

Dawid's veld school, thick with grass after good summer rains. © so

Kings of the Kalahari. © KS

Horned adder. © SO

Gemsbok. © KS

The rolling dunes of Rolletjies. © PG

Dawid's father, Regopstaan. © AP

Dawid's grandfather, Makai. © NF

Nat Farbman's 1947 photographs
of Makai and his clan. © NF

Sue Oxborrow. © PG

Patricia Glyn. © KS

Richard Wicksteed. © KS

Karl Symons. © KS

Priscilla, Queen of the Desert. © SO

family, and of him teaching children to stalk and shoot with their bows and arrows.

Four years after Farbman's trip, the French Capricorn Expedition – with a young Phillip Tobias on board as team doctor – arrived at Twee Rivieren, the 'threshold of the forbidden land'. Their intent was to find the legendary Lost City and film the Bushmen. They took photos of Makai against the wall of a building. He does not look amused, and who would be, positioned like a criminal and asked to turn and present all profiles for the photographer. His beautiful handmade shoes have been replaced by *veldskoene* and his loin skin is frayed and tatty.

Another visitor who took photographs of Makai was Jens Bjerre, leader of the 1958 Danish Kalahari Expedition, the purpose of which was yet more of the kind of 'anatomical research' into the Bushmen that obsessed scientists for centuries. Bjerre's book *Kalahari* contains damning impressions about the physical features of his research subjects but he was clearly impressed by Makai, describing him as 'a dignified and intelligent old patriarch, well endowed with humour and wisdom'. His photo shows exactly that – Makai much older now, but still a man with great bearing. And this time we get insights into his personality and thoughts. Makai is reported to have spent several minutes looking at his reflection in the wing mirror of the Dane's Land Rover, making faces and smiling at his reflection. When asked what he thought of 'all these wonders' he responded: 'Something belonging to white man [*sic*]. I do not think more than that. No good for my people, but too late, long ago too late.'

Bjerre then asked Makai if he thought he was good looking.

'Yes, very beautiful and very old,' he replied. When pressed for his age by another visitor in the 1960s – Marla Perkins of the United States TV show *Wild Kingdom* – Makai's philosophical response was: 'I am as young as the most beautiful wish in my heart and as old as all the unfulfilled longings of my life.'

So Makai, it seems, was indeed a polymath and a gentleman. How burdensome it must have been to grow up in the shadow of such a colossus. I felt great empathy for Dawid's destiny of being compared constantly with his legendary grandfather, and for being given what he called the 'bigger bag on my shoulders' of looking after the Kruiper family during a much more complicated time in their history. As our long interview with him neared its end, he looked into the distance and said, wistfully and almost to himself: 'If I had followed my grandfather's footsteps I would have been a better person. And then I would have lived long, and I would have been very amenable.'

About six months after our journey, I went back to Witdraai with copies of the photos I had found. On a moonless evening I propped my laptop on a chair outside the Kruipers' shacks and the family gathered around, jostling each other to get a good view of the small screen. Makai's gracious and beloved face looked out at them. Dawid wept quietly as Kabe bounced on his lap; Buks howled, 'My oupa, that's my oupaaaa! I loved him so much!'

CHAPTER 5

Patronage and Prejudice

During the next few days we crisscrossed the Contract Park in the Khomani's Land Cruiser to visit and document historical sites that the two old men wanted to put on record. I struggled to get used to the very slow rate at which everything took place but tried to bear in mind that Dawid was old and frail and that he should set the pace.

We returned to Sebobogas Pan, this time for Buks to talk about the endemic medicinal plants that his grandfather had shown him there. These days the pan is dry by autumn because of the many boreholes that have been sunk in the KTP, but in his youth Sebobogas was a dependable source of year-round water that remained in holes dug by the gemsbok looking for salt. In typical fashion Buks strode purposefully through the veld and unearthed his quarry with dedicated digging. 'This is a *poep uitjie* [fart onion]. You cook it and it blows you up, just like the porcupine. I will cook it tonight.'

Fab, I thought, now we will have farting as well as coughing for our camp chorus.

Among the Kruiper family on the journey were four teenage boys who alternated two-by-two throughout the trip so that we could maximise the kind of inter-generational knowledge transfer that Dawid was so keen to achieve. All four were qualified in cyber tracking, a means of field data collection using hand-held GPS devices for later loading on a database at the community's office. The boys were there to mark and document the plants, animals and heritage sites of our expedition.

The first two who joined us were Buks' son, Makai, and his cousin, Jeffrey. But they were lazing on the Land Cruiser's seats while Buks sweated in the sun. I could not understand why. Did they know about the plants he was talking about on camera? Or were they not interested? The next few weeks would reveal the answer.

Buks was born close to the pan but had not been back to his birthplace. Would he remember exactly where it was? No, but Dawid would, he said, and there would be evidence of the Kruipers having lived there: 'The tins are still lying there, and broken bowls. Bushmen always leave something to show where we've walked,' Buks told us, and I thought of Ouma |Una's plate shards.

'Tomorrow, I'm going to show you my museum,' Dawid said that night over our fire's dying embers. A museum? I could not wait.

I woke to the signature tune of our camp – sounds akin to a TB sanatorium and a blacksmith's forge. Am Am hammered away at a piece of wire, flattening it into what would become an arrow. Buks was putting his knife into the fire until it glowed red hot, then using it to burn images onto a bone pipe. His waistline looked as slim as always, so perhaps he had forgotten to cook the fart onion, I thought. Or maybe he had expelled the resulting gas during the night. I decided against asking him.

Very late, as usual, we got onto the Cruiser and drove to the highest dune in the area that Dawid had named Verdwaalskop (the hill that helps you find your way when you are lost). Because of its height and bright red crest, the youngsters of the community use it for navigation if they get lost while out in the veld, something they do fairly often for lack of experience. And Verdwaalskop's added bonus is that there is cellphone reception at the top of the dune, which makes it useful in case of emergency.

At the bottom of the dune was a very run-down thorn fence enclosing a small, threadbare grass hut. Dawid opened the barrier and welcomed us to his museum. I was touched by his pride in such a lowly place, but it soon emerged this was not due to the museum so much as the one artefact that it contained. He fumbled in a hidey-hole under the fence and came out with an old donkey stirrup, broken and bound up with wire.

'This was our forefathers'' and I remember it as a child,' he said, as he held the stirrup between two hands, moving his fingers lovingly over its rough edges. He sat down in front of his little hut with his cousin, Willem Swartz, whose mother, Anna, was one of Makai's daughters. Willem is fourteen years younger than Dawid but was also born in the Park and was part of the extended Kruiper clan who wandered these parts. He is a pastor in the Andriesvale community and spoke to the camera with all the flair and fervour of a practised orator.

'My first memories were of this place,' Willem told us, then added what he knew about this precious piece of family memorabilia: 'The stirrup is broken like this because of hammering gemsbok bones for the marrow and then someone tried to fix it. You can see that they didn't have pliers, he must have done it with a knife tip. When we find something like this it assures us that our ancestors moved here and that pack donkeys were their transport.'

The issue of not being allowed to have their dogs and donkeys in the Park still rankles the Kruipers because using them for hunting and transport is part of their tradition. In the past, the donkeys enabled them to cover great distances and the dogs to hunt big game such as gemsbok, which the hounds would track and keep at bay until the hunter arrived to finish it off with an assegai. The dogs were also useful in alerting the Bushmen to the presence of lions or other predators. But in the negotiations with SANParks over hunting protocols, Dawid agreed that no dogs should be allowed in the Contract Park because it would be hard to limit the amount of hunting the Khomani did. Now, years later, he bitterly regretted his decision, principally because of the community's shortage of meat.

But it was the right decision because dogs change the delicate balance of power between hunter and the hunted. Quite when the Bushmen of southern Africa started using dogs in their hunts is not known, but rock paintings suggest that it was a very long time ago. Nonetheless, there are still Bushmen who regard the use of dogs as a practice that erodes the hunter's tracking skills because the dogs can easily follow the prey's scent and the Bushmen merely follow them in turn.

Hunting buck – and especially gemsbok – without dogs takes great speed and endurance and was regarded by some groups as the pinnacle of the Bushman's field art. In the so-called running hunt the animal was chased and harried over a long period and distance until it stopped for the final coup de grâce or fell exhausted at the hunter's feet. Such high expenditure of energy did not happen often among the hunters of a clan, so there was seldom a danger of overkill. Other methods, such as one for which Makai was famous, were also the preserve of highly skilled experts and therefore seldom performed. Makai was known to climb a false camel thorn tree and wait for a gemsbok to be drawn to its shade in the midday hours, then he would swing down on one of the tree's branches, like a pole-vaulter, and stab the animal with his assegai.

Using dogs dramatically increases the risk of unsustainable hunting, and especially now that Bushmen do not migrate over large areas. However, the sad fact is that there are few – if any – Khomani hunters left who have the fitness or expertise to hunt without dogs. Although the men are highly skilled at catching porcupines, hares and other small game, at the time of our expedition not a single buck had been successfully hunted in the Contract Park. It seems that the elders have the bow-and-arrow skills but not the strength and the youngsters have neither.

There is certainly a strong case for the Khomani needing donkeys for transport inside the Contract Park but experience in Botswana's Central Kalahari Game Reserve has shown livestock's presence as having a devastating effect on its flora and fauna. Overgrazing and overkill turned the areas surrounding the settlements into dustbowls, and having access to donkey carts made it possible for small-scale commercial hunting for meat sales to town dwellers outside the reserve.

For many years Dawid's precious stirrup was lost in this vast piece of country, much to his anguish. But he was out one day with his grandchildren and, in a one-in-a-billion chance, young Makai found it at the base of a tree. 'Not a stirrup but *the* stirrup, the one I know,' Dawid said passionately. No doubt he saw great symbolism in the fact that it was found by the young lad who carries his famous great-grandfather's name.

Dawid hid away the stirrup and we headed up the hill. Verdwaalskop is part of the area that the Kruiper clan roamed not only before but after the Park was declared, and they were unique in being allowed to do so. In the 1930s, all other people who were living in the KGNP – fellow Bushmen, coloured farmers, BaTswana, Nama, and those who were products of these groups' intermarriage – were systematically evicted. They and their possessions were put onto trucks and driven far away enough to prevent their return. Some were dumped in Botswana, some became labourers for local farmers and many disappeared into the ghettos of nearby towns, where the Bushmen passed themselves off as coloured in the decades to come, both to avoid discrimination and to collect government pensions.

Grand apartheid's race classification system comprised four categories: 'native', 'white', 'coloured' and 'Asian', thus omitting any reference to South Africa's original inhabitants. Without an identification card stating to which group a citizen belonged, no state support was forthcoming. Most Bushmen chose to pass themselves off as coloured because the National Party government granted this group marginally better resources than they did the 'natives'.

Ironically, one of the initial reasons for the establishment of the KGNP was to provide a home for the Bushmen. Then Minister of Lands, P.G. Grobler, announced in 1929 that the Bushmen needed protection and specifically instructed that they should be allowed to live and hunt 'undisturbed' in their traditional territory – the land between the Auob and Nossob rivers – which was about to be declared a national park. Grobler faced vociferous objections to this idea from his fellow parliamentarians, one of whom said that the Bushmen would be an 'annoyance and irritation to the neigh-bouring famers'. Presumably he meant by this that the Bushmen would hunt game on land abutting the Park that had been sold at bargain-basement rates to poor whites. And, needless to say, that hoary old excuse that the Bushmen were not 'pure' surfaced again as a reason to get rid of them. Eventually the Park was declared without any protection offered to its first inhabitants.

Three years after the declaration of the Park, its second warden, Joep le Riche, was on one of his extended patrols in the Park when he met a group of roughly twenty Bushmen at Sewepanne (Seven Pans) near Mata Mata. The Kalahari was in the grips of a particu-larly bad drought and the Bushmen were dying of starvation and thirst. 'In spite of their wretchedness they wanted to flee at the slightest provocation,' he recalled. 'We had to lure them closer with tobacco and coffee to save their lives.' Motivated by a desire to save 'this special little nation with all its enemies', Le Riche per-suaded the Bushmen to move to Gemsbokplein, where he lived, so that they could be kept under his wing.

Makai and his family were not among this group and we do not know why they, too, found favour with Joep le Riche, but the Krui-pers and Malgases arrived a few years later and, again according to Le Riche, showed the other Bushmen for whom 'work was not their great love' how to provide diligent service to the Park. It is the descendants of these families – and about three or four others – who would later form the core of the Khomani land claim.

There was a degree of self-interest in allowing a few dozen Bush-men to stay, of course, because the new Park needed staff. Some of them were employed as trackers, borehole maintenance crew and in anti-poaching patrols but in those early years there were few re-strictions placed on the Bushmen. They were allowed to hunt with dogs, travel with their donkeys and live wherever they chose, pro-viding they could fulfil their work obligations. And because there were no fences around the KGNP for several more decades, they could wander into Namibia or Botswana to visit relatives.

Every couple of months the Bushmen who were not employed

would go back to where Joep lived – first Gemsbokplein and, in 1938, Twee Rivieren, sometimes travelling at night when it was cooler. Lions were a constant threat during these moonlit treks, but the donkeys and dogs warned them of danger. When they reached camp, Joep would fill their tins with rations of mealie-meal, coffee, sugar and tobacco and have them checked out by a doctor. And when far horizons beckoned, they would be on their way again.

The stories of the Kruiper and Le Riche families have been inextricably entwined for nearly a century and the relationships between the men from these two vastly different cultures and races is admirable and shameful by turn. Theirs is one of those complicated master/servant bonds that South Africa is so good at producing, where the lines are blurred between patronage and prejudice, affection and exploitation, respect and fear.

The first Le Riche, Christoffel, trekked to the Northern Cape in 1883 and opened a trading store near Rietfontein. Few men could have coped with the kind of isolation and hardship that the Kalahari offered at the time, and even fewer women. But the couple did well and soon bought a farm in the area where their son, Joep, spent his formative years in the veld, developing the knowledge that would one day make him an expert in the Kalahari's intricate habitat. When the Union government decided to establish a game reserve in that remote corner of South Africa, the Le Riches were the obvious people to run it because they were dedicated conservationists, and knew the people, politics and environment of the region so well.

In its first few decades, the KGNP was run rather like a family business. Joep's brother, Johannes, was its first head, and when he died of malaria only three years after the Park's declaration, Joep took over, ostensibly in a temporary capacity, but ended up leading the Park through its next quarter century. Eventually both of Joep's sons, Stoffel and Elias, were also employed as head rangers in different sections of the Park. Stoffel later died of a heart attack and Elias became Park head when his father retired.

Like Makai, Joep was extremely short and had the rare gift of the seer and the two men formed a fast friendship. To Dawid, Joep was his 'white father', a man he remembers with great fondness for his generosity towards the Kruiper clan. The two men spent many years in each other's company because Dawid was often confined to camp where he hand-reared springbok, gemsbok and eland lambs for sale to other Parks. 'If I asked him for anything he would have bought it for me. That was the kind of man he was.'

For decades the menfolk of the two families borrowed Joep's ring for their wedding ceremonies. Stoffel wore it on his big day then lent it to Dawid who in turn gave it to Elias. The ring makes for a fitting symbol of the relationship that the two families had, sometimes nurturing, sometimes tempestuous, rather like a marriage.

Elias and Dawid grew up together at Twee Rivieren and spent their early years playing on the sand dunes around the camp. Because Dawid did not know his date of birth, Elias gave him his – 1 September – so that they could celebrate together. The year of Dawid's birth is disputed, however. Elias maintains it was 1941, Dawid was sure it was 1935.

I am drawn to Dawid's view because a very elderly contemporary of Makai's concurred, and also because of a photo I saw of the Kruiper family taken in 1936. In the front row is a little boy the image of Kabe, Dawid's grandson, and the child bears a very youthful version of the features I grew to know so well on our trip.

The friendship that Elias and Dawid enjoyed as boys changed radically when they grew up, however, and as a man Dawid found himself at the receiving end of hidings by the old playmate who was now his boss. While the friendship lasted, and Dawid had real affection and loyalty for Elias, it was always a relationship between unequals that played out within the context of the deeply racist and divided country that South Africa was at the time.

At the top of Verdwaalskop we surveyed the endless dune country below us and I marvelled at the Kruiper ancestors' ability to navigate through this unchanging terrain, so devoid of unusual features or landmarks. The midday sun baked down on us and Sue and I shrank into what little shade was offered by the shrubs and grasses, but the Bushmen seemed impervious to the heat and glare. It was late, but Buks, Toppie and John decided to go hunting. The long shadows of morning were gone and tracking would not be easy with the sun directly overhead, but they shed their baggy Western clothes and changed into their *!xais* or traditional skin loincloths. In the blink of an eye, paupers became princes. Near naked one could see how well muscled and beautifully made they were, but so very small and thin. They grabbed their bows and arrows and trundled down the far side of the dune with Karl and his camera in hot pursuit. Disappearing into the distance they looked capable, timeless and so well camouflaged in their tawny wilderness. Makai and Jeffrey ran after them, their bright yellow soccer shirts soon the only means by which we could follow the hunters' progress.

It occurred to me that a stranger to this scene might dismiss the boys as not being 'real' Bushmen, so determined are some people to deny Bushmen their identity if they choose to adopt any aspects of other cultures. South Africans appear to accept that a 'real' Zulu is South Africa's current president, and that a 'real' Xhosa can be an IT geek. But throughout history people have tried to freeze the Bushmen in time and confine them to some notion of what or who they should be. Perhaps this is because of some knowledge, deep within humankind, that when we lost the kind of connectedness with wilderness that our aboriginal hearts once enjoyed, we lost the most important part of ourselves. By trapping the Bushmen in the state that we all enjoyed long ago we hope we can preserve some of the memories of a time when life was balanced and slow.

Craig Foster, a renowned film-maker who has worked with the Khomani and other Bushman communities in Botswana and Namibia, has experienced what it is like to touch again what we still yearn for: 'You will first confront yourself and then the most fantastic thing starts happening,' he told me. 'You are the same make-up of plants, the soil, the air, everything. It's just flowing and I believe that these early people ... were experiencing this state of grace as a norm.'

Being the victims of non-Bushmen's expectations is burdensome for the Khomani in many ways. The constant stream of anthropologists and tourists to the community has encouraged them to believe that the only thing worthy or interesting about them is how their grandparents looked and lived. Added to that, traditional activities such as dressing in skins, dancing and making crafts have become an important source of income for the community and this adds to their impression that the past is all that is valuable about them.

The question 'what is a real Bushman?' has long intrigued us and science has put forward many theories aimed at finding an answer. To date this has eluded us. In the early decades of the twentieth century, Raymond Dart, then Professor of Anatomy at the University of the Witwatersrand, believed in topographical analysis – the idea that one could look for anatomical markers in a skull or leg bone, for example, and declare whether its features were Bushmanoid, Negroid or various other 'oids'. That theory held water until the mid-1900s when it was disproved. It also became unpopular because of its overtones of Nazi eugenics.

If physiological characteristics do not answer the question of definition, then perhaps bloodlines do. Some Khomani have been genetically tested and have been shown to occupy the first and oldest branch of the human family tree. Their mitochondrial DNA reveals them to have a matrilineal ancestry stretching back 150 000 years. Studies of their autosomal – or nuclear – genes have linked them to probably the first modern humans in the world. But there is a lot of other blood flowing through the Khomani's veins today. Jan van der Westhuizen is one of the community's best traditional doctors and keepers of the old knowledge systems, but his ancestry is far from pure Bushman. His father was a German who slept with his mother when she was employed as a domestic worker in their house. Jan worked in the Park with Dawid, Buks and Jakob Malgas and, although he was much younger than them, he became one of a group of Bushmen that I call the 'Big Six' because their knowledge of the Kalahari and its environment set them apart from all others.

So if we cannot define a Bushman by his or her bloodline and ability to speak a Bushman language, should the hunter-gatherer lifestyle be the criterion? The problem here is that, like all peoples, the Bushmen have capitalised on what their neighbours had to offer – skills, technology, utensils and language – so at what point did they stop being 'the real thing'? When other Kalahari people first employed them, hundreds of years ago, to do non-Bushman things such as herding sheep? When they started using tin pots and mugs? When they decided to send their children to school? Another of the Big Six, Karel Kleinman or 'Vetpiet', believed that the Bushmen could comfortably straddle the two very different worlds that they currently inhabit. He was a legendary tracker whose veld skills were much sought after by management and scientific researchers in the Park. Among his many talents he could call leopards by imitating their cubs' distress calls. Vetpiet never wore skins, he lived in a house and loved rugby, beer and biltong on a Saturday afternoon and his grandfather was an Afrikaner. But on the dunes he had no equal in the intuition and experience he brought to understanding the ecology of the KTP.

So, is veld knowledge what entitles a person to call him- or herself a Bushman? Not necessarily, because there are other desert dwellers who are also proficient in living off the Kalahari's vegetation and animals – albeit perhaps to a lesser degree. Jan thinks it is about more than this: 'What makes you a Bushman is love of nature, the earth, the birds, the insects, the mountains, the sea, the springs.' Jan's point is that it is about love as well as knowledge.

Ultimately, there are Khomani people who regard themselves as Bushmen but who would not last a week in the dunes because they know so little about living off them. Perhaps that is the best of a bad bunch of 'qualifications': you are a Bushman because you know you are or you think you are. The idea of self-image being the key to identity has gained currency in the last few decades and it validates Khomani looking to answer questions about their 'Bushmanness'.

The hunters were gone for hours and I got bored and hungry

waiting for their return. At times I even wished I had gone with them, but knew that I would not have been able to stomach watching them kill anything. A vegan on a trip with the world's archetypal hunters, I thought to myself, bloody ludicrous! Not that the Kruipers viewed my eating habits that way. Curiosity and open-mindedness is a feature of their thinking, and our conversations around the fire during our trip often explored other ways of life and living.

Looking at Karl's footage later it was clear he had worked his proverbial butt off following the fast pace of the Bushmen and shooting their repeated efforts to get something for the bag. Try after try came to naught and they ended up raiding sociable weavers' nests in the hope of some snake for supper. Again, nothing. Much of his footage shows them compulsively scratching themselves on their legs as a result of a sticky, irritating substance exuded by one of the species of 'Bushman grass' in the Park. The abundant summer rains had resulted in a thicker than usual carpet of *suurpol* or 'acidic grass'.

How ironic, I chuckled to myself, Bushmen allergic to Bushman grass! Another good reason for wearing Western clothes like trousers!

We visited a hyena's den – Wolwegat – not far from Verdwaalskop, so that Toppie and John could show us some memorabilia that they had found while tracking with clients of the Wilderness Leadership School five months beforehand. A wide hole shafted into the sand at a 45-degree angle and its lip was covered with the spoor of porcupines. 'If the hyena doesn't have babies in the hole, then the porcupine will,' Dawid told us as he sat down with great effort. We had walked several kilometres from the vehicle and he was clearly in pain. While Toppie gently brushed away the sand under a small bush nearby, the old man challenged his youngsters: 'I want to know if any of these young Bushmen will go into this hole and kill the porcupine and bring it out? I used to go after Makai into the hole and when he'd killed it, bring it out of the dark, even if there were snakes in there.'

He knew very well that his dare would not be taken up. Nowadays porcupines are mostly hunted at night when they come out to forage, which is far less dangerous than going into their lairs. In the old days, Bushmen would tie a rope around their waist and dig into the den from the ground above. This was extremely dangerous because the sand could collapse at any moment and suffocate them. Porcupine meat is apparently sweet and succulent and is relished by the Khomani, so the temptation to overhunt these spiny rodents is huge. Indeed, they are severely threatened on the community's farms outside the Park. In Bushman mythology, the king of the Porcupines is pure white, and in the past Bushmen were terrified of seeing him because he visited when they had killed too many of his kind. Quite how 'too many' was determined I was not able to establish, and whether young Bushmen still fear the white king is debatable, but the old philosophy points to an understanding of sustainability that the Bushmen had long before it became the over-traded phrase of today.

The Bushmen's relationships with animals are at times so mysterious as to defy logic – even theirs. Dawid's brother, Petrus, once approached a porcupine hole with his uncle when he saw Am Am and John playing at its mouth. The men left the boys to their games and returned home – only to find the two children there. The adults in camp confirmed that they had not left the kraal and could not possibly have been at the porcupine den. 'This is what the porcupine king can do,' Dawid told us, 'he can change [into a human].'

Roger Chennells has an even more startling story involving an old Bushman song that tells of a lion being cuckolded by a Bushman. Every male lion allegedly knows the song, and finds it deeply humiliating. Roger was at the Molopo Lodge conducting meetings about the land claim one day and outside someone had parked a caged lion that was being driven back to Namibia after 'starring' in an advertisement. The lion was drugged and sleeping in his cage and a crowd gathered to gawk at the animal. The delegates then went into the conference room but soon afterwards the lion went mad, roaring, foaming at the mouth and flying around its cage. They rushed outside along with the lion's owner who was furious that someone might be teasing his pet. Nearby Tina and Dawid's sister, Rachel, were giggling.

'Did you make him mad?' Roger asked them.

'*Ja,*' was their reply. 'We'll show you later how we did it.'

The lion was given a steak laced with sedative and went back to sleep. Everyone returned to the meeting but Roger slipped outside a few minutes later to join the two girls. They put their arms around each other and started singing a discordant, funny little tune in Khoekhoegowab.

'And they hadn't sung three bars before the lion just went crazy again,' Roger told me. 'I asked them what they were singing and they said: "We started the words of the story and every lion knows how it ends."'

At the Wolwegat, Toppie had found what he was looking for – several shards of ostrich eggshell. In the middle of one of them was a small hole, clearly made by hand with a pointed stick or knife. 'This is like a little message that my ancestors left for me,' he told us with a broad beam on his quaint face. Toppie's forebears used to boil the juice of *tsamma* melons, then carefully pour the liquid into ostrich eggs, from which they had sucked out the yolk and then dried in the sun. Buried deep in the sand, the water would stay cool and clear for many years to be used by hunters and travellers in the dry months when the veld was devoid of *tsammas*.

Once again I was stunned by the acute memory it must have taken to remember where the egg was buried, and by how very little water the elders needed to rehydrate. 'We're going to leave them here so that our family can come and find them in the years to come,' added John, as they reburied the pieces.

The atmosphere in camp that evening was peaceful and we watched the sun going down behind towering cumulus clouds that glowed pink and orange like dyed cosmetic cotton-wool balls. Barbie-pink sunsets over a quintessentially masculine landscape – weird! I thought. Buks was *smeering* Richard on top of the dune, giving him a deep Bushman-style massage that heals as much through psychic energy as it does through the body. Richard had arrived with a sore back that had deteriorated to the point where he struggled to walk or sit. Willem strummed away on the guitar while the ladies cooked up another sheep stew.

I asked why they did not like braais. 'We old men don't have any teeth,' Dawid explained, his lips glistening with fat, 'so we like to suck on the bones.' By now it was clear that the Kruipers liked a limited variety of food – what I would describe as the diet of South Africa's poor: potatoes, pumpkin, bully beef, tinned sardines, bread and bottomless cups of tea and coffee. When we started the expedition I had told the family that there was to be no apartheid in the kitchen and that they were welcome to try our food and see if they liked it. Dear Buks was the one elected to come and tell us politely: 'We don't like overseas food, Mama, and especially those little green trees.' It took me a moment to realise what he was talking about. Broccoli!

We would be leaving the Park the next day for a week's break because Richard and Karl had work commitments in Cape Town. I called a meeting under a tree behind our camp to talk about the weeks ahead.

Would they like Sue to continue driving them? 'Yes, yes, she's slow and she's careful and we like her driving very much.'

Would they make sure that they brought enough tobacco and dagga for the trip? 'No problem, Mama, that's our job and we'll make sure we bring enough.'

I emphasised that the second part of our journey was much further north and therefore far away from the opportunity to re-provision should we run out of supplies. The Kruipers had been tucking into our stores with the kind of excess that is born of hunger, deprivation and the notion that Priscilla had a limitless pantry. I needed to make it clear that we would be on a go-slow on the next leg. Telling Bushmen how to manage on less was rather like telling grandma how to suck eggs and Dawid's retort was to say that the veld had everything they needed, right down to tea and coffee. He and Albert gave the group stern warnings that we would now have to look out for each other at all times because the northern area of the Park is teeming with game – and therefore lions – and we would be in unfenced camps. The children could not just hang out on the dunes with their headphones on and we would not be able to wander into the veld for a midnight pee. It sounded exciting and I was thrilled at the prospect of learning the 'Big History' that Dawid had hinted at so often and which lay somewhere in the wide, grassy bed of the Nossob River in the north of the Park.

CHAPTER 6

The String is Broken

The magic of the Kalahari vanished within an hour of us leaving Rolletjies. I went ahead in Priscilla, leaving Sue to drive the Kruipers home. At Twee Rivieren camp one of the guys sneaked into the shop and bought a bottle of cheap rum. Before they had left the Park there was mayhem on the back of the Cruiser: arguments, vile swearing and clothing being thrown onto the road. Fifteen minutes later they refuelled with booze at Welkom – the coloured township where Buks lived – and the pitch of the traded insults heightened, along with the women's pleas for their menfolk to behave. Sue stopped the vehicle and ordered them to shut up. When that did not work she took the car keys and started walking to Andriesvale, threatening to leave them to spend the night on the side of the road.

'Remember that The Devil always wins,' Richard had told me, but how quickly I had forgotten. It seemed as if everything we had carefully built up during the past week – mutual respect and affection – had been shattered. And I was devastated. The men we had grown to love and admire in the desert had vanished inside the skins of traumatised children, howling at the injustice of their lot.

Sue and I fled to the farm cottage that Phillipa and Grossie had lent us to lick our wounds and clean up our gear. We were utterly exhausted after just one week of our trip and I was not sure if I could handle more. Apart from the punishing temperatures and conditions of the Kalahari, we had done a great deal of hard physical labour in camp with no offer of help from anyone but Am Am and Toppie. The pace at which we worked was unnecessarily slow and the Kruipers' ruses to get home never stopped. At one point I even questioned whether they liked it out there at all. Snide comments had wafted our way if there was not enough meat, if we were not up early enough, if the sugar ran out. And the non-stop litany of requests from the Bushmen had also taken its toll: 'Mumsie, can I borrow your axe please? Mumsie, have you got some matches, a headache pill, a braai grid?' My gazebo was like an army quartermaster store with provisions being requested at all hours of the day. I had given a generous pre-payment to all of the Kruipers, but was constantly asked for more money based on the assumption, I presumed, that if I was white I was wealthy. More than that I felt as if I was being taken for a goat. So often on our trip the Kruipers had said: ''n Boer maak 'n plan maar 'n Boesman het 'n plan' (a white man makes a plan, but a Bushman *has* a plan). Now I understood what they meant. They had been five steps ahead of me all along. Craig Foster, a film-maker who has worked with them several times, is among some observers who use a foraging analogy to describe this behaviour: 'They've gone from foraging in the wild to foraging from outsiders. So they're manipulating you at one level, but they don't do it in a malicious way.'

Visits to Oupa Dawid during the break were even more trying. He was drunk and tetchy and snapped at me that he would have to abort the entire exercise if I did not provide the tobacco they needed for the second part of the trip, something that they had committed to do at our Rolletjies meeting. He wanted to go and see the doctor in Upington – at my expense – when we were meant to leave for the Park again, even though I had offered to do this for him long before our expedition; Toppie and John could not be there on the departure date either, and so on.

My audio diary of that week on the farm is filled with indecision and angst, and when Karin phoned to say that she had finally decided that she was too injured to rejoin us, I was crushed.

'The ancestors have spoken,' she said sadly, 'and I must release the dream.' Richard and Karl were doing a great job, but Karin had invested so much time and effort in preparing for this project that I had continued to hope that she could join us for the last few weeks of the trip.

Everything seemed to be going wrong – well, almost everything. On one of my pre-expedition recces to the Kalahari I had been standing at the washing line next to Oupa Dawid's house one afternoon when I felt a wet nudge on my hand. It was a young black dog with sweet eyes and dancing tan eyebrows. The white tip of his tail swished through the air and he had an air of friendliness that was unusual in the community's contact-averse hunting dogs. 'Hello, boy!' I greeted him, flattered that he had approached me and impressed that his tail was not curled between his skinny back legs. He was emaciated, like almost all the dogs at Witdraai, but had all the grace of a racing hound.

Nowadays many people in the Andriesvale community aspire to owning border collies, the herding dogs that white farmers brought into the area. Sadly, it will not be long before the Khomani's hunting dogs are a thing of the past and their mild-mannered genes are diluted by those of their highly strung European counterparts. *Canis africanis* is the umbrella term given to Africa's aboriginal dogs, a land race that has adapted to different regions' specific conditions. Those from the Kalahari are generally short-haired, whippet-like animals that can survive on very little food and even less water.

I have been a fan of *Africanis* dogs since I picked one up after a long walk through Zimbabwe in 2002. Three years later Tapiwa walked from Durban to the Victoria Falls with me and I rescued another puppy from sure death during that trek – Mpho, my little Botswana Babe. Ours is a continent plagued by millions of starving, neglected and abused dogs and I am now an enthusiastic advocate of giving them homes rather than paying thousands of rand for dogs that conform to some European notion of canine beauty and functionality.

The next time I went to the Kalahari, the black-and-white dog was still there but was much thinner. When scraps of food were thrown onto the sand by the Kruiper womenfolk, he was chased off by the other dogs and fled with a whimper. 'What's his name?' I asked. 'Blits – because he's so fast.' He looked far from it.

Now, during our break from the expedition, I was back at Witdraai. Next to a grass *skerm* (enclosure) lay Blits, so weak he was unable even to lift his head. 'I think your dog is very sick,' I said. 'Let me take him to a vet.'

You will already have guessed the ending of this story, but the fact that Blits lived was thanks to his will far more than my intervention. After two days of feeding and attention at our farm cottage he was still listless and pale-gummed, so Sue and I took him to a vet in Upington. I stood next to Dries Lategan's table while he examined the timid creature, tense with fear that he would recommend euthanasia. 'This dog has tick bite fever and it's very bad,' was his diagnosis. 'But give me a few days and I'll see if we can pull him through. If he makes it I'll take him to a kennel and you can collect him when you've finished your trip.'

Quite when we would finish our trip was still moot. Driving to and from Upington on our Blits mission, Sue and I chatted about what to do. Should we abort the expedition? No, I was in too deep financially and the South African media were following our progress. Could we manage this group of dear but damaged folk for the rest of the trip? Only with a very different approach. Would I be able to put these recent events behind me? Maybe not. I phoned Phillipa and Grossie and moaned down the phone about how difficult we were finding things. They offered to call Dawid and ask for the low-down from his point of view and tell him how much planning and money I had put into this exercise. It would be his last opportunity to go to the heritage sites and he needed to be reminded of that. 'I know how hard this can be,' Grossie comforted me on the phone, 'but they chose you and we supported their decision because we know you're tough – and mad – enough to get through it.'

The trap I had fallen into is a common one among outsiders, particularly whites, who come to this community and offer their help. We were thrilled – and secretly smug of course – that we were going to spend time with 'Africa's First People, the gentle, noble Bushmen' and we arrived bright-eyed with naivety, ignorance and guilt. But it is only a matter of time before our rose-coloured spectacles were crunched underfoot. Looking back, I am surprised I felt hurt and betrayed. The Kruipers' behaviour was not about me, nor the trip. It was their means of coping with the hopelessness of the lives they were heading back to. And once they got home they devolved again into the pained, angry people that historical circumstances have made of them.

Someone who knows this syndrome very well is Nanette Flemming, who was employed after the land claim by the South African San Institute, among others, as a development facilitator for the Khomani's many projects. She and her partner, Lizelle Kleynhans, lived and worked with the Bushmen for eight years and got to know and love them deeply. Nan is a tall woman with a calm, hippy-like air mixed with old-fashioned Afrikaner grit and an earthy sense of humour. She is, unquestionably, one of the most tolerant and compassionate people I have met. After my journey with the Kruipers, Nan and I sat together for many hours as she translated the interviews we had done into English, breaking off every now and then to tell me about her time with the Bushmen. She described visitors to Andriesvale as a circus that pulls in to entertain the community. The Bushmen get their seats for free and watch us contort ourselves, jump through hoops, fly trapeze, perform all sorts of acts that make them laugh and cry. But it is just a show and they sit there politely until it comes to an end and then go back to their lives.

I told her about my crash in faith and confidence. 'You mustn't be offended by their behaviour,' was her earnest recommendation. 'It's not personal. What goes on at Witdraai is so abnormal, so absurd and ironic that eventually you have to laugh – otherwise you'll go mad. It's very Shakespearean, you know, drama and tragedy playing out all the time.' Was it possible, I asked, that the Kruipers were deliberately trying to wear me down?

'Oh yes,' said Nan, 'you're the centre and they draw energy from you. And they know how to do that well. They just suck you dry.'

'Are they aware of that?'

'Yes, they are.'

'And why do they do it? Is it a test? Because sometimes I felt I was being tested by them.'

'It's a test to a certain extent but it's also not knowing really how to manage this situation and wanting the best. You must imagine: suddenly someone comes and takes them on a trip and they don't know who this person is. This person says they've got very good intentions and all of that, but the Bushmen don't know that and they've been bitten before.'

The test of love that Nan endured was extreme at times, especially for the first three years when she was living in a grass hut at Witdraai. Virtually every night she was woken by a Bushman in crisis: they were being abused by their husband, their house was burning down, they needed to get to the clinic to give birth. Nan got a cat to control the rats and snakes around her hut and left it in the care of two young men while she went home for a week's break. When she returned, one of them was wearing her cat as a headdress. '*Ag* sorry, Nannies, we were hungry!' was their excuse.

There are some good-hearted folk who have run for the hills after spending time in Andriesvale, vowing that they never want to see another Bushman for as long as they live. No doubt the Khomani feel similarly about us outsiders at times. But seldom do foreigners escape being bewitched by these intriguing, eccentric individualists. 'Every person that has stayed there has gone through a process of healing and moved to a higher level of being through that experience,' Nan told me. 'In the beginning I thought I was there for them, and then I realised I would never, in any other place, have learned the soul lessons that I learned there,' she said. 'Why?' I asked. 'Because the exchanges are so unmasked, uncovered, so naked to the bone, to the marrow there's no way you are left in any doubt about what you had to learn. It just slapped you in the face: to love, to really love people, unconditionally. And that wasn't so difficult because I could see their souls. And their souls are pure.'

Claire Barry is another volunteer who has worked for years for the Khomani's betterment. She has a programme called 'Keep Kids in School', in which donors get involved in the education and welfare of a few children at boarding school, making sure they have the books, clothing, pocket money and support that goes some way towards them achieving good marks, and preventing them from being taunted by their coloured classmates. I asked Claire whether she felt she was part of a human circus. 'It was like falling in love,' she said. 'I think it's the very ancient quality which underlines people. It's the acceptance of everybody, in a way, besides all the warring and people's jealousies of each other.'

We chatted about the state of mind that results from long-term abuse of poor-quality alcohol and dagga. 'Every drug has its own personality, and alcohol tends to lead people to violence,' Claire believes. 'And there is enough research to prove that routine use of dagga has its own set of demons. People are quite psychotic in the way that they change all the time. One minute it's this and the next it's that, and then there's that convoluted, weird way of thinking that doesn't follow any logic and doesn't come to any conclusion.'

The primary reason for substance abuse among the Khomani is certainly psychological trauma and escapism from it, but there are people who believe that drinking also provides the Bushmen with a kind of dumbed-down experience of being in trance. The slow demise of the clan's culture was marked by several significant body blows and the loss of the trance dance was the most devastating. The ability to heal by this means is a gift to which many Bushmen aspire but few are given. It is an altered state of consciousness that is induced by rhythmical clapping and singing by people around the fire, and, when reached, the healer can diagnose a patient's sickness and draw it out of their body by laying his or her hands on their head. Nowadays the Bushmen can buy a pale imitation of that glorious sensation with 2 litres of Gordonia 'special' wine at a price of R9.

Ironically, the Kruipers' greatest skills have fuelled their substance abuse. Throughout their lives, all of them, particularly Dawid, have been much sought after for photographs, films, documentaries and advertisements, not only because of their quintessentially Bushman looks but because they are very talented actors. With the slightest prompting, Buks knows exactly what hackneyed 'hunter' pose to adopt for the lens, staring into the distance as if he has spotted his quarry, his hands tense and expectant on his bow string. It is a common misconception that Dawid starred in Jamie Uys' very famous film *The Gods Must Be Crazy*. He did not, although he did have a part in its sequel and he has many other good films on his credit list. In one of them Dawid had only one line, which he liked repeating for comic effect. 'I had to go over to a white lady, take her in my arms and say, "Darrrlink, I luff you!"'

To this day both national and international crews arrive at Witdraai almost on a monthly basis. Some exploit and underpay for the Khomani's services and most of them pay cash, resulting in the Bushmen having a great deal of money to blow on booze and luxuries for a short time, before it runs out and then they are back to square one. On one occasion they cleared the Molopo Lodge Bottle Store of every brand of liquor on sale. On another, the recipient of movie wages set fire to thousands of rand rather than continue seeing it wreak havoc in the community.

Underlying a lot of the substance abuse at Andriesvale, however, is pure boredom. Long gone is the physical outlet of hunting and gathering. There is employment in the area for a mere handful of people so the vast majority wake up every morning to another day of sitting on a dune, contemplating their miserable existence. I remembered another piece of Richard's advice: 'Suspend all judgement when you come into this community. They have suffered more than you could possibly imagine.'

They also know exactly how to find each other's bruises. The

Bushmen may live in an extended family that is generally loving and supportive, but because they have known each other virtually since birth they know precisely how to irritate and hurt each other, and they frequently vent their anger or frustration with their treatment by outsiders on one another. A well-targeted comment around the fire can incite a violent fight within a split second and it is terrifying for participants and onlookers alike.

Like Bushmen throughout the subcontinent, the Khomani's suffering goes back so far that its psychological hallmark must be branded on the strands of their DNA. For four centuries they have known constant persecution, and from all peoples. The first 'newcomers' to South Africa were Khoekhoe sheep-and-cattle herders – once pejoratively labelled 'Hottentot' – who migrated here from Namibia or Botswana roughly 2 500 years ago. They settled initially on the coast and near rivers and eventually arrived in Gordonia – or Siyanda, as this area of the Northern Cape is now known – about 800 years ago. The Khoe languages are characterised by 'clicks' – like those of the Bushmen – and relations between the two groups were generally cordial, in part because there was still plenty of land to go around and the Bushmen could retreat to less hospitable areas when tensions arose.

The real trouble started with the arrival of Nguni and Sotho agro-pastoralists, who met the Bushmen with a set of completely foreign attitudes and habits. These people were herders, like the Khoekhoe, but they also grew crops, had social hierarchies and settled in one place for years at a time. How strange it must have seemed to the Bushmen that a society was not egalitarian, like theirs. How curious they must have thought it that a man should have to till before he could eat, and that an animal – or land – could be owned and tamed.

And of course once people have staked out and claimed territory, they need to defend it, so relations between some farming groups and the Bushmen degenerated into war, displacement and sometimes slavery. Other groups, such as the Xhosa, enjoyed better relations with the Bushmen and intermarried with them to the point where Bushman culture was subsumed into theirs and survives today only in the clicks of their language and some of their spiritual practices such as rainmaking.

This period of their traumatic history is keenly felt by the Khomani and affects their relationship with black Africans to this day. Richard Gordon, a FOKS, who works for Wilderness Leadership School and takes people walking with the Bushmen in the Contract Park, remembers a moving encounter between Toppie and a visitor in 2009. Toppie had told Richard some time beforehand that he had had a dream that a Zulu would one day come into his life and that they would be able to dance together to heal the pain of the past. When he saw Sipiwe he stopped in his tracks for several moments before walking on without comment. But that night for the first and last time ever, Richard saw the Kruipers dance spontaneously – a healing, joyous and powerful dance in which Zulu and Bushman united in forgiveness and tolerance.

When the Dutch colonists arrived in the mid-1600s, followed by the English, unrelenting disaster befell the Bushmen, and from then on they were regarded as little more than animals, vermin and anatomical curiosities. Virulent European diseases such as smallpox wiped out whole communities and dozens of 'Bush People' were shipped off to Europe for display in circuses and fairgrounds. *The Times* of London reported on an exhibition of these 'sullen, silent and savage aborigines' in Piccadilly in May 1847: 'Nothing … is more curious than this stunted family of African Dwarfs. In appearance they are little above the monkey tribe, and scarcely better than the mere brutes of the field.'

Back home, the 'brutes' were putting up the best resistance to foreign occupation that they could muster, armed only with bows, arrows and hit-and-run tactics. From about 1700, disaffected and land-hungry trekboers started moving out of the Cape in search of grazing for their herds and freedom from the restrictive laws of the Dutch colony. As they moved northwards, they commandeered waterholes and shot out game that the Bushmen relied upon for their survival. The trekkers' livestock trampled on their food and medicine plants and overgrazed their plains and valleys. Militias and posses of farmers rooted out Bushmen with such ruthless efficiency that their activities can only be regarded as genocidal.

Decades of running battles ensued, with the Bushmen putting up the kind of passionate opposition that had not been expected from these 'Stone Age people' and they gained renown as warriors who would fight to the death rather than face capture. They set fire to farmhouses and crops, raided cattle, shot and sometimes tortured the trekboers before retreating into the mountains or vleis where their pursuers' horses could not follow them. More often than not, however, they were defeated by the enemy's superior firepower, and their women and children were taken away for a lifetime of slavery in the kitchens and fields of the victors and as concubines in their bedrooms. Now the Bushmen had been expelled from even the drier parts of the country – such as the Northern Cape – to which they had retreated during the Nguni and Sotho incursions.

When the British took over governance of the Cape from the Dutch at the end of the eighteenth century, Bushman policy changed from one of annihilation to assimilation. The view now was that the 'little people' should be introduced to the wonders of Western civilisation by missionaries and that a new breed of farmer should give them cattle and goats and encourage them to forgo their wanderings. The government even declared a reserve for the Bushmen, bordering the Orange River in the far north of the Northern Cape, where they could live in peace. That did not last long because the herders continually defied laws that forbade their incursions into the Bushmen's territory. Then it was discovered that merino sheep could thrive in the area's dry and scrubby conditions, so now the foreigners were definitely there to stay.

The Khomani's ancestors retreated into even drier parts of the 'Great Thirst', the largest expanse of sand on the planet, the semi-desert called the Kalahari. Its extreme heat and aridity would provide some defence against the land grabbers, they hoped, for this was no place to grow crops or foster herds. The Bushmen began to acquire the skills and knowledge that enabled them to survive in this most inhospitable of places where surface water was rare, there were fewer edible plants and fruit-bearing trees and, in the driest time of the year, their prey animals would migrate. Here the foreign invaders could be avoided by moving in small, mobile groups.

But trouble came to find them in Gordonia with the arrival in Rietfontein of the Basters in the 1860s. Those Bushmen who did not stay and work for the new settlers moved off to areas that were still impenetrable to the herders.

Moving around in the late nineteenth century became increasingly dangerous as the region was destabilised. Not long after Germany occupied South-West Africa in 1884, it began a systematic genocide against the indigenous peoples of that country. Eighty per cent of the Herero were slaughtered, along with 50 per cent of the Nama. It is not clear how many Bushmen died, but those who were not killed were displaced, and their horror at the depravity and violence they witnessed is unimaginable. The Khomani, along with other Bushman clans, fled. But safe nooks in which to hide from these brutal colonisers became fewer and fewer.

In the early 1900s, relations between Britain and Germany deteriorated rapidly and when the First World War broke out in 1914, its tentacles spread throughout all the colonies of the two nations. Several clashes between them took place in the Kalahari, and the local people either fled or hid.

After the First World War, farmers, hunters and traders arrived and brought famine to the Bushmen by over-hunting the local game. They also hunted the Bushmen – legally and with permits – until 1927 in South Africa and in neighbouring Namibia until 1937. In fact, hunting Bushmen became something of a jolly Sunday afternoon sport and some farmers were alleged to have strings of Bushman ears hanging over their hearths, taken as mementoes of the days' outings. One settler who took much more than ears was George St Leger Gordon Lennox – alias, Scotty Smith – a renegade trader in the Northern Cape who had a hugely successful business exporting Bushman skeletons and body parts to the museums and laboratories of South Africa and Europe. Smith's exploits are described in a riveting book by Martin Legassick and Ciraj Rassool called *Skeletons in the Cupboard: South African Museums and the Trade in Human Remains*. The authors show how mistaken it is to view Smith as merely a swaggering, somewhat admirable, Robin Hood-type, as so many sources do. They write of how Smith found his 'specimens' by attending Bushman funerals then returning later to steal the bodies and that there were also rumours that when demand for bodies exceeded supply, Scotty would shoot his victims. I trawled through Lawrence Green's notes, letters and articles to find out whether this was in fact the case. It is a private collection that has been meticulously preserved by Joan Yates-Benyon, and a 1957 letter sent to Green by Scotty Smith's close friend Stuart Smith says: 'As for the bushmen skellitons [*sic*], I [Scotty Smith] had shot and buried hundreds of them when living at Luitlantspan and so it was no trouble to dig them up again.' It is fitting but somewhat macabre that Smith's farm, Scotty's Fort, is one of the farms that the Khomani won in the land claim, where Petrus Vaalbooi and some of his family now live. At the time of writing this book, efforts were underway to have Scotty's victims' bodies returned to South Africa for burial.

The big squeeze for the Bushmen just kept on coming in Gordonia. The Park was declared in 1931, and, at the same time, 25 farms next to the KGNP were proclaimed the Mier Coloured Settlement Area, a communal reserve set aside exclusively for the coloureds, some of whom were descended from the Basters and were already living there, others who migrated to the area in the years to come. Small settlements grew, and, in 1979, the apartheid government sold off units of land in Mier that were fenced into livestock camps, making traversing it difficult for the Bushmen. 'It kills my soul,' Dawid's father, Regopstaan, said of that time. 'I walked all over there, but now if a Baster sees a Bushman's tracks he calls the police. Everything is closed now: I have no land, no water, no meat.'

By the 1950s borehole technology had advanced sufficiently to enable the plumbing of even deeper water reservoirs, so the farming of animals such as cattle became more viable and widespread, and increasing numbers of white farmers moved into the Kalahari.

The Bushmen's hideaway was now fully occupied, and the years that lay ahead of them would be characterised by continued exploitation and degradation. By the 1970s it was estimated that fewer than 30 'pure' Bushmen were left in South Africa – almost all of them Khomani. About a century beforehand, a /Xam Bushman had described the experience of being wrenched from the land of his birth, spirit, succour and memory in a song called 'Song of the Broken String':

> *Because of a people,*
> *Because of others, other people*
> *Who came breaking the string for me,*
> *The earth is not the earth,*
> *This place is a place now changed for me.*
> ...
> *Because the string is broken,*
> *The country feels as if it lay*
> *Empty before me,*
> *Our country seems as if it lay*
> *Both empty before me,*
> *And dead before me.*
> ...
> *This earth, my place is the place*
> *Of something – a thing broken –*
> *That does not stop sounding,*
> *Breaking within me.*

For the Khomani, the string had now been well and truly broken. What they had suffered in the preceding centuries was not only physical annihilation but psychological subjugation, too. For a long time hence they would see themselves as ugly, stupid, backward and well deserving of being on the lowest rung of South Africa's human hierarchy.

Craig Foster is well acquainted with the deep psychic pain that most of the Bushmen carry and attributes it also to the extremely fast pace at which the Bushmen have had to leap-frog periods of human 'development' to which the rest of us have adjusted over thousands of years. In no more than a few centuries they have been wrenched from the peaceful, independent world of the hunter-gatherer through pastoralism, agrarianism, industrialisation, and now the era of technology.

Making allowances for people's personal narrative and psychological map is difficult at the best of times, but I knew that if we were to complete this expedition successfully I would have to find a different way of managing myself and the Kruipers. Our first week in the Kalahari had been a useful look-see, a chance for us all to weigh each other up and fine-tune our interpersonal tactics. I had no doubt that the Bushmen's intuition and insight were far superior to mine and that they had got my measure within a couple of days. Now I had to temper the attitudes I have as the product of a stable, relatively affluent, educated family. I needed to limit my expectations, wash the scales from my eyes and find a balance between compassion and firmness. Above all, I had to humble myself before the deep trauma and self-sabotage that saturates every action and decision of the family I was trying so hard to help. I had to try to understand what Dawid described to me long beforehand as the Bushman's capacity to 'dig a hole and jump into it'.

By the time we left again I had my tongue under control and was armed with quiet resolution and my succour in times of stress: a carton of cigarettes.

CHAPTER 7

Standing Up Straight

Our departure date for Part 2 of the journey was Friday the 13th and the day lived up fully to its superstitious reputation of causing mishap and mayhem. When we arrived at Dawid's hut he could hardly greet us. His older daughter, Oulet, looked daggers at me, and when the rest of the family emerged from their shacks no one was packed and no one would get onto the vehicle. Eventually the old man broke his silence with a list of reasons why he could not go back into the Park: 'I need to collect my pension, my legs are sore, I've got a legal case pending, I need to phone my agent …'

I smoked and seethed while Phillipa tried to broker a deal on the phone. He wanted this trip, she reminded him, I had bust a gut and my overdraft to make it happen, so what was the problem? They had no *twak*, he said – *twak* being tobacco, as opposed to *Boesman's twak*, which is dagga. 'But we agreed that you'd get it!' I fumed. But he would not budge, so I agreed to a compromise – I would buy the *twak* and take it off their salaries at the end of the trip. Now, could we please get going because we had a long way to go?

The issue was more than just a shortage of tobacco, of course. Dawid had once again been subjected to the twaddle of the naysayers in his community who had told him that he should not carry on with the trip. A lot of this was motivated by pure jealousy because Dawid had not chosen them to join the expedition. I had

86

decided to put a large chunk of the proceeds from this book into a trust for the Kruiper family's heritage preservation. Some of the family felt excluded and were trying their damnedest to scupper my efforts. But Phillipa's persuasion eventually worked, Dawid rose to his feet and said, 'Okay, let's go.'

It was late morning and our destination was a full six or seven hours away so I tried to hustle everyone onto the vehicles. It was like trying to catch a feather in a gale, but eventually we headed out, Dawid clinging to a huge roll of newsprint paper that I had bought the family so that they did not suck black ink into their lungs along with their *twak*. Our destination was one of the Park's major tourist camps, Nossob, which is named after the dry riverbed on which it is situated. We reached it after navigating a deeply corrugated road that curls up and down the dunes like a lazy roller coaster, until the terrain suddenly opens up to reveal the beautiful tree savanna and grassy plains that are characteristic of the northern KTP. It is different country from what we had seen in the dummy, not nearly as dry and forbidding, and around every corner were vast herds of grazing springbok, wildebeest and gemsbok, so Lilliputian by comparison with their surroundings that they looked like plastic animals scattered in a sandpit. The Kruipers' silhouetted heads turned this way and that on the back of the truck as they pointed out one natural wonder after another to each other.

Park management had allocated us a site on the landing strip outside the camp so that we would be away from the noise of their visitors and the temptation of the liquor on sale at the shop. But this meant we would be outside the fence and without its protection against a pride of lions resident in the area. We made camp, ate and collapsed into our tents. I gazed through my gauze window at a bright near-full moon and made a wish that we would all be restored by the extraordinary beauty around us. 'Please don't let me down, Dawid, you old bugger!'

While I slept, two jackals played on the runway about 10 metres from my tent. The next morning Willem and Buks showed us their busy little tracks and reconstructed the story of what they had been up to. 'You see, Mama, they had a lot of fun chasing each other, but here is where they saw us and ran away,' Buks gestured at the sand, and I marvelled again at the skill that enabled him to interpret what for me were just chaotic drags and splodges. Big Six member, Vetpiet could even glean an animal's vocalisations from its spoor and Professor Anne Rase had seen him do it. Anne is a biologist and became one of Vetpiet's closest friends during the years she researched meerkats and invertebrates in the KTP. She taught him about insect tracks, he schooled her in mammal spoor and they had set each other little tests out on the dunes. One day Anne was asked to reconstruct the story of a steenbok and her lamb for her Bushman teacher. 'This is where the lamb tried to drink from its mother,' Anne told Vetpiet. 'It tried again here but both times she kept on walking.' Cracked that one! she thought, as she turned to him in triumph. But all he said was, 'You must look again. Look carefully now, you've missed something.' After she failed to find the information that the master was hinting at, Vetpiet said: 'Look, here is where she stretched her neck and called her baby.' And there, in the prints of the steenbok's front toes was the faintest increase in the depth of the track, showing how her torso lowered into the sand as she called.

Dawid was not well after our journey to Nossob so we decided to rest that day and Sue and I used the time to sort out the stores we had carted during our week's break and left in the camp's workshop. We had joked about running the second phase of the expedition like two female guards in a Nazi concentration camp but were already like kittens in the hands of our amusing travel companions. Not that we were without renewed tests of our patience, mind you. A couple of the Kruipers were mildly drunk that evening and the long meeting we had to sort out timetable issues was hijacked by the Bushmen's concerns about their stipends. Would they be paid on days when we did not do any work, when would they get the balance of their money, and so on. I went to bed mildly miffed that the precious heritage work we were here to do seemed to be less important to them than their salaries.

By nightfall the next day, however, my mood was entirely different and I recorded an end-of-day diary entry that went thus: 'It's Sunday and all I've got to say is, fuck, these people take you to the brink, you know. They've taken me to the absolute brink and this morning the gems started to arrive again. Suddenly this project appears to be working.' Perhaps it was no coincidence that the moon was now a full, brilliant ball in the sky, moving over the Kalahari bush like a trophy for my staying power.

The gems involved the story of another of Dawid's ancestors, his mother's brother, Agerob Bladbeen. In the veld behind the tourist camp was the camel thorn tree under which Agerob had lived and worked, but all that remained of his presence there were a few small pieces of coal from his fire and the large stone with which he stretched the skins of buck he hunted. Toppie pressed his hands to the stone and then smeared his chest, drawing in the spirit of another hero from his past. Buks picked up some charcoal and proudly handed it to Dawid to show the camera. Our interview with Dawid was interrupted for a tape change and I watched as Dawid marked the place where he had been standing before walking away for a smoke. 'Positions please!' he called to everyone when Karl was ready to resume shooting. 'Are you sure about your lighting?' Dawid asked Richard. 'The sun has gone behind a cloud now.' I giggled quietly to myself about the old man's familiarity with the demands of film-making after so many years of working with movie and advert producers.

Grossie tells of an incident when Dawid and Vetpiet were being filmed on a particularly hot day in the Kalahari. Dawid glared with exasperation at the film-maker, Andy Spitz, and instructed her: 'Only one *donnerse* [damned] take, so get it right!'

The Bladbeens were fellow Khoekhoegowab-speaking Bushmen who shared this territory with clans like the Kruipers for many decades, so it was inevitable that at some point they would intermarry, and they have continued to do so. Both Dawid and Buks were married to Bladbeens. Like Makai, Agerob was a brilliant veld doctor and hunter, but he is remembered principally for his love of solitude, his bravery and cheek. I am told that he could catch leopards with his bare hands and would chase them off their kills and steal the meat. Agerob was extremely short, even shorter than Buks, but a man of great bearing and athleticism. Nat Farbman's photographs for *Life* magazine in 1947 show him to be small, certainly, but muscular. His face is square and smiling and his aura, proud. One of the shots captures him poised to throw an assegai at a gemsbok that his dogs are keeping at bay. He looks like an Olympic javelin thrower, all tensed muscles, gleaming skin and keen concentration.

Dawid and Buks served something of an apprenticeship with Agerob when they were teenagers, and he was not averse to beating his nephews if they were not up long before dawn to go and find his donkeys. It was then that the boys learned to control their fear and to use intuition as their ears and eyes on the dark, cold dunes, navigating their way back to the tree by means of the stars. 'It doesn't help to be scared.' Dawid told us. 'Nature and a Bushman are one, so why would you be scared of it?'

It was this oneness that developed the Bushmen's extraordinary intuition and when it is honed they truly do know when something is about to happen, or is happening beyond sight or sound. Jan van der Westhuizen once had a stomach bug that was so severe he stayed out in the veld for about seven days. Eventually he consulted Agerob who told him, 'You have made a girl pregnant and she's going to have a boy and you've now taken on her pains.' When Jan returned to camp the girl confirmed that she was with child, and, months later, gave birth to a boy. Richard Gordon recounts a story of sitting with Dawid around the fire one very dark night when the veld was as quiet as a tomb. The old man was recounting one of his very long stories when he suddenly stopped mid-sentence and said, 'There comes the lion. Don't worry, he's just coming to drink some water. I'll show you in the morning.' Five minutes later, plovers screeched their alarm at the lion's presence. Dawid had since had cataract operations, but at the time his sight was so poor he could not see further than a few metres. The next morning he took Richard's arm and walked him through the lion's activities, reconstructing what had transpired. 'Here is where he came down the dune. Here is where he drank. Smell this bush, this is where the lion pissed.' What Oupa had told Richard the night before was substantiated by the tracks, each and every time.

This highly developed intuition and oneness with nature made the Khomani elders completely fearless in the veld. 'It's only when I came amongst people in the city that the fear came,' said Jan. If his grandsons are to be believed, fear was definitely not part of Agerob's vocabulary either. When he was missing his wife or wanted to buy a *dop* (drink) at Twee Rivieren, some 140 kilometres south as the crow flies, he would simply set off and run through the night, either until he got there or was caught by the Le Riches and returned to Nossob, where he was employed. In the early decades of the KGNP, Joep le Riche was allowed to keep sheep in the Park because, being so far from shops, there was a shortage of fresh meat. It was Agerob's job to look after the herd at Nossob and his kraal was around the tree under which we were standing. When Elias took over the reins from his father, the sheep stayed, according to Elias because he had permission from the Botswana authorities to keep the herd on that side of the border as it was not yet declared a national park.

In those days the Twee Rivieren office would radio ahead with tourists' bookings at Nossob camp, so Elias always knew when they were coming. Agerob would then shepherd the animals across the riverbed and hide them until the tourists had gone. For modern urbanites it is hard to imagine the bravery it took to defend sheep from lions and hyenas with nothing but a bow, arrows and an assegai. Night after night, Buks recalls, the men would light fires on each corner of the huddled sheep and patrol the kraal, throwing burning logs at the lions to keep them away. And if the donkeys were tied up it was often them who fell victim to the lions and were dragged away for the pride's supper.

The strength of character required for this dangerous job was also one of Dawid's father's prominent traits, and he was given the

Afrikaans nickname 'Regopstaan' (Standing Up Straight). Given that Kruiper means 'Crawler' in English, the translation of his full name is therefore somewhat absurd: 'Standing Up Straight Crawler'. Regopstaan's stepdaughter, Lena Witbooi, who later married one of the Big Six trackers, Jakob Malgas, remembers him hitting a lion with a knobkerrie. The animal was so enraged that it jumped into the kraal and broke the backs of a dozen sheep.

Regopstaan, like his father Makai, is remembered by the Khomani with a fondness that borders on adoration. 'I never met anybody who knew Regopstaan who didn't speak in reverential terms about what kind of man this was,' Nigel Crawhall told me. 'A man of bravery, of dignity, of honesty, an impeccable man.' As we have come to expect from the Kruipers, Regopstaan had great veld skills and healing abilities but he was also a gifted water diviner and located the first well at Twee Rivieren for Joep le Riche, a feat he performed blindfolded. He was also an athlete, it seems, and would run 40 kilometres every morning to fetch Joep's newspaper. Regopstaan's photographs show him as having had a face that is arguably even more kindly than Makai's but it is careworn, perhaps because it was in Regopstaan's lifetime that the Kruipers began trying to straddle the vastly different worlds of their past and future. By all accounts, Regopstaan led them through these confusing times with sensitivity and wisdom. He did not drink or smoke, did not keep company with rowdy people and was slow to anger, unless his children lied to him. He often used his pension to buy food for Khomani families who were struggling to survive after their eviction from the Park, and it seems he had a special affinity with children.

Lena relates a touching incident when she was walking through the veld with Regopstaan in deep winter. The sand was covered in ice and she soon accumulated a thick layer of it on the bottom of her feet and was slipping and tumbling down the dunes. When they got to the shop, her stepfather bought her a pair of shiny, black shoes, which so embarrassed her that she refused to try them on. Regopstaan saved Lena's life several times, using his superb tracking skills to find the little girl when she had run away from his stock-post to visit friends at other kraals, sometimes a day or more after she had disappeared. She remembers being half dead from thirst on a particularly hot day and him digging into the cool layer of the sand and burying her there until he could return with some water.

Regopstaan's kraal was on a high red dune west of Houmoed (Keep the Faith) Pan and it was there that Dawid was born. But this area was very definitely within the boundaries of the Park and although Elias le Riche denies having kept sheep there in what would quite likely have been a contravention of both Park rules and responsible environmental management, the Bushmen say otherwise. They maintain that the Le Riches' sheep eventually numbered several hundred and that they were instructed to hide the sheep when National Parks big bosses visited the Park during the 1970s and 80s. 'If you hear a plane you must fall flat on the ground so that they don't see you,' Elias instructed them, so that he could claim that the sheep were untended and had wandered into the Park of their own volition.

Sheep farming in a national park. Only here could people get away with that kind of illicit activity because it is so far from head office, I thought as Dawid told us his story. It appears that the Le Riches' sheep were an open secret among the Park's staff, but whether or not the authorities sanctioned these activities I have not been able to establish. When Rocco Knobel retired as head of National Parks, however, I am told that huge trucks arrived to drive the Le Riches' sheep out of the Park, which suggests that the herds had had his tacit approval.

'But what about the tourists?' I asked Dawid. 'Surely they could see the sheep's spoor?' 'Tourists know nothing about animals,' he said with mild disdain. 'They don't know the difference between springbok and sheep tracks.'

The concept of owning animals was foreign to Bushmen of old, and I asked Dawid for his views on this issue, given that so many of the Khomani are moving into stock farming. By way of an answer, he gave us this declaration about the bounty of the natural world and his people's place within it: 'Like the farmer that has dogs and cats, the Bushmen also has everything. If he wants pigs, he has bush pigs. If you talk about cows, our cows are the eland. That is a cow that's a bit bigger. He's got everything that a pastoralist has … The first law is in heaven and then there's the Bushman. If you go according to the animal history, the Bushman is second after the Lord. But the Bushman gets put back second, third, sixth, tenth. So if they can just fix that little matter and give the Bushman recognition … then the land will have rain like there is now and there'll be peace again. His heart will not be sore and even the pastoralist will be happy because his sheep will have rain and he can market them.'

If we could just fix that little matter. I swallowed hard.

I saw Brenda sitting on the ground near Agerob's tree writing something while her daughter Mefi hung on her shoulders and watched. On a small, white stone she had written the words 'Oupa Agerob Bladbeen' and looked up at me to say how glad she was to see where her grandfather had lived and worked. Because of the forced removals, she had never known about this place and was clearly deeply moved by being there. 'I can go and show my other sister who is at home and tell her where I picked it up,' she said, turning the stone over in her hand. She explained to me that Bladbeen is a translation of |Galakab, the Khoekhoegowab surname of this family. It means shoulder blade and is a reference to the puberty rituals that a young girl went through in the old times. She was secluded in a hut for two weeks when 'she gets her health every month', as Dawid put it, and during that time was only allowed to eat meat from the front of an animal. Quite why the family was named after this ritual no one could remember.

The two new cyber trackers, Isak, and Toppie's son, Klein Dawid, diligently marked the humble heritage site on their GPS devices and talked wistfully about how Agerob's generation had been so free and how impossible it would be to retrieve those days and ways. Like the other two youngsters who had joined us on the first leg of the journey, they are very aware of the dangers of excessive drinking because of the domestic abuse they have witnessed since childhood. 'I've got big hopes that we won't be like we were in the past,' said Isak. 'We are a few young people who sit around the fire and say that we don't want to live like our parents. We decided this is it, no further. We are not going to let the culture die … so that the Khomani people do not become extinct.'

I asked Buks if he wanted to take any medicinal plants from Agerob's kraal before we moved on. 'No, Mama, there have been too many people here and their shadows have fallen on the plants. If that happens they do not work. Because Nossob is so busy we will not extract here, we will get from places where there are only animals.' Suddenly I understood the curious directions we sometimes took in the veld – it was so that our shadows were behind us and our 'darkness' did not alter the efficacy of the plants they were picking.

The following day we were taken to a small gravesite not far from Agerob's tree. Two of the graves had glass bottles pushed into the sand as makeshift headstones, the third was covered with white calcrete rocks. The family moved past it in procession, each picking up some soil to scatter on the rocks before standing behind Willem in silence. 'This is where my father lies,' he began, 'and for a long time I didn't know where he was buried.'

While it appears that the Le Riches were happy to break some Park rules by farming sheep, they were swift to enforce others. One of these was capturing 'wild' Bushmen, Nama and BaTswana people for poaching. When Dawid and Buks were working in the Park as young adults, they had the unenviable task of tracking and arresting these men, some of whom turned out to be members of their own extended family. 'When I was sworn in and employed by the Park,' Dawid told us, 'I had to swear an oath that I would even catch my mother or father, my daughters and sons for game poaching … It was for the game we did this.'

Richard asked Buks how he felt about doing this: 'In your heart you feel a bit sore, but it's your job. And even if it's your own blood you must do it, because you eat through doing your job as a game ranger.'

Tales about catching trespassers in the Park make for awe-inspiring testimony to the bush skills of both the poachers and the game rangers – 'the Le Riches' blood hounds' – as Jan called them. Buks tells of a Bushman who they were sure was a poacher but who was caught with no weapon and no meat. They went back on his spoor and on one footprint noticed the faintest sign of an irregular movement in his heel. Sure enough, they found his gun in some nearby bushes, the heel print having been a give-away of the force with which he threw the weapon. Sometimes the best poachers became the best anti-poachers after they were caught. One of these was Optel Rooi, another of the Big Six whose first name means 'picked up'. Optel was arrested after many months on his tracks and a three-day chase that has remained legendary in the Park's annals. The trick that enabled him to escape capture for so long was his ability to run along the top two wires of the Park fence, jump down onto a tuft of grass on the other side and disappear into thin air, leaving no trace of where he had gone. Optel was adopted by the Kruipers and became a sought-after guide and ranger in the KTP until he was murdered in 2004 by a local policeman.

It took some time before the KGNP was cleared of people, and those who were caught hunting illegally faced two bleak options: either go to jail or work for Park management, for a few months, a few years and, in some cases, for life. I was told that some of these men never saw their families again because they had illegally crossed the border into Botswana or Namibia and did not have passports to get back. Willem's father, a Damara Nama named Demapanjani, was arrested for poaching in the 1930s. He decided against going to jail and for the rest of his life worked as a 'convict' in the Park. 'He was very obedient,' Willem told us all, 'a sensible person who was very forgiving of the way he was treated.' When Demapanjani was on his deathbed Willem was summoned from the farm he was working on, but his employer refused to allow him to go. The old man died in hospital in Upington and Elias flew him back to Nossob in his private plane to be buried there. Some years later Willem worked as a ranger at the camp, and in all the five years he was there, no one told him that his father was buried less than a kilometre from his house. 'We are the First People but we are still the spare wheel,' Willem added bitterly. 'If it wasn't for our forebears the Park wouldn't be as tame as it is now, or as successful.'

The Bushmen elders are always quick to say that if it was not for the Le Riches the land of their ancestors would not have been protected for their children. The KTP is probably the most difficult of South Africa's national parks to maintain because of its porous international boundaries and unforgiving terrain. Under the Le Riches, the Park's roads, fences, pumps and camps were meticulously maintained, and poaching was kept to a minimum.

The Le Riche men, it seems, were as resilient and tough as the land that produced them. The Bushmen I interviewed all agreed that while Joep and Stoffel were hard men, they were just and kind. Stoffel's right-hand man was a Bushman called Tokolos, or Marthinus Org, and he described his old boss as generous and soft-hearted and thoroughly enjoyed the many years they spent together on patrol. Tokolos is also one of Anna's sons – and therefore one of Makai's grandsons – and another of the Big Six trackers. He, too, has that special prescience or foreknowledge of events. When Nan went to find him for our interview, which I could not pre-arrange because he does not have a phone, he was waiting at his house. 'I sent my son out to look after the sheep today because I had a feeling that a visitor would come and that I should wait here,' he told her.

While the Bushmen still have great respect for Joep and Stoffel le Riche, I am told that they are united in their loathing of Elias, and they bitterly resent the dark deeds that were committed in the course of 'taming' the KGNP. All except the Kruipers, that is, who remain unfailingly grateful and loyal to him, either out of fear or good neighbourliness, as Witdraai borders his farm. I wondered what his white staff thought of Elias and it appears that most were terrified of getting on the wrong side of him. 'The Le Riches were a law unto themselves,' one staff member remembered. 'Their whole aura was that no one else could run the Kalahari … so we must put up with whatever they do.' Anne Rase has a different view. 'You know, Elias wasn't an employer, he was a parent, and a very involved one at that. He was very much loved and respected and when he left that Park fell apart. His people just went, they refused to work for the next person.' I have also been told that Elias was meticulous in his attention to the Bushmen's health, and because he completed all but the final year of his medical degree he would even perform minor operations on them.

The Le Riches' methods of dealing with poachers in the Park differed as much as their personalities did. 'Joep was a good man and when he caught people he would ask them if they were hungry or thirsty so that their fright would lessen a bit. But Elias would come with a big bang, make noise and use violence and all of that,' Dawid told me.

Jan van der Westhuizen tells a story of Bushmen who had stolen some horses and fled through the Park from some white Namibian farmers, who had impregnated all three of the family's daughters. When Elias and his trackers eventually caught up with the group after three days of hard tracking, all hell broke loose as the Bushmen tried to escape capture. Their blind grandparents cowered in the sand as two of the women fled through thorn bushes that cut them to shreds. Another started running in a different direction with the children. Seeing their chance to get away, three panic-stricken young men mounted their horses, hoisted their grandmother onto another and rode away. When granny slowed the men down, they cut her horse's reins and left her to her fate. The chase was long and hard. One Bushman and two horses died of exhaustion, another was captured along with one of the women whose feet were so badly cut that she could go no further. When the anti-poaching patrol returned to where they had found the Bushmen, all that was left of one of the children was his little skin waistband. He had run in a different direction to the rest and straight into a pride of lions.

Jan was utterly horrified by what he had witnessed, and when Elias wanted to take the young Bushmen in for punishment he begged him not to because their grandparents were blind and needed to be cared for. His pleas fell on deaf ears. The young men were arrested and worked as 'convicts' at Nossob for three years. In their camp under the stars that night, Jan left Elias in no doubt about what he thought of his conduct. 'You're a two-faced bastard,' he ranted, 'look at this trunk here. We have everything we need: coffee, sugar, tinned meat. We have jackets when we're cold and soft bedding. How can you do this to people who have nothing? How can you kill this kind of life?' The two men went to bed and at 4 o'clock in the morning Elias woke Jan up. He had tears in his eyes and said he had had a dream in which his forefathers came to him and told him that what he was doing was not right. 'What have I done with my life?' he sobbed to Jan. Sadly, in the years to come I am told that Elias' conduct towards the 'wild' Bushmen remained the same.

Jan is one of several Khomani who believe that Elias was 'a monster'. 'He was really terrible, but you must forgive him because his father spoiled him,' Jan said. 'We brown people suffered under him. He treated us like slaves,' remembers Tokolos. The Bushmen were subjected to beatings and petty cruelties, and Dawid's step-sister, Lena, recalls an extremely hot day in the veld when Elias made a Bushman kneel down and then sat on his shoulders so that he did not have to sit on the hot sand. 'We others had to stand around him and make shade for him,' she told me.

In the grass alongside the runway that afternoon I had a long chat to Tina, Brenda and Galai about their lives in Andriesvale and the violence that the Khomani women endure. 'We don't walk a straight path like our forefathers, we are out of line,' was Brenda's contribution. She talked about how difficult it is to live with the see-saw syndrome of alcohol abuse, as some women in the community do, being with men who beat them when they are drunk and cannot remember doing so when they are sober. And then there is the persistent threat of white hunters and farmers who trawl the ghetto for some young brown flesh. The brother of the manager of the Molopo Lodge has a child by one of his Bushman waitresses, and another employee had a long-term relationship with a Khomani woman, to whom he at least gave the dignity of public acknowledgement. But when the Khomani come and visit their pals working at the Lodge, or have a dip in the pool on a hot day, they are thrown off the property. Such were the contradictory cross-cultural relations of apartheid South Africa that remain pervasive in the Northern Cape to this day.

I asked Tina why it is important to know how to make porridge from *tsamma* melon pips when nowadays they can just go to the shop and buy flour. 'We don't have money every day and work is scarce,' she replied. 'Our parents taught us not to beg, we had to make a plan. So then we go into the veld and find food.' All three women expressed great delight in being on the trip and wished it could happen more often. It is like a little present in your heart, we agreed, and when times are bad we can think of this journey. But they confessed to feeling 'stressed' by having to work so hard in camp. 'What do you think is the biggest difference between your lives and mine?' I asked them. They giggled and looked down at their laps, but eventually Brenda decided to answer: 'You probably had better opportunities ... and your parents never had to work for other people,' she said. 'Yes,' I agreed, 'but it's also that no man tells me what to do!' They nodded enthusiastically and we all laughed.

When I raised the subject of the Kruipers' female ancestors and asked why they are so neglected in the family's historical lexicon, it was a line of questioning that soon came to a dead end. My concern about the skewed way in which the genders of the family's past are remembered and honoured was clearly not theirs. 'What did your mother and grandmother teach you?' I enquired. 'Any stories or legends?' 'They taught us how to find food and make *tsamma* pap,' was the only answer.

I wish I had talked to them about Dawid's mother, Lys, who was, somewhat unusually, the sister of Makai's wife, Sakas – so father and son married two sisters. Neither did we chat about Dawid's wife, Gais, one of the strongest women that the Khomani have produced. Gais – or Sanna as she was also known – was straight talking, direct and Dawid's anchor until her death in 2006. 'When she smiled it was like the sun was rising,' Nan told me. The Kruipers squabbled, like all married couples, but loved each other deeply, and were always quick to point out when either of them was on the wrong track. Elias encouraged Dawid to marry Gais in church and he used the famous ring for the ceremony. But his courtship of Gais was traditional and ritualistic and her father insisted that Dawid had to kill a leopard and bring him the skin before he would agree to the marriage – which Dawid did, lying in wait for one, ambushing it and clubbing it to death.

Pinpointing Dawid's religious beliefs is difficult and I was left with the impression that, like his forefathers, he drew something from each of the philosophies that crossed his path and suited his purpose. He could be scathing about Christian hypocrisy and piousness, yet married in a Christian church and, like many of the Khomani, believed that the religion's essence tallied with Bushmen's spirituality.

Academics call this melding of different beliefs syncretism. It is quite a common feature in religions and cultures that have been subjugated, and is a means of facilitating coexistence between the conquered and the conquering. One of the Bushmen explained it like this to Nan: 'We didn't know about Jesus, we just knew about love, and when people came and told us about Jesus we realised that this love must be called "Jesus".'

The women and I rose from our seats in the grass and went back to camp where they started cooking supper. I watched the Kruipers chattering around the fire and longed to understand more Afrikaans. 'It's this awful knowledge that three quarters of what goes on there is unknown to me,' I muttered into my recorder. 'I feel awkward going to sit with them because I don't understand enough and they feel inhibited by me. When they have to translate everything the conversation is stilted.' I had enough of the language, however, to gauge something about their relationships with one another and found its tone alarming at times. 'You know it's the kind of frank interaction which one is not really used to when you wear the kind of masks that we wear in town and censor everything we say. Here it's no holds barred.'

I also did not need fluent Afrikaans to notice the improvement that was slowly happening in our camp's atmosphere. I had put all of the Kruipers onto a liver tonic and multivitamins and their faces already looked less pinched and tired. Tensions were beginning to dissipate and I had begun to relax: 'It's taken a long time to get over my impulse, my compulsion to be efficient and speedy and on top of things, which is not to say that things are falling apart but I'm just less harried than I was. And I realise now how good it has been to have the guys here. Richard knows the family well and Karl is quietly dependable and even-keeled.'

As had happened before, however, my contentment would not last long.

Scientific Studies and 'Cultural Curiosities'

uks was waiting for me as I emerged from my tent in the morning. 'Please, Mama, can we have some pills? Me, Toppie, John, everyone, we're all sick.' Maybe they have got food poisoning, I thought, as I opened up my first-aid kit and patients began to line up at Priscilla's mobile clinic. But their complaints differed one from the other and I soon had to abandon my diagnosis. Toppie had a bad chest – I had heard him coughing during the night – Buks had sore kidneys and John could hardly walk from back pain.

The car accident that had so badly injured John, Buks, Dawid and Toppie remains one of the Kruipers' most painfully acute memories. It happened during the phase of their post-eviction lives when Regopstaan was trying to make a living for the family by capitalising on tourists' interest in their ancient culture. In 1987, a tour operator called Lockie Henning came into their lives and he appeared to be a godsend for the beleaguered family.

Lockie invited the Kruipers to move to Kuruman where they would earn money by making movies, performing traditional Bushman songs and dances and selling their crafts. With the proceeds he undertook to buy the family a farm on which they could live out their lives in peace. It all went horribly wrong, and, according to the Kruipers, Lockie reneged on his promises to them.

The family split up to find jobs wherever they could, and some went to work at a similar operation in the Magaliesberg where they had an even worse time of it. There they were allegedly all but imprisoned on the premises and denied the right to mix with local people.

In 1991 another invitation came, this time from a nature reserve in the Cederberg mountains of the Western Cape called Kagga Kamma (Place of the Bushmen). The Kruipers regrouped and about 30 of them took up the offer of limited rights to hunt and gather on the reserve in exchange for entertaining tourists. While performing their old dances and making their old crafts did to some extent preserve some of the Khomani culture that was being swiftly eroded, whether their displays can be labelled anything more than shallow mimicry is debatable. What Kagga Kamma marketed as unique and genuine 'encounters' with unique and genuine members of a fast-disappearing culture was patently false, but, knowing them as I do now, I have no doubt that what the Kruipers presented was informed by their ability to 'read' what their visitors wanted and give it to them. Performing like circus acts, night after night, cannot have been easy, but they became masters at perfecting the illusion that the outside world wanted of them. And at least the visitors' interest fostered some pride in the family's 'Bushmanness'.

Dawid maintained that the Kruipers were not altogether unhappy at Kagga Kamma and at least they were able to live together as a family, unlike other Khomani who were scattered across the Northern Cape. After a while, Kagga Kamma's manager, Michael Diaber, started an informal school on the reserve where children such as Am Am and Galai got a rudimentary education. What the family really struggled with at Kagga Kamma was its terrain and weather. For the first time they experienced bitterly cold rain and snow, so foreign to these desert dwellers. Their 'houses' were little more than pieces of plastic and canvas strung between poles and lamentably inadequate to protect them against the elements.

Not surprisingly, tourists were forbidden from visiting them there and management's promises of proper housing for them never materialised. The region's rocky mountain terrain made tracking extremely difficult, and its animals and plants were foreign, so they relied on Western foods on sale at the local shop. One of the Kruipers' comments has become well known as a rueful encapsulation of their experience on the reserve: 'I went out hunting today and came back with a tin of fish!'

Relationships within the group suffered under these adverse conditions, so far from home and the home people. They fought a great deal and many left when things got too much for them – only to be joined by other Kruipers who were suffering on farms elsewhere. Regopstaan's health started to deteriorate and Dawid took over leadership of the clan. With daily reminders of the mercantile value of Bushman features and culture, he allegedly kept a tight control over who the youngsters married, insisting that their partners had to be Bushmen. Many people have criticised Dawid for deliberately orchestrating the Kruipers' marriages. It was done in order to keep the family's 'Bushmanness' intact and therefore attractive to film-makers, but it is also important to bear in mind that his motivations were a result of a sense of being persecuted, of knowing that they are the last of their kind. The Kruipers, quite understandably, have an 'us-and-them' mentality after centuries of genocide and prejudice, and they understand the imperatives of keeping their genes alive.

Kagga Kamma provided Dawid with his first tests of leadership and a position that was traditionally foreign to the Bushmen. In the past, decisions were made by consensus and no member of a group was allowed to stand out above the rest. As the intermediary between the family and the reserve's management, his authority was constantly challenged by those who felt they were not getting enough out of the deal. Without any real power, the Kruipers opted for go-slows and non-cooperation when they felt aggrieved – techniques with which I had become all too familiar on our expedition.

It was while the family was at Kagga Kamma that Regopstaan made a prediction that has since become famous: 'When the sun goes dark a sick man will come and help us return to our land. And when that happens it will rain and rain and rain in the Kalahari.' The year was 1994, South Africa became free and democratic and one of the first laws the new government passed involved restitution for those who had lost their land under the apartheid regime. The winds of change that were blowing through South Africa swept into the Cederberg and they brought with them a 'sick man', who was introduced to the Kruipers by an ethno-musicologist who was studying their music at the time, Cait Andrews. That man was lawyer Roger Chennells, who was suffering from ME (myalgic encephalomyelitis) at the time and he arrived at the family's shacks on the day of a solar eclipse. Regopstaan grabbed his mouth bow and started singing a song describing how the moment for change had now arrived. With Roger's help he began the long process of claiming back the Khomani's land; his brief to his lawyer: 'We want a place where the sand is soft and clean and the water is sweet.' When Regopstaan's health started to deteriorate, Dawid took over the onerous negotiations.

During the following year, the Kruipers were driven from Kagga Kamma to Andriesvale several times for meetings and the land claim was officially lodged in August 1995. Roger remembers the journeys as being highly entertaining because of the Bushmen's ability to tell stories that would last for hours, and it was on one of these journeys that their lives were tragically altered. While they were filling up with fuel at a petrol station, Dawid noticed that one of the back wheels of the minibus was very hot. He pointed this out but was ignored.

A short while later the tyre exploded and the combi careened down a slope, rolled five times and eventually came to a stop. Toppie's wife, Maria, lay at the side of the road, motionless. He staggered over to her, held the bloody mess that was once her head and wailed: 'Is this you? Is this you?' She was dead, as was her baby in utero. His young daughter had broken her leg. Buks' son, Baliep, was dead. Anna and Gais had broken their hips and Toppie and John had severely damaged their spines. Dawid's legs and head were so badly injured that it took many pins, screws and plates to put him together again. Buks had damaged one of his kidneys, and Oom Segraan, the last of the Khomani's trance dancers, was permanently brain damaged.

So the tragic accident not only claimed lives but severed the last thread connecting the Kruipers with their past as healers and rain-makers. This was the means by which they brought rains, which in turn brought their food, and, as Robert Gordon points out, it was 'one of the most important mechanisms that Bushmen have for coping with the vortex of change that is sweeping them off their feet'.

Since the Kagga Kamma accident, the Khomani have had many more fatal and near-fatal car crashes – so many that a superstitious person would call them cursed. Given that so few of the community drive, it is tragic that they have had so many traumatic experiences on South Africa's roads. And it is also sadly ironic that one of the worst accidents happened when several of them were on their way back from Springbok after an Alcoholics Anonymous meeting.

'Buks is peeing blood,' Richard came to tell me. I put him onto an antibiotic and hoped for the best. Was he feeling well enough to go into the veld? It seemed so, and we set off for a place he wanted to show us. After an hour or so we stopped on the side of a small Park management road and he started his story. The year was 1958 and Buks was a teenager. News came in to Nossob camp that a car had been found deserted in a remote part of the Park. In it was a note from its owner saying: 'No water for the car, no water for myself, no food, following this road. H. Schwabe.'

Petrus Kruiper, Demapanjani, young Buks and the Le Riches set off to find the car and begin tracking Schwabe's hapless spoor.

'Was the car right here?' I asked Buks.

'Yes, Mama, exactly here.'

'But how do you know it wasn't 50 metres further up the road, or down? After all you were only a boy at the time!' I teased him.

'We Bushmen have GPS in our heads,' he replied, 'and our memories are good because we can't write. The car was here, I know for sure.'

Contrary to Hans Schwabe's note, his car radiator still contained water and the rescue team smelled a rat. They set off on his tracks, which were at first strong and confident. Then there were signs that he was stopping often to dig small holes in the sand. Eventually the German's footsteps became erratic and halting, he was dragging his feet and sitting down often. After some 40 kilometres, the trackers made a grisly discovery at the foot of a small camel thorn. Around the tree was the spoor of a pack of hyenas and signs of a struggle. Schwabe's body was mutilated and his left forearm – with a gold watch on it – had been taken by the scavengers. As Anne Rase is wont to say, 'That's why deserts are so addictive – they're black and white. If you do good you'll survive. If you make mistakes you'll die.'

The Bushmen stayed with Schwabe's remains for the night, beating off hyenas that were attracted to the bloody scene, and the next morning Joep returned, said a short prayer and his staff buried what was left of the adventurer. They made a cross of camel thorn branches and placed Schwabe's prospector's hammer, his little tin of Marie biscuits, a few cigarettes and his pill box on the grave. It would be over half a century before Schwabe's family came to visit his burial place and Elias took them there recently.

Schwabe was one of the many dreamers who have been attracted to the Kalahari throughout history in the belief that their fortunes lie beneath its sands. He was looking for diamonds, hence the evidence of prospecting that the trackers found along his route. He was neither the first nor the last of the fortune seekers to come here. Others have searched for the legendary Lost City of the Kalahari, the towering, turreted settlement that had allegedly been discovered in this area by the explorer William Hunt – better known as Farini – in the late 1800s but never seen again. Since the proclamation of the Park there have been at least 30 expeditions mounted to find the Lost City, and they have used everything from donkeys to planes in an effort to locate it. Many of the teams employed Joep le Riche as their guide, although he remained skeptical about the existence of the city, and, like other Kalahari natives, he believed that what Farini had seen was probably an outcrop of calcrete formations, most likely on a farm in the area called Koppies Kraal.

There are many other legends that swirl around this region, stories of gold, of giant, subterranean snakes and tiny, tiny Bushmen who can shape-shift and whose language sounds like the chirping of birds. The legends lie deep within the Khomani's oral history and they have perfected avoidance techniques when outsiders' curiosity gets too close for comfort. In time I learned when to desist and change the subject.

By the time our interview ended Buks was clutching his back and wincing in pain. We called it a day and headed back to camp. John was now unable to sit down and stood at the back of the Cruiser, clutching the canopy bar to lessen the impact of the bumpy road on his spine. I dosed them both and they went to bed before nightfall.

It was Dawid's turn to take us to a historical spot the next day, but Buks and John stayed in camp to rest. We walked to a flat-topped dune not far from Nossob that provided an endless horizon against which Dawid wanted to talk about Bushman law. 'So now,' he began, 'as far as your eyes can see, except for the shepherd's trees and grey camel thorn trees, there are black thorn acacias. In those trees is where Bushmen were punished for breaking the law.'

What slowly unfolded in our conversation were details of the methods by which Bushmen once conserved their resources and kept their families stable. As he spoke of these traditions it occurred to me how useful it would be if we all aspired to their ancient environmental ethic. In essence, the greatest crimes a Bushman could commit involved greed and over-consumption. Never was a hunter allowed to kill an animal in the field and not bring it home to his family. 'If you kill a hare you can eat the head but you must bring the rest back,' he explained. 'You are not born to eat alone while others go hungry. And if a hunter makes the mistake of killing a hare and chucking it away that's big punishment because you are not allowed to waste or squander.' Dawid related an incident in which two Bushmen killed four gemsbok calves and a gemsbok cow and only took their colons and some bones for marrow. Joep le Riche caught them and brought them to Makai and Regopstaan for punishment. The group's decision was that they should be sent to Namibia, never to be seen again.

'But there's another punishment,' Dawid added, 'if [a Bushman] doesn't listen the second time you must take him, throw him in the black thorn and then he must see how he gets out of there.' I shuddered at the thought – the hook-shaped thorns could rip a man to shreds.

'Even today [as traditional leader of the Khomani] they hit me if I'm doing wrong, because that is the Bushman law,' Dawid added. Indeed, to this day when traditional members of the Khomani clan transgress, there are cries for them to be stripped and hauled through the *haakbos* or the *!nooibos*, the equally lethal candle-pod thorn. Nan was horrified when they first suggested this in her company and pointed out to them that they could not be in tatters when they greeted tourists. 'Can't we have something else?' she asked. 'Okay, take away his salary,' was the answer, '[lack of] money also hurts them.'

I asked Dawid for his thoughts on white hunters and their rules, or lack thereof. 'Those men shoot everything, but a Bushman is not like that. He'll just take that little one and will go and share. You know these machine guns, it's the gun of the white man, he fills it with 20 bullets and there are lots of buck standing there and there are no guides or trackers with him. He pulls the trigger and *da da da da*,' he imitated the sound. 'How many are killed through the stomach? And he only goes to the ones that are dead. He doesn't follow the tracks of those that are wounded. And that's why any hunter that comes here must ask us for trackers. We have real trackers that could find that wounded buck. A Bushman looks very carefully and is aware. A Bushman will look at the track and will know which one is wounded, even if there's no blood in the track. This is how a Bushman tracks and the standards are so high.'

And what about modern hunting's habit of taking the biggest and best trophy animals, I asked him. 'A Bushman is just happy for what he gets. I wouldn't want the biggest just because it's the biggest, but because it means that I have more meat and can survive on it for perhaps fourteen days.'

It was now mid-afternoon and I felt limp and sweaty. We walked down to the truck but just before boarding it Dawid called me. Hang on, we need to go and sort out something in a meeting, Sue translated. Brenda's eyes rolled and she muttered, 'Oh God, we've had all this before.' I knew then we had hit another hiccup and prepared myself for the worst. Sure enough it was yet another ruse to try to get back to Andriesvale the next day. The Kruipers wanted to vote in case they were prejudiced by the local municipality for not doing so.

Yeah, I thought cynically, and you would get the meat and booze that the ANC has laid on to persuade you how to vote. And then I will have all the mayhem again of trying to get you back here, hangover and all. I listened to Dawid with my head bowed and when he was finished, took off my sunglasses so that he could see the cold anger in my eyes.

'Okay, guys, here is my line in the sand,' I said, dragging my finger through the sand for extra effect. 'This year you have to choose between your heritage and voting. We can leave the Park tomorrow but we will not be coming back. I'm going to the car now so that you can discuss this and I'll wait there for your answer.'

In five minutes they were clambering onto the truck. 'Well?' I said. 'What's it to be?' 'We are going to finish this work,' Toppie said. 'We are not stopping until we've reached the end.'

I sighed. A little more of my heart had hardened, and I whispered into my recorder that night: 'I think what really hurt is that this was all planned. Apparently they discussed it last night, took us out, we had a really nice day, really good interviews and they knew that they could hijack us out there, prevent us from getting back on the bus and tell us what they wanted.'

I dreaded the atmosphere in camp the next day but the incident was never mentioned again. 'It's very weird,' I noted in the following day's audio diary. 'You can say things with the utmost force and it's not taken amiss at all!'

Looking back, the 'line' meeting was a turning point in my relationship with the Kruipers. It was as if I had been tested, assessed and then accepted as someone who genuinely wanted to contribute to their heritage preservation but who was no bleeding-heart sucker. Literally from the next morning onwards, the ambience of our camp started to change and over the next couple of weeks it became increasingly harmonious, even loving. Laughter and teasing filled the fireside chatter, the Kruipers' health continued to improve and I decided to babble away in my lamentable Afrikaans, regardless of how it sounded. Even Galai managed to overcome her shyness and speak to Sue and me without Brenda as go-between. I had managed to suspend at least some of my world view and mindset and we could continue towards the 'Big History', as Dawid called it, with a common goal and vision.

The Khomani's ability to size up strangers is a survival tactic that they have been honing for more than a century in the face of a constant stream of curious visitors. But for researchers such as myself, the information from these visits is frustrating in its inability to help fill the gaps in the Kruipers' – or indeed any other of the Khomani families' – stories.

Farini's visit here in the late 1800s was followed by that of the famous Austrian anthropologist, Rudolf Pöch, in 1909, who made some recordings of the Bushmen's language that survived, unlike his diaries, which were tragically lost. A few years later, in 1911, Dorothea Bleek, daughter of the highly respected linguist Wilhelm Bleek – and a talented ethnographer in her own right – visited the Bushmen living at Ky Ky on the lower Nossob, just north of Twee Rivieren, and did further work on the N|uu language. Dorothea also did not note down the names of her subjects so there is no way of knowing whether the Kruipers were among that group at the time, and her photographs are too indistinct to identify her subjects. A prospector called Fred Cornell made movies in the area just before the First World War, and in the 1950s and 60s he was followed by Jens Bjerre and Marlin Perkins. Because the family was, by now, corralled into a settlement near the Warden's house at Twee Rivieren, they also had to get accustomed to a tsunami of academics flowing into their lives because they were easily accessible. Several major local and international expeditions came to study South Africa's First People and the group became arguably the best-documented Bushmen anywhere on the continent.

A champion of the Khomani's cause came into their lives in 1936 in the form of Donald Bain, a big-game hunter – and a big man – whose work with the Bushmen has been the subject of fascinating books and articles by Robert Gordon. Bain was horrified by the fact that Minister Grobler's intention for the KGNP to be a place where the Bushmen could live undisturbed was already being undermined. He wanted to lobby government for a dedicated Bushman reserve outside the Park, but he had to confirm their 'purity' in order to strengthen his argument that they were a precious – and fast-disappearing – cultural treasure. Knowing what we know now about the intermarriage of the desert clans, it was a delusive exercise but Bain organised for a team of scientists from the University of the Witwatersrand (Wits), led by the renowned anatomist and archeologist Raymond Dart, to visit the Khomani and conduct extensive research on their physiology, language, cultural practices and family relationships.

Those Bushmen who were not yet living at Twee Rivieren were enticed there with promises of food and tobacco, and five professors in fields such as anatomy, anthropology, linguistics and musicology arrived at Twee Rivieren, set up a state-of-the-art camp comprising creature comforts and a 'laboratory in the desert'. Each of Dart's 'living fossils' was given a tag, and over the next four months the scientists measured, probed and documented every inch of the Khomani's bodies, beliefs and society, later publishing their findings in a journal called *Bantu Studies*.

The volume is revealing of the contemporary obsession with physiological hallmarks as proof of race and contains a series of

PATRICIA GLYN

intimate measurements of noses, chests and genitals. Photographs
of buttocks and breasts abound in the plates, along with those of
faces that purportedly supported the racial stereotyping of the day.
Even more invasive – but not published in the journal – is a series
of photographs of two women's labia. For this unimaginably invasive procedure, the women were made to squat in front of the cam-
eraman so that he could capture their genitalia on film for eternity. I found some of those photographs in a dusty cabinet at Wits
Medical School. When I put them on the light box I felt my own
womanhood contract in revulsion at the insults they had endured.
Was the scientists' work akin to Nazi eugenics? Looking at their
research with the benefits of that arrogant facility called hindsight
one almost concludes so. But while the findings have all the hallmarks of cultural imperialism and racism, I doubt this would have
occurred to Dart's team. And I believe that Bain's motives, while
informed by the somewhat patronising contemporary views about
these 'children of nature', were largely admirable.

Raymond Dart's contribution to the scientific findings of that
trip was a study of what he called 'hut distribution', meaning an
examination of which family members each household comprised
and how they were related to those in other households. He identified six different 'tribes' living together, among them the Khomani, and his extensive genealogy also shows them to be sometimes
intermarried. In fact, he cites many cases of 'inbreeding', saying:
'It is clear from our table alone that these several groups of people
have been mingling with one another by cross-marriage for the last
century. They have probably been inbreeding in this way from the
remotest times.'

Ah, I thought, so this charge has historical precedents. The six
ethnic groups of the Wits study were people such as the N‖n+e, the
|Auni, the |Namani and the ≠Hanasen and while they might have
had close ties with each other, they did not necessarily share the
same clan loyalties – something that would become a divisive issue
in the post-apartheid land claim 60 years later when they, and others, were all thrown together for that process.

114

Some of the clans were hunter-gatherers who spoke Bushman languages, like the 'Home People' or N‖n≠e, whose language was N|uu. Others were not Bushman at all but Nama pastoralists, and still others were hunter-gatherers who spoke Khoekhoegowab, like the Kruipers and the Bladbeens. The Wits scientists labelled the latter two 'outsider clans', perhaps on account of their not speaking N|uu. Bushman languages rarely survived when they rubbed up against those of their neighbours and it is likely that because the Kruipers and Bladbeens had a symbiotic relationship with Khoekhoegowab-speaking clans for whom they tracked, herded and found water in the Kalahari in exchange for money or goods, they eventually abandoned their Bushman tongues. Culturally, however, they adhered to Bushman beliefs and customs.

Nigel Crawhall had the unenviable task of picking through the Wits study and conducting many hours of interviews with Khomani elders to make sense of where the Kruipers fitted into this complicated web. He concludes that they were ≠Hanasen, which means Kruiper in Afrikaans and 'Crawler' in English, a reference to a defining moment in their family history, which we will get to in Chapter 11.

The linguist on Dart's team was Clement Doke and he provided the first detailed description of N|uu, a language he mistakenly called 'Khomani'. None of the N‖n≠e elders whom Nigel later interviewed had any idea what the term meant or where it came from because it turned out to be a Khoekhoegowab word meaning 'speakers of the Bushman language that we do not understand'. Having applied this umbrella label to the six clans, it stuck, and, in the land claim decades later, became entrenched.

I first saw the 1937 Wits report when I was doing post-expedition research in South Africa's libraries and archives. The moment the librarian put the journal on my desk I tore through the photographs, desperately hoping to see Makai or Regopstaan. The faces that stared back at me looked obliging but vulnerable, and the only man pictured in the report that I had heard of was |Galakab – Agerob's father. He looked proud and strong, like his son, but cynically amused at being photographed, and the number 69 pinned behind him makes him resemble a museum specimen.

Dart described |Galakab as having an 'Australoid-Boskop' type of face, with 'Mongolian features and possibly some Mediterranean ones'. How confusing, poor chap! But the volume contains no photographs of the Kruipers. Why were they not part of the Wits study? Some have suggested it was because they were not deemed 'pure' Bushmen. But that does not explain why the Bladbeens were included, because they were also Khoekhoegowab-speaking hunter-gatherers. Others think it was because the Kruipers were employed by the Le Riches and could not be excused from their duties. Given the praise for their work ethic in Hannes Kloppers' book about the Le Riches and their contribution to the KGNP, this might be the reason. The Kruipers were certainly living cheek-by-jowl with the scientists' subjects, and Donald Bain took a photo of the family with his translator. Donald's son, John, and his grand-daughter, Judy Orpen, have a precious box full of his letters, photographs and memorabilia. I trawled through it with Judy's help, but came away empty-handed as to why the Kruipers stayed at home. Bain does write that he had collected 99 Bushmen and about 30 to 40 dogs and it was not feasible to take them all. 'In the end,' he continues, 'it was decided to leave 29 of the Bushmen behind to look after the dogs and that 70 would accompany me.' Elsewhere in the collection he says of the 99 who gathered in the camp that 'it was quite obvious that fifty per cent were not true to type, or would measure up to Museum standards'. Whether the Kruipers were among those regarded as 'not true to type' we do not know, but either way, the lack of attention to them by the Wits expedition eventually served the family well.

After the academics were finished their work, Bain loaded the Khomani onto trucks, with the exception of the Kruipers, and took them to Johannesburg, along with a couple of hunting dogs that one of the Bushmen smuggled onto the vehicle. I could find no reports on what the dogs hunted in the big city! Ouma |Una Rooi was one of the children included in the group and told Nigel how excited they all were to be going. After all it was an Englishman who had invited them, and their view of society's pecking order was that God came first, then the English, the Afrikaners, the coloureds, the blacks and finally the Bushmen – so they felt honoured to be taken along by someone so high up on humanity's hierarchy.

The Khomani went on show as a 'Bushman Display' at the Empire Exhibition of 1936, and they were arguably the most popular 'exhibit', providing what one writer has described as 'a feeding frenzy of the eye' for photographers, academics and the general public. Their stand was pejoratively described in the brochure as a 'nest' and was far from authentic. It was surrounded by corrugated iron and some sand was thrown on the concrete floor to make their dancing easier. The Khomani were forbidden from wearing anything but skins and from speaking anything but N|uu, and they would forfeit their rations if they were caught speaking Afrikaans or Khoekhoegowab. When not 'on show', the Bushmen were on the Wits research farm at Frankenwald where the scientists continued their examinations.

A few accounts survive of how the Bushmen reacted to their city experiences. 'Where do you get all the water?' asked their 'leader', Abraham Witbooi. The Khomani were taken to see the Union Buildings in Pretoria but were reportedly much less impressed by its grandeur than they were by its fishpond – and started scooping fish out of it. Bain recalls that 'the city's lights never ceased to fascinate them and the buses left them speechless'. They went 'completely mad over the cinema', and only ate ice cream once they had melted it in the sun. Some beautiful photographs survive of the Khomani at the Empire Exhibition but the Bushmen largely look bored, awkward and irritated. They also look far from overwhelmed by the experience.

Bain came in for some criticism for taking the Bushmen to Johannesburg, his detractors saying that it was a money-making mission and that they had found it hard to readjust back to life in the Kalahari without plentiful food and water. One article raised the old complaint that these were not 'pure' Bushmen, but, generally speaking, the public's response to 'Bain's Bushmen' was positive and he received welcome popular support for his idea of a Bushman reserve.

But he needed to petition parliament, so he took the Bushmen to Cape Town where they were put on show at the Rosebank showgrounds and marched on parliament in one of the most eye-catching demonstrations that South Africa has seen: dozens of tiny, barefoot Bushmen led by a giant white man. The acting prime minister at the time, General Jan Smuts, and six other cabinet ministers were in favour of the Bushmen being able to stay in the Park and hunt with traditional weapons, but they faced great opposition from the National Parks Board who wanted them out. Smuts' opinion was echoed by Colonel Denys Reitz a few years later when he was appointed Minister of Native Affairs, but the KGNP management still wanted the Khomani removed. After a few years' worth of acrimonious debate, the state allocated a very dry farm next to the KGNP – near the dummy – as a reserve for the Bushmen, but it was on Mier land and the Department of Coloured Affairs objected. So the Bushmen had to stay on in the Park with their increasingly hostile 'hosts'. A decade or so later the farm Struis Zyn Dam, also in this area, was allocated to them. But in a bureaucratic bungle the land was sold to a white settler, and, again, the Bushmen were left in the Park, strangers on their own land.

But those events were still far in the future. Before leaving Cape Town, the Khomani suffered another assault on their human dignity. A couple of the group's womenfolk, notably Abraham Witbooi's daughter, |Hanako, had the steatopygic frames that so obsessed Western physical anthropologists. |Khanako's family was taken to the Cape Town Museum where they posed for casts to be made, much like those that formed part of a glass-cased display at the museum for many more decades. Worse still, |Khanako had casts made of her head and genitalia at the University of Cape Town's Matthew Drennan Medical Museum. To this day, the casts still have her body hair attached to them.

Bain and 'his' Bushmen left Cape Town empty-handed, so they

went to Port Elizabeth and Durban to try to garner more publicity for their quest. The Bushmen bankrupted Bain – or rather white South Africa's apathy did. Instead of raising 30 000 pounds, as he expected to, he got 60 pounds. He took them home to the Kalahari and continued to feed them because the veld was in the grips of an extremely dry period. 'A month or so later I received the disturbing information that the Game Warden refused to allow the Bushmen to remain in the reserve and that the police were arresting them for killing gemsbok,' Bain says in his papers, adding that the government had no authority over the reserve because the rights to the area had been vested in the National Parks Board by act of parliament. His hands and those of his allies – such as General Jan Smuts and Sir Abe Bailey – were tied and they could do nothing further to protect the Bushmen who had been taken to the Empire Exhibition. In a letter to Smuts, Bain added that 'it [is] the avowed policy of the Magistrate of Upington to force them to take service with the farmers as soon as possible'. So now the Kruipers and their relatives were the only Bushmen left in the Park, and so the clan deemed 'outsiders' by the 1936 study eventually spearheaded the land claim. Within a couple of years Bain had retreated from public view to lick his impoverished wounds. Another Bushman rights campaigner, whatever his flaws, had been defeated by a cruel and indifferent system.

Since the Wits expedition of 1936, researchers have continued to dissect the Khomani. It is a sad commentary on modern academia and the poor status that it occupies in places of power that none of their investigations have made the slightest difference to improving the community's day-to-day lives, with the exception of the work of Nigel Crawhall and Hugh Brody that culminated in the Khomani's successful land claim. As I paged through *Bantu Studies* and all the reports, books and theses that I have since read, I wondered what it must feel like to be a cultural curiosity, how I would respond if my identity was dependent only on whether I could remember how to do copperplate with a quill, or speak the Gaelic of my ancestors. And how I would like it if my individuality was subsumed by a group whose interest to the wider world lies only in a collective experience that is all but extinct. I could find no answer.

CHAPTER 9

Like a Little Bird

The day after the line meeting it was clear that Buks' health was deteriorating, as was John's back, and that we would have to get them to a clinic. Brenda's little daughter, Mefi, also needed to get home so Sue got the unenviable job of doing the ten-hour round trip to Andriesvale. Driving after dark in the Park is prohibited so I rushed over to Nossob for permission from the section ranger, Brent Wittington, for her to do so. They set off down the runway, Mefi curled up on Buks' lap and John lying on one of the bench seats at the back of the Cruiser.

Richard, Karl and I left camp soon afterwards to interview Dawid at a game-viewing spot overlooking the Nossob River, which brings life to the southern Kalahari, notwithstanding the fact that it flows on average only twice a century. Dawid had seen this happen only once in his 76 years, about 30 years beforehand, when the Nossob and Auob both flooded and claimed one life in the Park. He showed us the beacons in the middle of the riverbed that demarcated South Africa's portion of the Park from Botswana's and followed by describing how, even in the old days, Bushmen had their borders, too. 'You can walk to those high dunes over there and from the top you can see very far. You'll look and see there's a tree on that dune and you'll know that's your border.'

Pre-Park and pre-fence 'borders' were a matter of a gentleman's agreement between neighbouring clans and varied greatly according to rainfall. If the rains were good and the *tsammas* and game plentiful, the Bushmen tended to congregate near the Nossob and Auob because these areas provided enough plants and game to sustain them. When the dry season came, small family groups spread out and hunted their particular patch of Kalahari. The 'patches' were vast because the southern Kalahari had so much less surface water and available resources than further north. But the sense of ownership of these areas was founded on mutual tolerance and reciprocity in resource utilisation. 'Not like today,' Dawid said, 'when people say "this is my land and it's not your land". Previously they used to say "this is our land".'

During the dry, hot months contact between the various family groups was infrequent because of the large distances between them, but it was not unknown for the Bushmen to walk hundreds of kilometres to visit their relatives.

Richard asked Dawid if he remembered any exciting incidents that happened near the Nossob and our conversation veered off to the subject of poachers once again, but with an interesting twist. It seems that Joep le Riche's means of catching these men relied on methods other than just tracking. Like Regopstaan, Joep was a 'seer', a man with finely honed instincts. It was his habit to drive around the Park until his intuition told him to stop. He would then tell the rangers on the back of the bakkie that this was the place from which they had to track the poacher. And he was invariably right.

Regopstaan's method of divining centred on his *dolosse* – bones comprising predators' vertebra, stones, sticks and other artefacts that he had carefully selected as representing different aspects of health, life and fate. Regopstaan was a master at 'throwing the bones' and diagnosing his patients' problems. The pattern the *dolosse* made when they were thrown onto the sand would show whether someone would die, go to jail, what they suffered from and how to cure them. 'It's like a letter,' Dawid told us. 'You can see what's written there.'

When Dawid entered manhood, Regopstaan started teaching

him how to use the *dolosse* and one of his final tests involved Lockie Henning. 'My dad said, "Look at the bones and see if he will stay with us or leave us",' Dawid recounted. 'So I threw the bones and said to my father, "Once he has finished helping us he will just disappear and he will take everything including money." And my dad also saw that in the bones.' Quite why the Kruipers went with Henning if they knew it would all end in tears Dawid puts down to a combination of blind hope and desperation.

Regopstaan's *dolosse* became a great source of power and comfort to the Khomani and before he died he elected Dawid as the next generation's custodian of this precious divining tool. But tragedy soon befell the bones. A Bushman healer from Damaraland, Namibia, borrowed Dawid's *dolosse* twice and kept badgering Dawid to sell them. The third time Dawid capitulated and the healer then sold on the bones to a woman in a Kuruman township. 'After the man sold the *dolosse* I heard the woman's voice, very deep like far off through a pipe. That woman looks in a mirror and tells fortunes.' The *dolosse* were never seen again and their loss still pained Dawid greatly. 'I didn't feel I'd learned enough to make my own *dolosse* so I decided to doctor people using herbs. I can say that from that day on I was not the man that I was supposed to be. It was very heart-sore for me and that's when my strength broke.'

Why on earth would he part with such an important item? Was he in dire straits at the time? Was he drunk? He had no answers for us. It troubled Dawid that, in his mind, he was not the man his father and grandfather were, and that his leadership of the Khomani was less than perfect. 'How will people remember me after I'm gone?' he asked us earnestly.

Dawid was often referred to as an anarchist in newspaper articles. I think of him as an iconoclast on whom authority did not sit comfortably. He was eccentric, self-deprecating and immensely humorous. Roger has a very fitting description of him as a trickster, the impish figure in Bushman mythology who was difficult to pin down and was always challenging norms and assumptions. 'He knew he was revered and admired and he quite liked it,' Roger told me, 'but he also didn't like people taking him too seriously.'

There is no doubt that Dawid will not be remembered fondly by some quarters within his community and even by a few members of his family. He always had an eye for a comely female thigh, was an incorrigible flirt and was sometimes led astray by the women he associated with after Gais' death. In fact he called himself the 'Old Ram'. Under the influence of alcohol he could be petulant and abusive, and on a few occasions he signed away access rights to Khomani land to people who plied him with brandy and promises. Some people believe him to have traded his spirituality for more worldly diversions, and on our trip Oupa certainly never struck me as a particularly spiritual person.

That may have been more as a result of my lack of awareness than his lack of beliefs and Nan is of the opinion that my very poor Afrikaans also prevented me from accessing the deeper, more esoteric nuances of what the Kruipers were saying. Craig Foster, who has spent time with Bushmen who are deeply connected with the spirit world, maintains that 'there's a look, there's a way about them, a peace, and Dawid didn't have it'. But Craig is also quick to point out that for Dawid to have seen his grandfather and father living traditional and then quasi-traditional Bushman lifestyles only to have them ripped away from him 'is such a massive affront that it's going to cause huge psychological damage'.

It is in the context of the land claim, however, that Dawid has – and will – come in for the most criticism. Some of the claimants believed that the Kruipers did not have the right to lead the claim because they did not speak N|uu, a situation I have described in the previous chapter. Dawid felt rejected and wounded by the researchers who switched their attention to the N|uu speakers soon after their arrival and dismissed him as knowing almost nothing about the Khomani's heritage. Others in the district maintained that the Kruipers were in Botswana at the time of the forced removals, which disqualified them from being part of the process. This is not true. A lot of the criticism centred on the belief that

Dawid sold out the traditional Khomani by not negotiating for more land in the Park.

Belinda Kruiper, a coloured woman who married into the family, co-wrote a book about her time with the community, *Kalahari RainSong*, which contains some scathing criticism of Dawid's leadership, describing him as having been 'caught up in a game too big for him, a pawn in other people's agendas'.

My own view is that this is uncharitable, because how people remember Dawid must be tempered by considerations of the complexity of the task that the land claim presented, and its importance in the 'new' South Africa's political genesis. For the first time in his life, Dawid found himself sitting at boardroom tables with the most powerful and educated of our country's society and facing the huge challenge of wending his way through volumes of paperwork and complex negotiations. He could neither read nor write and had to depend on intermediaries to translate and explain the material. And he had the equally difficult job of explaining what was happening in the talks to his largely ill-educated and profoundly damaged community, and balancing their occasionally opposing demands and expectations. Added to this, while Dawid was intelligent, perspicacious and wily, he was also a man with a forgiving nature who was anxious to share the spoils of this hugely significant event.

Ouma |Una Rooi said that three principles should guide the land claim process: land, water and truth. The claim was lodged by the 50 or so people – the Kruiper extended family – who had been left in the KGNP after 'Bain's Bushmen' were refused permission to stay there in 1936. But Dawid added the names of some of the Nama people who had been stock farming in the Park before it was proclaimed and who were now also destitute. This was permissible because the claim was not an ethnic one, in other words not restricted to Bushmen but meant to recompense all those who had been evicted from the Park. The list was complicated further by people taking the name Kruiper even though they were only related by marriage. The family misled the researchers about their genealogy out of fear that their claim would be weakened and it may be that a similar motive prompted them to say that they were !Gabe-speaking.

This brought the number of claimants to about 100, but when their petition was presented to the Department of Land Affairs, the officials' response was that these were far too few people to be awarded such a big tract of land. 'Look for more Bushmen' was their order. 'If you are able to include other Bushmen we'll raise the value of your claim from R8 million to R15 million.' Added to this, as the country's first citizens, the Bushmen theoretically had legitimate claims over the whole country, and the last thing the government wanted on its hands was a series of future legal battles. Best it was settled once and for all.

And so the Northern Cape was scoured for people with Bushman ancestry, as far back as six generations. The numbers began to swell, in part because some people – with absolutely no Bushman blood – bought their way onto the list. 'Vote for us in the first election,' they were told by corrupt community members, 'and we'll see that you get land.' Others, who should have been included, were not. Eventually some 300 'Bushmen' lodged their papers in 1995 in what was a patently pragmatic decision by government to include as many people as possible so as to prevent further claims. And so the lengthy and stressful process began.

But now the majority of the claimants were not people who wanted to preserve Bushman culture, and 'traditionalists' like the Kruipers (sometimes called 'revivalists' because they have lost many traditions that need to be 'revived') were sidelined by 'modernists' who wanted to move into farming and business. Many of the modernists also had friends in high places in the Northern Cape province and it was not long before they started flexing their political muscle. Roger Chennells and Nigel Crawhall were tasked with managing the claim's evolution and were soon joined by experts appointed by Derek Hanekom, then Minister of Land Affairs. Grossie and Phillipa were employed to assess the sustainable economic opportunities that the farms and the Park land offered,

and to help support the community in the complicated imple-
mentations that lay ahead. Roger set up the South African San
Institute, a non-profit, non-governmental support agency through
which funding and resources could be sought and channelled to
the Khomani for these projects and for legal representation.

Dawid now found himself pulled this way and that by people
who wanted very different things from the land claim. Valiantly
he tried to accommodate the dreams of all sectors of his newly
formed 'community'. The Kruipers and the four other families
that comprised the original claimants vilified him for having included 'outsiders' in the claim. A date for the signing of the transfer documents came closer and closer but no deal was yet in sight.
National Parks stood firm in their refusal to grant any land inside
the KTP and matters were further complicated by a very late claim
put in by the Mier coloured community around Rietfontein. They,
too, had used the Park as traditional hunting grounds in pre-KTP
times and had also been progressively disenfranchised by the
apartheid regime right up until 1987 when they lost more of their
land because the KTP's southern boundary was extended. Some of
the Park land must go to them, too, they rightly insisted, but their
claim overlapped and competed with the Khomani's.

The relationship between the two groups had been adversari-
al for decades and the coloureds were also resentful that the researchers were only interested in the Bushmen. Assuaging this
community was essential in ensuring future peace and the Bushmen decided not to object. The goal posts had changed and talks
had to start anew, now in an even more intense and emotional
atmosphere.

Throughout the negotiations, Dawid and his family had been
updating Regopstaan on their progress or otherwise. By now the
old man was bedridden and in great pain, lying on a mattress in
a small shack in Welkom and being cared for by the women of
the family. 'Have you had some gemsbok?' Roger asked him in
their last conversation. 'Yes and it was good. So good.' He died
just a few hours after hearing the news that the Khomani would be

compensated for their historical loss. He was 96 years old. Regopstaan's death was deemed so important in South Africa's history that notice of it appeared in the obituaries of *Time* magazine. Now Dawid would be without his father's guiding hand in the tumultuous events that followed.

The day before the designated handover ceremony there was still no agreement. Pressure mounted on Dawid to sign the papers. Outside the hall his people waited. They were exhausted after decades without a home. They had endured five years of travelling up and down from Kagga Kamma and had had a tragic car accident. Night came and the talks continued, Dawid's small, tired frame surrounded by suits and spotlights.

'By the time Thabo Mbeki [then deputy president under Nelson Mandela] arrives tomorrow you will either have accepted this offer or you'll get nothing,' the negotiators threatened. Eventually at three in the morning the deal was done. Dawid had been coerced into signing something that he would forever regret. But at the back of the Molopo Lodge, the Khomani changed into their skins, made a huge bonfire and danced with the kind of fervour that they had not felt in decades. For the first time in almost a century, Khomani families that had been spread all over the Northern Cape were together again and the community was suffused with unity, hope and the joyful expectation that life was going to get much, much better.

The agreement conferred 25 000 hectares of Park land to the Khomani and a further 25 000 hectares to the Mier people. As for the land outside the Park, Derek Hanekom insisted that the six farms – which totalled some 40 000 hectares – were allocated in such a way that the legitimate claimants' rights were not usurped by the more worldly wise 'late-comers'. The farms were divided up so that three went to the modernists for stock farming, one would be shared by both sectors of the community, and two would go to the traditionalists. There the latter could live in as traditional a way as they chose and make a living out of eco-tourism, hunting and other wildlife-related endeavours. These farms are Witdraai, where the Kruiper family now lives, and Erin, a farm on the other side of the main road that, at the time, was stocked with a million rand's worth of game. According to the agreement, government would assist the Khomani in optimising the benefits accruing from their land by supplying a manager, training, infrastructure development and other material support.

The handover ceremony was timed to coincide with Human Rights Day – 21 March 1999. It was widely covered in the local and international press and well attended by communities and government officials from all over the Northern Cape. On a hot, cloudless day, Thabo Mbeki flew in by helicopter and made a congratulatory speech to the huge, expectant crowds. 'This land claim … is about the rebirth of a people,' he told the crowds. 'This is your land. Take it. Care for it. Thrive on it,' he counselled.

Dawid replied by saying: 'A key has been turned. A thick chain has been clasped fast together.'

What happened when the official handover was finished has gone into the annals of the Kalahari's great legends. Several elderly Bushmen women began singing and, out of nowhere and completely unpredicted, it began to pour with rain. Mbeki rushed for his helicopter and only just managed to take off. The Bushmen looked at the sky and believed that Regopstaan's prophecy had come true – that when the drought was finally broken the Bushmen would at last live in peace and prosperity.

But Cait Andrews believed differently. 'They're not actually getting their land yet,' she said to Roger. 'This is just symbolic. Wait till the land is transferred.' In December 1999 the first farm, Scotty's Fort, was handed over. Petrus Vaalbooi and a group of Khomani marched along the road towards the farm and it began to rain. It rained solidly for two weeks in the Kalahari. The Nossob and the Auob rivers flowed for the first time in fifteen years, the skies were thick with moths and insects and birds of prey ate so well that they could hardly fly.

Tragically, peace and prosperity did not come to the Khomani and particularly the traditionalists. Having seen that the Kruipers' needs were in danger of being overlooked in the allocation of farms, and in recognition of their founding role in the negotiations, Derek Hanekom allocated about R500 000 to be held in trust for the family so that they could buy their own farm if they needed to in the future. During the celebrations, he lent over to Dawid and whispered in his ear: 'Be careful of the vultures.'

In the years that followed, the vultures gathered and circled. Dawid was routinely exploited by those he had tried to help, and it was not long before corruption, jealousy, greed and materialism hijacked the benefits of the land restitution for which the Khomani had waited so long. Community tensions rose steadily. The modernists scorned the 'backwardness' of those Bushmen who wanted to live as much as possible like their ancestors. They laughed at Dawid if he wore his skins to gatherings and deliberately kept him ignorant of meetings. Phillipa remembers arriving at Witdraai one day to find Dawid crying over a letter someone had just read to him. It accused the traditionalists of being 'you heathens that stink of piss and *kak* [shit], who wear skins and sleep in grass huts'. The years that followed broke Dawid's heart. He watched from the sidelines as his and his father's dream devolved into a dogfight. Eventually he retreated into cynicism and the bottle. 'I was driving the Land Claim bus,' he famously said, 'and I kindly invited other people onto it. Then they decided where the bus should go and soon I found myself chucked off it and hitching on the side of the road!'

The sad story of the Khomani Land Claim debacle played out like this. The farms allocated to the Bushmen were bought on a willing buyer, willing seller basis from white farmers in the area and were to be handed over fully stocked with whatever game and fixed assets they contained. The farmers were given a roughly six-month grace period to wind up their businesses on the farms. But during that time some of them stripped their land of as many assets as possible: pumps, tanks, fencing and wood stockpiles, none of which had been inventoried by the Department of Land Affairs. By the time the Khomani took possession of their land it was all but bare.

Collective ownership of the farms rested with the Community Property Association (CPA) – of which all claimants were members – and they now voted in their first Management Committee (MC) to oversee the day-to-day functioning of the properties. Dawid and some of the other traditionalists were on the MC. It was chaired by Petrus Vaalbooi and the first treasurer was Andries Steenkamp – both stock farmers who had not grown up in the Park. The first few meetings were constructive, with Phillipa and Grossie helping the committee to establish policies and guidelines for things such as land use, stock-carrying capacity, grazing rights and resource ben-eficiation. Two of the farmhouses were earmarked as guesthouses and things were looking promising. But it was not long before the meetings became abusive, with the churchgoing ladies and gentle-men on the committee saying, 'We can't work with these pagans, savage pagans.'

Dawid and his people would often abandon the meetings after being ignored and insulted. Sometimes matters would be finalised while he and his traditional colleagues were caucusing outside the meeting rooms so as to reach the kind of consensual decisions that were typical of Bushman society. Dawid's cynical recollection of the meetings was that 'they would start and end with a prayer and they'd lie in between'. Without approval or warning, MC members and other stock farmers occupied the farmhouses and claimed them as their own. Sheep and goats were moved onto the proper-ties before it had been decided how many the farms could support. In addition, in flagrant disregard for the agreement, some com-munity members poached game on Erin, which was allegedly sold by MC members, and some leading-light modernists then put their herds onto the farm. Allegedly, members of the MC also started fleecing and mismanaging the interest from the 2.5 million rand development fund meant for the properties' improvements. I am told that money, assets and equipment worth hundreds of thou-sands of rand were either stolen or mismanaged. All efforts to see the MC's books were evaded and within months the broader com-munity's rights to benefit from these resources lay in tatters. The

Vaalbooi brothers moved their herds onto the modernists' farms, herds so vast that they eventually accounted for 80 per cent of the livestock, thereby preventing equitable access to what were meant to be the community's resources. By the end of 1999, a forensic audit had been conducted at the behest of the Department of Land Affairs. Due to its findings of mismanagement, fraud and corruption, the first MC was removed from power. Petrus Vaalbooi and Andries Steenkamp were barred from holding office again.

In 2000, a second MC was appointed, chaired by Andries' sister, Magrieta Eiman, whose husband became the new treasurer. This MC did deals involving the sale of game, which the community regarded as unlawful, and under their noses the animals were captured, hunted and, on occasion, poached. Game died of thirst because the MC had not paid the farms' electricity bills, so power was cut off and water could not be pumped from the boreholes. The stock farms were being overstocked, overgrazed and mismanaged. To make matters worse, unbeknown to Dawid, his fellow traditionalists and most of the community, Petrus and Andries ran up personal loans offered to them by the former white owner of Erin, Attie Avenant, allegedly using the farm as collateral. When the money they owed grew to about 300 000 rand, Attie called in his loans and obtained a court order for a sale in execution that the second MC inexplicably did not oppose. Erin was within a whisker of being returned to him when Phillipa and Grossie heard about the matter from Dawid and brought it to the attention of key people in the Department of Land Affairs. On the latter's instructions, Dawid's trust money was used to repay Petrus' and Andries' personal loans and save the farm. The Trust was much later reimbursed by government. By means of a court order in November 2002, the Department of Land Affairs removed this committee on charges of corruption and took over administration of the estate and the MC's duties. They never revealed their findings and unfortunately a forensic audit could not take place because, most mysteriously, Magrieta's car burst into flames with the MC's books and paperwork in the boot. Evidently, nothing was saved. To date Petrus and Andries have not been asked to repay their debt to the CPA.

After nine months with no one at the helm, a third management committee was elected in 2003 that Jan van der Westhuizen was meant to chair. Within a few days, however, he had been sidelined and replaced by Gert Bok as chairman and Arrie Tieties as vice chairman. Neither of them is a registered member of the Khomani CPA, yet they were in office for the next five years, during which time fraud, bribery and corruption allegedly reached new heights. To date – and despite many letters and appeals – not one MC member has been prosecuted and not a cent recovered.

Then matters in Andriesvale took a more sinister turn. In December 2003 a community member named Deon Noubertson made the long journey to Johannesburg to visit the South African Human Rights Commission and present video evidence he had that allegedly showed a policeman named Lieb Liebenberg driving around the district threatening, '*Ek gaan 'n Boesman dood vrek skiet*' (I am going to shoot a Bushman dead dead). It being 23 December, the Human Rights Commision offices were closed and Deon was advised to return in the new year. But before the offices reopened, Optel Rooi was dead, shot in the back in January 2004 after trumped-up charges that he was stealing liquor from the Molopo Lodge Bottle Store. Like many other cases in Andriesvale, the incident was not properly investigated and charges were not pressed initially, so Phillipa and Grossie turned to the Human Rights Commission. A national outcry followed the release of Stef Snel's and Richard Wicksteed's documentary, *Death of a Bushman*, which was aired by the South African Broadcasting Corporation, and the Human Rights Commission announced their intention to conduct a full investigation of the matter and the plight of the Khomani community.

In August 2004 Dawid's frustration at the lack of government attention to his community's problems and the MC debacles reached a peak and he decided to hitchhike to Cape Town and speak to Thabo Mbeki in person. Fortunately, Grossie was in the

Kalahari at the time so five of the Kruipers jumped onto the back of his bakkie and drove to Cape Town through the night. Dressed in their skins, they kept vigil outside parliament where their presence attracted considerable attention. Thabo Mbeki was unable to meet with Dawid but, with Derek Hanekom's assistance, he got an audience with Thoko Didiza, Minister of Land Affairs at the time, who promised to look into the situation at Andriesvale. Among the concerns that Dawid discussed with her was the fact that the settlement prescribed that a manager be appointed to oversee the farms, but that this still had not happened. Nothing further was heard from Minister Didiza.

Two months later, in October 2004, however, the Human Rights Commission conducted a three-day hearing in the Kalahari. Their subsequent report recommended that Optel's murder be investigated properly and the perpetrators prosecuted. The case finally received the attention it was due and Lieb Liebenberg, the senior police officer who was charged with the murder, was acquitted. His subordinate was found guilty but given a suspended sentence, and, to this day, the verdict rankles the Khomani.

The Human Rights Commission report is a damning critique of all levels of government involved in this 'sad story of neglect and indifference'. Of the debacle surrounding the first MC, the report states that '[MC] members were found responsible for gross mismanagement of funds by an official audit called for by the Department of Land Affairs. This audit found funds in excess of R150 000 unaccounted for, and recommended criminal investigation against senior office-bearers. No prosecution followed, as the director general of the Department of Land Affairs declared it was by and large a lack of capacity and knowledge that contributed to the degeneration of the CPA's financial affairs.' Grossie remembers the Human Rights Commission's advocate expressing loud incredulity when he was informed by Sugar Ramakarane, Land Commissioner of the Northern Cape, that the director general of the Department of Land Affairs had 'condoned theft and fraud'. He asked what kind of message this sent out.

Most of the recommendations of the Human Rights Commission's report were ignored, with the exception of the establishment of a local court at Witdraai and school transport for the children so that they could avoid boarding at the Askham Primary School hostel as there had been incidents of sexual abuse. What the report fails to recommend, however, is prosecution of the MC members who had allegedly stolen so much from the community.

The Human Rights Commission's visit was followed by a special rapporteur from the United Nations' Rights of Indigenous People, who investigated the Khomani situation in 2005. In his testimony, Dawid said poignantly: 'I'm like a little bird and I could sit nowhere on the ground, I had to stay in the trees. And then the Land Claim happened and I thought, okay, now I can land on the ground. But now I'm in the air again and I'm very tired, I've got nowhere to go and nowhere to sit.' The United Nations pleaded with government to respond to the situation, but again there was nothing but silence from South Africa's politicians, with the exception of Pallo Jordan, then Minister of Arts and Culture, who was reported by the *Sunday Independent* as saying: 'We have to acknowledge also the imbalances created by apartheid. While all Black people, including the Khoikhoi and the San, were oppressed and deprived under apartheid, it was nonetheless also hierarchical. The most oppressed and deprived were the Africans. The Khoikhoi and their descendants had the right to own and purchase land in virtually every part of South Africa not set aside as a "White group area". Africans were compelled to carry passes that controlled their movements and made them subject to a system of constant monitoring by the state, the Khoikhoi and their descendants did not suffer such indignities.'

Some kind of legal redress has now been sought for the Khomani. At the time of writing this book, the Department of Land Affairs – subsequently renamed the Department of Rural Development and Land Reform – was being taken to court by the community over its failure to honour its contractual obligations. It is hoped that government intervention and funding might restore justice and provide redress to a now profoundly disillusioned group of people who had high hopes for the land restitution but who have been routinely let down by the organs of state meant to help them.

Not surprisingly, the land claim debacle resulted in seriously deteriorating social affairs in Andriesvale. The rivalry between the modernists and traditionalists became a bitter war of attrition and relationships within family groups on both sides of the Capulet/ Montague divide were – and are – deeply scarred. The Welkom Declaration that the traditionalists wrote in February 2004 was in essence a motivation for them to break away from the rest of the community. That did not happen and the horrors of life in those dunes have, if anything, escalated. Rape became commonplace in the community, as did assault and verbal abuse. The abused became the abuser. The Witdraai police continued to victimise and harass the Bushmen, and, at the time of writing, there were ten unsolved murders in the area that the police had failed to investigate. They are alleged to have the attitude that as long as it is 'just Bushmen killing Bushmen' that is fine. It must be said, however, that in many cases the Khomani do not want offenders to be prosecuted because they are family, so the police's probes are scuppered by uncooperative witnesses who choose to exact their own punishment against perpetrators.

Since the land claim was initiated, Phillipa and Grossie have been working as technical advisers to the community and their moral and practical support for Dawid became invaluable to the old man. Several times a few members of the community tried to get rid of their services because of the bright light that the two ecologists were shining on the murky corners of the community's affairs, but Dawid insisted that they should stay. Those early years of their involvement took a heavy toll on their lives and hearts. Often they would do the long drive back to Johannesburg in a state of shock and despair. 'It was the sense of disappointment because there had been such hope and enthusiasm that finally justice had been done and the land had returned, and a vision about what we were going to do,' Phillipa recalls. 'And it just went down the tubes so rapidly with all the thievery, corruption, deception, jealousy, racism, discrimination and the criminals just getting away with it. And people were starving. They didn't even have enough money to build shacks.'

In the intervening years some 30 or 40 original claimants and elders have died waiting for redress and, again at the time of writing, there is no CPA executive as required by the relevant Acts. Infrastructure development remains a dream and on several of the farms, including Witdraai, the Khomani live as they have for centuries. Their toilets are behind a bush in the veld and they cook over open fires. The one borehole at Witdraai yields water that is so high in fluoride it has rotted the Kruipers' teeth. Fourteen years since being awarded the farm there is still no electricity, no waste management, no sanitation, no road to speak of and no houses. But across the road there is plenty of the Khomani's favourite rotgut which they call 'Killing me softly'. After nightfall, however, the 'killings' are anything but soft.

Dawid's decision to settle the Kruipers at Witdraai is seen by some as contravening his father's wishes. Regopstaan wanted the family – and other traditionalists – to live on three remote farms closer to the Park. There, he believed, they would be far from the temptations of the liquor store and the insults of the modernists. The farms are extremely dry, so they would be forced to live off the land as their forefathers had and the area would be ideal for traditional conservation. Perhaps those, like Belinda Kruiper, who believe that Regopstaan's prophecy was a parable are right – that the rain he predicted and which would heal the Bushmen is symbolic. The long drought in the southern Kalahari is within the Bushmen's hearts and the rain they need is a return to their traditional ways and historical reputation as the gentlest people in the world.

Andriesvale's torrid odour returned with Sue late that night. She had had several fractious interchanges with Dawid's family while trying to get some things from his hut. The jealousy of those left behind made them obstructive and rude, and they seemed to care little for the welfare of an old man in need. Karl, Richard and I huddled in the mess tent sipping hot coffee while she related the day's news. The Kalahari's brutal winter had now arrived and the temperature at night was consistently below zero. Our tents were crusted with a thin layer of ice in the mornings, and I was piling jackets and jerseys on top of my sleeping bag to compensate for its paltry insulation. The next morning we would move our camp once again and I dreaded not having the use of Nossob camp's hot showers. But we would be one step closer to hearing Makai's secret, should Dawid choose to divulge it to the outside world, and I hoped against hope that he would.

CHAPTER 10

Santa Claus at the Human Rights Commission

I f the wild and limitless southern Kalahari were to have a symbolic capital, Union's End would surely be it. It is a scenically unremarkable place on the Nossob's southern bank and is the point where Namibia, Botswana and South Africa meet. The spot is marked by a signpost with wooden flags giving directions to, and distances from, various towns and cities in the three countries. They are all hundreds of kilometres away, the pointers told me. We were now as far from 'civilisation' as we had ever been on the expedition and I felt elated and privileged to be there.

Next to the signpost, an information board supplied useful facts about this remote no-where-land: 'The name Union's End comes from the association of being the most northerly point when South Africa was still under British Rule from May 1910 to May 1961. This is the point where the dry Nossob River enters South Africa from Namibia. The border fence from Union's End south, separating what was then the KGNP from South-West Africa/Namibia, was finally completed in 1966. Union's End is also referred to as World's End on account of its remoteness.'

Just as I like it, I thought.

Nico van der Walt, the KTP's head, had designated us a camping spot on a management road that runs along the border fence, south of Union's End. There, our camp would be safe to leave while we explored the area's Bushman history. The fence runs in a dead straight line for 750 kilometres and then a further 400 kilometres after a small east-west kink, making it the longest straight border in the world. It is a relic of the imperious disregard for landscape and tribal affiliations with which Africa was carved up during the nineteenth-century European race for her resources. We chose a high point overlooking the grassy plains, next to a camel thorn tree that hosted enormous sociable weavers' nests. The birds darted in and out of their holes, chirping and chattering, while we hastily erected our tents and cleared an area for fireside gatherings.

Our arrival had been delayed because of the lengthy process of getting water from one of the Park's boreholes. Am Am had spent an hour lying on top of a tank holding a hose pipe into the water while Sue patiently siphoned off what we needed for the next few days. It was after 10 p.m. by the time we had all eaten and I settled down to star gaze with a cup of honeybush tea.

The Kalahari's night sky is one of its greatest assets. A vast dome of deepest blue velvet serves as backdrop to a twinkling display of diamond-white stars. In Bushman mythology they were created when someone threw coals into the sky to light the way home for the hunters. The effect of this stellar grandeur has always been to diminish my puny human compulsions and incite my most precious of dreams.

It is a sight that stimulates reflection, encourages balance and stills the ego, and on the journey I came to cherish those quiet end-of-day moments. By now I had also learned to adopt at least some of the Kruipers' unhurried, contemplative ways. The elders of the family have a remarkable ability to be fully aware in every moment, observing and absorbing movements in the wind or clouds, facial expressions and body language, bird sounds and subtle changes in temperature. These are skills that come with stillness, and we city dwellers have largely lost them.

I lay under the weavers' nests, watching the busy little 'republican birds', as they were once called, come and go from their homes. The warm sand cushioned my shoulder blades, the grass cradled my head and I felt the pure rush of elation and peace that being in the wild brings. For the previous weeks I had been so obsessed with the minutiae of providing and provisioning that I had failed to relish the great privilege of being in this unique landscape with its aboriginal inhabitants.

It is common for people who do not appreciate the restorative value of nature to dismiss the Bushmen as 'backward'. Too often the politically powerful who hold the fate of Africa's First People in their hands fail to understand just what the Bushmen lose when they are ripped away from the wild places that bring them joy and balance. The argument is put forward – particularly in modern Botswana – that Bushmen must change, must modernise, must become part of the educated citizenry. Some of that reasoning is a result of misplaced embarrassment about 'bush people' and their pre-literate lifestyle. Urban-aspirant Africans want no reminder of where and how we once lived. For we were all Bushmen once upon a time, and their all-knowing oneness with the Earth, its systems and inhabitants is what we lost when we left the 'bush'.

Our psychological trauma at this separation from source manifests in dysfunctional and violent societies, wholehearted disregard for nature's bounty and a terrifying assault on her creatures. And nowhere is this trauma more extreme and keenly felt than in the people who have been recently cut off from that which is so important to human sustenance. Perhaps this is the reason for the alcohol abuse and social ills that beset aboriginal people the world over. The brutal severance that we experienced centuries ago and whose agony is just a faint memory for us, is fresh and monstrously painful for these people. The more time we spent in the Kalahari, the more I came to understand just how much the Kruipers lost when they were evicted.

We spent the next day in camp so that Oupa Dawid could tell us about his days patrolling this area. A man on a horse approached the fence from the Namibian side and he and Dawid stood and chatted over the international boundary. It struck me what a telling image this was of how fences have wrecked the lives of migratory humans and animals. The man knew Dawid's sister, who still lives in Namibia, and promised to send her Dawid's greetings. Later, two boys arrived on a cart to say hello, their horses drenched in sweat after being ridden too hard. Both mares had deep sores on their chests and mouths. Their pitiful state highlighted how our treatment of animals has deteriorated since we moved away from a hunter-gatherer lifestyle where animals were not viewed as property to a state of being where fences proclaim our ownership of land, animals and resources. Christians call it 'dominion'; to me it's ignominy – for man and beast alike.

I stormed back to camp before I completely lost my temper with the cruel boys and huffed and puffed in the mess tent while Sue baked another batch of her delicious wholewheat bread. The two Kruiper youngsters, Dawid and Isak, were at the top of the camel thorn. Great, I thought, they are really getting into this now and are looking for game to hunt on the plains. But when I approached the tree it turned out that they were up there trying to get cellphone signal.

My how we have reversed roles! I chuckled to myself. Here am I all gleeful to be away from contact with the outside world and they are desperate for it. Priscilla's chargers were being used every day to juice up the kids' cellphones so that they could listen to music. 'Bizarre that they don't want these gorgeous bush sounds,' I recorded in my diary. 'Kids living on a cultural cusp, I guess.'

In retrospect, that was not entirely true. What the Kruiper youngsters want – quite understandably – is both electronic *and* bush music. And never mind a cultural cusp, they sit on a cultural knife-edge because theirs is the generation whose decisions will determine like never before how much of the Khomani's knowledge and tradition survives. There are those who maintain that it is a romantic and futile dream to try to preserve this heritage, and that outsiders like me are not only patronising the Bushmen by trying to 'save' them, but guilty of preventing their culture from developing naturally into whatever shape it finally assumes.

What I was learning on the trip, however, was that while the community at Andriesvale has severe problems that need to be addressed by a full gamut of social interventions and services, when the Khomani are out in the KTP they are far from in need of saving. If anything it is the other way around.

My time in the veld with the Kruipers had given me some understanding of how masterful the Bushman ancestors – and Kruiper elders – were in resource management and conservation, but the family had also taught me about those two most important principles: 'eat when you are hungry', and 'eat to live, do not live to eat'. For the first time in my life I had felt daily the gurgling, acid pain in my gut of real hunger – but without the despair of not knowing where my next meal was coming from, of course. I could not get over how long the Kruipers could go without food when we were in the field, and how great their self-control was in waiting until a meal was ready before snacking on whatever they could lay their hands on.

To this day, if the Khomani are short of food they use their *maagbands* – a belt or strip of material that they pull tighter and tighter around their tummies to stave off hunger. The Kruipers were certainly champion consumers of tobacco, coffee, tea and sugar but ate small amounts of food, spaced very far apart. And portions were meticulously measured out so that everyone got the same amount of food. Several times I had seen them storing leftovers for the following day, even though they knew that Priscilla was stocked with adequate provisions. Theirs is an attitude towards eating from which we have much to learn in our chef competition- and cooking show-obsessed society. For the Bushmen, food is a necessity and a pleasure, but it is not put on the culinary pedestal that modern consumers have erected for it.

By this point on our expedition my attitude towards our planet's most precious resource – water – had undergone something of a revolution thanks to the Kruipers' mentorship. Even though they have had access to water on tap for some periods of their lives, it remains a commodity that they respect and use sparingly. They drink far less water than the average 'townie', who cannot seem to move 10 metres without a plastic bottle of water in hand. Are the Bushmen products of environmental adaptation and natural selection? I am not equipped to answer that, but I suspect that, apart from their size and skin colour, they have no special attributes other than the self-discipline that comes from centuries of survival master classes in the Kalahari's arid terrain.

And of course their consumption of 'virtual water' is also extremely low – at least traditionally. Virtual water is that which is involved in the growing and processing of food and it is the part of our water usage that we must monitor and reduce with the greatest vigilance. Yet we still cling to the belief that it is in doing things such as showering rather than bathing where we can conserve best. James Workman's book *Heart of Dryness* is a masterful account of what the Bushman values can teach us about the strategies we need to cope with this, the worst hot dry era in 30 000 years, and a time in human history when two thirds of the world's population will face water shortages. His – and the Bushmen's – teachings are particularly apposite in southern Africa, which has been identified as the continent's region that will be worst affected by this water-stressed time in human history.

The Bushman old-timers embraced everything we are now trying to re-teach ourselves: eat local, fresh and seasonal food so as to lower our carbon footprint and water consumption. The greatest amount of virtual water embedded in our food is to be found in meat. I had witnessed on our trip just how hard it is to harvest animal protein when you have to hunt it yourself, and, in the old times, this made the Bushmen's consumption of animals very low by comparison with ours, in a society where meat is mass produced and factory farmed.

And there was another great lesson I was learning on my journey with the Kruipers. The family elders have little to no regard for material possessions. A scarf that I gave Dawid was on Galai's head the day after I gave it to him, then back around his neck a few days later and, after that, given to whoever needed it. With few exceptions, the older Khomani have a genuine non-attachment to 'things'. This is, no doubt, a by-product of extreme poverty as well as their culture of egalitarianism and it has the benefit of making them look and feel equal. It has its downsides in that there is something of a 'tall poppy syndrome' within the community – people who get beyond themselves are subjected to ridicule, although this is beginning to change as more and more youngsters emerge from the damaged days of the post-land-claim period. Certainly, things are sold or swapped for a *dop* but I have never been in the company of people who lack vanity as much as the Kruipers. They arrived for both legs of our trip with little more than a single change of clothing each, and all of the possessions that Dawid held dear were contained in a small tin box. The family's clothes were almost without exception tattered and outsized, although the womenfolk did their best to keep them washed and clean, and I often envied the Bushmen their sweet scent – a result of powdered roots used as deodorant – when I was feeling self-conscious about what I must smell like after several days without more than a basin bath.

The Kruipers' habit of giving away, losing or selling their possessions has been the source of anguish to donors who give them expensive presents, never to see them again. Similarly, money is hardly ever saved; it is shared and enjoyed until it runs out. It remains to be seen if the younger generations of Khomani forgo the lure of tinsel and trash, but, for now, it is liberating to be with people who are so genuinely lacking in greed and social aggrandisement. The Kruipers are self-accepting and self-deprecating, they sometimes dress for deliberate comical effect and have a finely developed sense of the ridiculous. On one of my pre-expedition visits to Witdraai, Oupa greeted me wearing a white man's grey wig and clearly could not wait for my reaction to his new 'look'. Grossie relates the story of how Dawid testified before the South African Human Rights Commission in a Santa Claus hat because he felt he had given the land away like a Christmas present.

The Kruipers' thinking is subtle and sophisticated, as well as perspicacious as to what rubbing up against European culture can – or cannot – do for them. Craig Foster worked with Toppie for many months at a time while making his film *My Hunter's Heart*. He offered to buy Toppie a set of false teeth to which Toppie responded: 'If you give me teeth you'll take away my wildness. It would make me tame like you.' As Craig correctly interpreted about this statement: 'If he actually becomes money orientated and drops the last vestiges of hunting and gathering and that immediate return economy his last bit of wildness will die.'

Because of their work in films, and because Dawid was the representative of traditional Khomani issues, the Kruipers are well travelled and well aware of what happens in the world outside the Kalahari. They are neither cowering nor subservient when faced with the noise of Western cities or the 'sophistication' of their inhabitants. Dawid went abroad several times and in 1994 was invited to Geneva to address the United Nations Working Group on Indigenous Rights. He insisted on wearing his skins on the flight and Roger Chennells recalls a Swiss woman in the seat next to him being most indignant about him being semi-nude. 'What's wrong?' Dawid asked, knowing full well. 'Doesn't she like me?'

He proceeded to walk into the United Nations building with a skin bag full of dope – and got away with it because Roger told the security guards that he was a 'traditional king'. On one occasion Roger got hopelessly lost in the city's streets and Dawid guided him home, telling him at each juncture what they would see when they rounded this corner and then the next – a cat on a dustbin, some red flowers on a windowsill. That fail-safe Bushman GPS is not limited to the Kalahari, it seems.

On a subsequent visit to Europe, Dawid was taken to a porn peep show. It remained a vivid, and oft-described experience, not because the spectacle horrified him but because he was so amused by the clients' rapt attention to what they were watching. 'I could have been on fire and they wouldn't have noticed,' he told me with a grin.

The Kruipers also know exactly how to capitalise on their Bushmanness, albeit in a charming manner. Nan Flemming took them to Cape Town to perform in a FIFA World Cup ceremony in 2010. They were booked to stay in several double rooms at a luxury guesthouse, but the Kruipers chose to sleep all together in two of them. The guesthouse's management evicted them four times for transgressions such as smoking joints at the front door, waking up other guests with their parties and falling down the carpeted stairway, which Toppie referred to as a 'very high, green dune'. They went to Greenmarket Square where the group spread out to enjoy its stalls and cafés. When Nan caught up with them, a gathering of Rastafarians had given the Kruipers a whole arm of dope and a tobacconist had donated packets of *twak*. Next, they went to the factory shops in Muizenberg to buy cheap clothing with their per diem allowances. Their presence caused such a stir there that they came away with more clothes and mattresses than they could fit into the bakkie.

Throughout our journey, Richard, Karl and I had been recording profile interviews with each of the Kruipers, and it was now time for Toppie's son, Klein Dawid, to tell us about his life. Klein Dawid has the nickname Tankies, which means 'the footpath of the animals' in Khoekhoegowab. It is the footpath into nature and his feelings, he told us, and he is very proud to have the name. Like many of the community's youngsters, he has seen a great deal of domestic violence in his life and, as a five-year-old, was in the terrible car crash that killed several members of his family, including his mother. Since her death he has been brought up by an aunt and, more recently, by Tina. But the turmoil of his life does not show in his face – it is beautiful, open and gentle with a wide smile and even, white teeth.

The more I listened to Tankies speak the more hopeful I felt about the Khomani's future. His dream – like those of the other teenagers we had interviewed – was to become a field guide and eventually a game ranger in the Park. He seemed determined to avoid drowning his life in alcohol and drugs and was immensely proud of his heritage and culture. 'I don't know why they gave me

Oupa's name, but most probably as the years go by there will be a big job that I must do. I want to make myself strong, to make myself a man so that when the time comes I will be ready. My dad, Toppie, is also a legend,' he said. 'Our people didn't have much education, like my dad, but they've got it inside them. The centuries-old knowledge.'

'What would you like to say to the people of South Africa?' Richard asked him.

'To tell them to look a bit deeper,' said Tankies. 'It's a big privilege to still have the Bushmen on Earth. You won't get better people. If you look at Earth a little bit deeper there are secrets that the Earth won't show you unless you respect him. I'm very proud of being a Bushman.'

I watched some sheep grazing on the Namibian side of the border through the ugly fence that gashes this otherwise pristine landscape. When the National Park was declared in 1931 there was no fence here, and while that had its benefits for Bushmen and herds on the move, the lack of protection for the animals of the KGNP was a constant source of worry for Park management. It was thanks to the Le Riches that no fence was erected along the border between South Africa and Botswana, down the middle of the Nossob riverbed, despite the pressure they were under from National Parks to do so, and despite the fact that its absence would always make protecting the Park difficult. At the end of the Second World War, petrol and bullets were widely available and what the Le Riches called 'the era of mass killing' began. By this stage there were not many windmills in the Park to provide sufficient water to keep its animals sedentary and as many as 15 000 springbok would migrate out of the KGNP to its neighbouring countries. Sometimes as few as 3 000 would return. On occasion, Joep would have to drive lions back into the Park that had wandered out to eat local farmers' donkeys and sheep.

Mier residents would poach regularly along their border with the Park, but because they used donkeys for their transport they were often not fast enough to get away from the rangers, and in a period of seven months during 1948 Joep caught 22 poachers and confiscated 52 donkeys, 18 dogs and 11 guns. The biggest damage to the Park's game was done by white farmers from Namibia. They came in well-organised expeditions, equipped with powerful rifles and 4x4 vehicles. At one point Joep came across 100 springbok in a 50-metre radius with only the best biltong meat cut out of them. The poachers were also fond of shooting game such as lions and leopards. They would skin the animals – for later sale – and leave the meat to rot in the veld.

Joep kept pressing for a fence along the Namibian border to stem the slaughter on that side of the Park. In Makai's time, a land surveyor demarcated the border with beacons but it was over 30 years before the fence was erected. Park management set up a post at Union's End, staffed with one ranger and some camels to aid swift track and chase, but out there alone there was little he could do to curb the poaching in this vast area. The KGNP's road infrastructure was minimal and the shortage of vehicles and staff meant that Joep had to do the anti-poaching work himself, aided, of course, by his coloured and Bushman rangers. And if the vehicle broke down – as it did on occasion – they had to walk the 120 kilometres or more back to Twee Rivieren.

By the late 1950s the KGNP's staff numbers had increased and the border was patrolled regularly by Dawid and Buks, among others, who spent many days with Stoffel or Elias, driving the border and camping out for nights on end, trying to catch the hunters. It was work they far preferred to their other tasks, such as erecting windmills, fixing roads, making tourists' beds and shepherding animals, and they were often joined on these missions by other members of the Big Six. Their patrols were sometimes fuelled with high excitement and adrenalin, and gave the Bushmen the opportunity to use their superb tracking skills and every other trick up their sleeves to catch the culprits.

'The nicest thing I ever did when I was in the service of the Park was that I caught policemen,' Dawid told the camera with an impish grin on his face, before relating a long tale about this incident.

He is particularly proud of the fact that the policemen tried to dupe Stoffel into staying in Mata Mata camp one Saturday by saying they were coming for some beers and a braai. Dawid sat quietly nearby and watched the poachers' faces carefully.

Once they had gone, he said to Stoffel: 'Oubaas, Saturday those police are going to go hunting. You'll wait and wait and they'll never arrive.' It took a great deal of persuasion for Dawid to convince Stoffel to go deep into Namibia the following Saturday and lie in wait for the poachers, and once there, Stoffel reminded him: 'Remember, Dawid, you're the one who might have brought us here for nothing!' The rest of the tale made for hilarious listening: interminable waiting until they saw the reflection of the sun off the poachers' vehicle's windscreen, quickly dousing their fire, Stoffel with his foot caught in a plate of food, a high-speed chase through the bush, one policeman getting such a shock at seeing them that 'his pants and hands were full of piss', and finally the arrest of the three white policemen from Namibia who lost their jobs and 'paid a hell of a fine'. It was Dawid the storyteller at his very best, his gap-toothed grin wrapped around his words and his wracking cough punctuating every paragraph.

The day came, in the early 1960s, when construction of the fence began and Dawid said to Vetpiet: 'We are being cut out. We are now sitting in the Park but there will be a day when we'll have to go out of the Park, and where will we go then?' It was a prescient comment about the rootless life the family would endure within little more than a decade. 'We wandered around and wandered around but my heart was in the Park, and wonderfully I am sitting in the Park today. Not as Park owner but as a partner of the Park. So I thank the Park that we can sit here today to follow up on this history that I'm busy with now. I say thank you very much to the Park.' His gratitude was touching and his seeming lack of resentment even more so.

The benefits of being back on their land were beginning to show in the Kruipers' demeanour and faces by this point of the expedition and I was deeply thankful to have been able to bring them on this trip. I recorded my diary entry of 20 May while waiting for Sue to finish having a wee in the bush late at night. We had to go out together after dark so as to stand guard for each other: 'A really nice atmosphere in camp once again today. The old man gets more and more relaxed the further we go on and his memory is definitely improving. I showed the ladies what they look like in Priscilla's wing mirror and they agreed that they are looking wonderful by comparison with how they did when we left. Amazing what good nutrition and no booze can achieve. Suzi! What are you doing there? A monumental movement? Beethoven's ninth? Just get your pants up, I'm bored now!'

The next day was Saturday, 21 May 2011, and for some of the planet's crazier sects it would herald the end of the world. As Richard commented: 'Well, if it happens we're better off on this massive mattress of sand than anywhere else in the world!' The planet did not implode, of course, but I shall always remember that date. It was the day I witnessed an old, tired man finally released from a secret that had kept him prisoner for his entire adult life.

CHAPTER 11

Released from a Secret

Dawid's day of the 'Big History' dawned brittle-crisp and it took me several hours to thaw after another cold and restless night. It was mid-morning before we headed back along the KTP's main arterial road on the west bank of the Nossob River. After an hour or so we reached one of the Park's exclusive self-catering tourist camps, Grootkolk. The camp was empty, save for its resident ranger, whom we were required to inform that we would be on foot in his area. 'Watch out for the lions,' he said. 'I've just seen a big male and a female wandering through here.'

Grootkolk (or Geinab, as the Nama people call it) is a legendary place in the southern Kalahari. It is named after a small hollow, which retained water after the rains and provided the Kalahari's people with the only surface water within hundreds of square kilometres of this particularly arid region. The *kolk* is gone now, along with the reeds that fringed it, and a solar-powered borehole 50 metres away provides water for the tourists in the camp.

Makai and his fellow Bushmen were not the only desert dwellers who found the *kolk* useful. In the eighteenth and nineteenth centuries, the area was home to several different peoples, such as BaTswana and Nama, who wandered across what were to become international borders, in search of grazing and water for their horses, cattle and goats. Grootkolk became one of their favourite places, albeit not in the driest months of the year, by which time

152

the water had evaporated. Some 35 kilometres further south at Polentswa (or Poronswab in Khoekhoegowab) there was another rare source of water, but it lay deep beneath the sand in pits that the Bushmen – and later the Nama – had excavated in the chalky crust of the site.

We parked the Cruiser on the camp's access road and climbed a high dune nearby, our feet slipping backwards with every step in the dry, fine sand. It was about midday and the heat was shattering.

'It just sucks at your marrow,' I noted later in my diary. 'We were completely buggered but the Kruiper elders seemed to be impervious to it.'

From the top of the dune it was clear that this was the highest point in the area, as a concrete trig beacon at its summit confirmed. Karl set up his camera, positioned Dawid, and the old man began his seminal family story.

'This is Spioenkop [Spy Hill],' he began, 'but we also call it Kanonkop [Cannon Hill]. My grandfather Makai used it in the old days because it was his compass.' The sleeve of his old tracksuit flapped around his bony arm as he drew a broad semi-circle across the horizon. 'All of these [surrounding] dunes are very low, so if he came here he would know exactly where he was … and he could look for game … But then the Germans came and the fighting started.'

The Germans came to southern Africa in April 1883 to the country known today as Namibia, which is only a few kilometres away from Grootkolk as the crow flies. A twenty-year-old trader sailed into a bay on the west coast of Africa, which he promptly bought from the local Nama chief, and named after his equally young employer, Adolf Lüderitz. In exchange for money and rifles he also purchased a small patch of land surrounding the natural harbour.

Back in Germany, the Chancellor, Prince Otto von Bismarck, remained wary of acquiring colonies that his nation could neither afford nor defend, but eventually relented under pressure from traders wanting to do business in Africa, and from a public that was suffering from extreme poverty and landlessness as a result of an unprecedented population boom, urbanisation and industrialisation. If Germany could settle some of its citizens in a satellite state with plenty of space for both humans and livestock, raw materials and an unlimited source of cheap labour in the form of black Africans, many of its problems would be solved.

Bismarck's intention to acquire colonies was greatly assisted by the decisions made at the Berlin Conference of 1884 and 1885, which notoriously sanctioned European nations to carve up Africa into dominions that they could exploit at will. The diplomats allocated this corner of Africa, among some others, to Germany. And occupying this land would have the added benefit of keeping it out of British hands, something that Bismarck was keen to do.

By the end of 1884, this vast, dry territory was under German control, at least on paper, but it took the rest of that decade before the country's African citizens could be persuaded to sign the vague 'protection and friendship' treaties that the colonists offered. By the standards of the day, the treaties were lenient and the Germans made no attempt to seize land from the country's inhabitants. This was partly due to the fact that the new colony was proving to be unattractive to German settlers, and it took ten years before a mere 1 200 of them had decided to make a home in what had now been renamed German South-West Africa (GSWA). It took a similarly long time for Germany to put sufficient troops onto the ground to enforce its plans for the colony, plans that became increasingly – and alarmingly – evident to the local people.

At the time, GSWA was home to about five groups of people, two of which became the primary focus of German oppression. The Herero numbered about 80 000 and were pastoralists who had migrated to the country roughly 3 000 years beforehand and lived largely in the most fertile parts of the territory – its central and northern areas. Their fellow pastoralists, the Nama, were a mixed group of people who had fled the Dutch colony of the Cape in the eighteenth century and settled in the more arid, southern parts of GSWA, an area known as Namaland. Their population was roughly a quarter of the size of the Herero's.

The GSWA's Bushman population was much the same size as the Nama group and they had the added disadvantage of being loathed by settler and Herero alike. The Germans deemed them to be like wild animals and treated them as such. Some of the Bushmen fled the area when it became clear what sort of 'masters' the Germans would make, but many were unwittingly caught up in the horrifying events that ensued.

Herero society was organised like those of other herding nations in southern Africa in which large groups of people lived in well-established settlements and submitted to the laws and rulership of chiefs. They had been in contact with the outside world since the early 1800s, owned ox wagons and were well armed with the latest weapons.

The Nama, by contrast, comprised loosely affiliated, smaller clans, each with their own *kaptein* (captain), a name for their chiefs that they had picked up from the Dutch in the Cape and which had military origins. The title was appropriate because the Nama men were as much soldiers as they were herders. They were brilliant horsemen and marksmen, were disciplined and courageous in battle and often wore military tunics similar to those worn by the Boer commandos in South Africa. By the time the Germans arrived, the Nama had perfected guerrilla-type hit-and-run techniques against their enemies. Because the sale of hides and ivory was a major source of their income, they were also hardy and re-sourceful, having lived in the veld for long, tough hunting expeditions.

Nama society was egalitarian and women enjoyed equal rights with their menfolk, they could own property and were viewed as the head of their households. Namaland was communally owned and clan boundaries were fixed and strictly enforced. The *kapteins* who headed these clans were literate and intelligent, politically astute, charismatic and Christianised. Their home language was Khoekhoegowab but many of them spoke Dutch and English as well. Almost all of them enjoyed reputations that bordered on legendary in southern GSWA, and should have far greater renown outside the country alongside the world's other great resistance fighters.

Two of the most powerful of the twelve *kapteins* were Hendrik Witbooi of the Kowese, or Queen Bee, clan, who were also known as Witboois on account of the white headbands that they wore around their hats. Witbooi was only five feet tall, but was a man of great presence and leadership. His fellow *kaptein*, close friend and equally gifted leader, Simon Kooper, was the leader of the yellow bandana-wearing Geelkams (Fransman or !Kharakhoen) clan, who were named after Simon's father – their previous leader – Willem Fransman. The sequence of events that led up to what happened at Grootkolk involved these two remarkable men.

It was fortuitous for the Germans that at the time of their arrival the Herero and Nama were at war with each other. They had been so, on and off, for over twenty years as a result of the Nama encroaching on some of the Herero's prime grazing land and stealing their cattle. The Herero therefore regarded a treaty with Germany as a useful way of protecting their herds from their southern neighbours, and they signed the Germans' offer of 'protection' in May 1890. But it was little more than a trick by the colonists who then went on to try and sign up the Nama to the very same conditions. The *kapteins*' response was mixed. Only three of the twelve signed the treaties, and Hendrik Witbooi responded to the German offer by up-scaling his war against the Herero.

Meanwhile the new German settlers were far from happy. They resented the bargains that their leaders had struck with the Herero, in which the colonists could only rent, and not own, the land they farmed, and that they had to buy cattle from people they regarded as their subjects. Stories began to surface about the settlers appropriating land and seizing livestock. Worse, were increasingly frequent tales of abuse, severe beatings, rapes, forced concubinage and murders, committed by farmers and soldiers who were invariably let off by the German-controlled courts.

A formal declaration of peace between the Herero and Nama was signed in August 1892, but tensions in the colony continued to escalate and the local people developed a deep contempt and loathing for their colonisers. The Germans exerted pressure on the Nama clans to sign the treaty, without success, and then decided to teach them a hard lesson by destroying Witbooi's clan.

On the night of 12 April 1893, 200 German soldiers encircled Witbooi's camp, Hoornkranz, and opened fire on his people while they slept. Witbooi and his men were taken completely by surprise and he ordered them to flee the village so as to draw the German troops away from his womenfolk. But the Germans did not follow the Nama soldiers. Instead they fixed their bayonets and slaughtered all of those people who would not be of further use to the colonists: the elderly, children and the infirm. They set fire to the Witboois' houses with dead and injured occupants inside, looted the camp and left, taking 80 women with them who were distributed as slaves for the troops in Windhoek's fortress.

News of the horror of Hoornkranz spread quickly. Now it was clear that the Germans would have no hesitation in including noncombatants as targets in their war against the country's indigenous peoples. For the Nama and Herero this was utterly repugnant but even in the ensuing skirmishes and battles they resolutely protected German women and children, and non-German white men, from harm.

The battle had the effect of galvanising Witbooi and his guerrillas into seeking revenge for what had been perpetrated against the defenceless of their clan at Hoornkranz. For the next seven months they conducted raids against Windhoek, attacked German convoys and roads and caused havoc with their supply lines. But the Nama's supply of weapons was no match for that of the Germans. Eventually Hendrik Witbooi capitulated and signed the treaty, followed by Simon Kooper and the rest of the *kapteins*, most of them under considerable duress.

The following decade was devastating for the Herero because an outbreak of an infectious viral disease called the rinderpest wiped out 30 000 of their cattle within six months. As a result, many of them were forced to sell their land and go into the service of the Germans.

In the south, though, the Nama stuck to their treaties with Germany, and some *kapteins* became very wealthy on the proceeds of land that they sold or rented to the settlers. They slowly rebuilt their cattle herds and some received an annual stipend from the colonists. GSWA was stable, if not peaceful, but the tinderbox of tensions in the colony needed only a small spark to set the whole country aflame.

That spark was the murder of the *kaptein* of the Bondelswartz Nama in October 1903, who said with great prescience as he died: 'Now the war starts.' His people revolted, and ignited a rebellion that spread quickly throughout the south of the country. At exactly the same time the Herero mounted a huge uprising in the north. This presented a problem for the German authorities, who could not deal with both revolts at the same time. The Herero capitalised on their disadvantage and killed over 100 German soldiers and farmers within days.

What started as a rebellion turned into a war by early 1904, and Germany sent more troops to help crush the uprising in June of that year. With them arrived Lieutenant-General Lothar von Trotha, a man who was described by a soldier who served under him as a 'human shark' and 'the most bloodthirsty animal in his [Kaiser Wilhelm's] war arsenal'. By June, Von Trotha had started implementing his iron-fisted approach to the people he described in his diary as *unmenschen* (non-humans). He declared a state of martial law, let it be known that Germany would no longer negotiate with her adversaries, and demonstrated his intransigence by lynching, beating and hanging the rebels that his troops caught and leaving their corpses swinging from rudimentary gallows as a warning to others.

The Herero, to their great cost, did not recognise this fundamental change in Germany's response to local politics and thought they could still negotiate a settlement. Fifty thousand of them, with an equal number of cattle, withdrew as far as possible from the German settlements to the last waterhole before the forbidding Kala-hari – a plateau called the Waterberg (Water Mountain). There they waited for a German rapprochement, but it never came.

Instead, Von Trotha and 6 000 of his men headed for the Herero's Waterberg settlement, encircled them, and, in an almost carbon copy of what happened at Hoornkranz, rained down their guns on the settlement at dawn on 11 August 1904. The result was mayhem. The Chief, Samuel Maharero, and his men, tried to draw the German soldiers by fleeing into the Kalahari through a gap in the German lines, followed by some of his people. But the Schutztruppe stayed in situ and proceeded to massacre every man, woman and child who remained. They then sealed the area's wells and set up guard posts along a 300-kilometre line to prevent the escapees from returning. And in that dreadfully dry part of the Kalahari, the Herero survivors were faced with a desperate struggle to survive. Many did not.

As if Von Trotha had not made himself clear enough at the battle of the Waterberg, on 3 October 1904 he issued a proclamation that was nothing less than an extermination order. It was an explicit command, in writing, for the commitment of genocide in which Von Trotha instructed that: '… every Herero, with or without a gun, with or without cattle, will be shot. I will no longer accept women and children, I will drive them back to their people or I will let them be shot at.'

For two further months the Herero were hunted down in a series of 'cleansing patrols' that were instigated the length and breadth of Hereroland, and many Nama and Bushmen also became victims of the campaign.

Some harrowing oral testimonies survive about what happened during the battles and patrols under Von Trotha's leadership. The eyewitness accounts were collected by British investigators when that country wrested control of GSWA from Germany during the First World War and were released in 1918 in a parliamentary report, or 'Blue Book'. The book has recently been republished with the title *Words Cannot Be Found*, taken from a statement by one of the survivors who was interviewed about the treatment of the weak, starving and thirsty Herero who eventually limped back from the Kalahari after the battle of the Waterberg: 'Words cannot be found to relate what happened; it was too terrible. They were lying exhausted and harmless along the roads, and as the soldiers passed they simply slaughtered them in cold blood. Mothers holding babies at their breasts, little boys and little girls; old people too old to fight and old grandmothers, none received mercy; they were killed, all of them, and left to lie and rot on the veld for the vultures and wild animals to eat.'

Notwithstanding the fact that the Blue Book is riddled with British bias and pious moral outrage, and was produced by a nation that knew about the gross human rights violations happening in GSWA at the time and remained silent about them, it is a valuable collection of accounts of the extermination by the African peoples of that country. The book makes for deeply disturbing reading: soldiers throwing a baby to each other like a ball, then catching it on a bayonet to roars of laughter; young Herero women and girls being raped and then bayoneted; floggings, hangings, people being burnt alive. Accounts of these terrible acts pervaded the furthest reaches of GSWA and its neighbouring countries and filled the local people with terror – a terror that is still vivid in the memories of elderly Khomani Bushmen, who told Nigel Crawhall of the dreadful screams that filled the Kalahari, which they would never forget.

'Her fear was frightening,' Jan van der Westhuizen said of his great-grandmother's recollection of these terrible times. 'Every morning she would stand on the dune and sing "Bethlehem Star" like a prayer as the sun came up and the morning star appeared … Then she would hide in an aardvark hole the whole day.'

In December the Herero capitulated and surrendered to Von Trotha, but at precisely the same time the Nama decided to consolidate their uprising against the Germans. Their decision was prompted by what Hendrik Witbooi had witnessed at the battle of the Waterberg, where his troops had fought alongside the Germans, and his disgust for their treatment of the Herero's innocents.

Simon Kooper and all but two of the Nama clans joined forces with Witbooi and started attacking German patrols, farms and depots in south-western GSWA. For two further years they continued their brave and desperate raids, but superior – and much more plentiful – German weaponry eventually proved too much for them. One after the other the clans surrendered and their livestock was confiscated.

Hendrik Witbooi died in battle in October 1906 – he was 80 years old at the time – and his death was the last blow for the exhausted and demoralised Nama. The uprising was well and truly crushed – in no small measure because the Herero and Nama nations had not managed to put their differences aside and coordinate their efforts to expel the colonists. The war officially ended on 31 March 1907.

But one resilient and defiant Nama *kaptein* remained unbowed – Simon Kooper. Kooper was a small, stern man who smiled seldom and was reported as being 'old, somewhat shaky and decrepit' in a British dispatch of the time. 'But [he] still maintains his dignity as chief,' the report adds, 'and is treated with great respect by his followers.' Kooper was a godly man who had a pastor in his camps to lead the Sunday service and prayers before battle; as well as a multilingual clerk who handled all his correspondence and a schoolteacher who ensured that the Fransman children got an education during the clan's constant migrations. But Kooper exerted ruthless discipline over his men. His Khoekhoegowab name was Gom!ab, meaning an impenetrably dense thicket of thorn bushes, and he was given it because he was a reticent, difficult man who was very hard on his men. His only living grandson, Daniel Kooper, told me that Simon would punish his soldiers severely – sometimes they faced capital punishment – if they wasted bullets by only wounding – and not killing – their opposition. Kooper (sometimes spelled Cooper, Copper or Kopper, but his family used 'Kooper' on his gravestone) rode a striking white horse with red spots and a very long tail and he was a brilliant field tactician. As testimony to his wily battle techniques, the Germans christened him the 'Fox of all Foxes'.

One of the Bushmen at Kooper's right hand was Makai Kruiper. 'Makai was an errand boy, tracking for them,' Dawid explained to us on top of Spioenkop. And when his grandfather was not assisting the Nama fighters with reconnaissance, Makai and other members of his extended family, such as Agerob, looked after the Fransman womenfolk, minding their livestock, hunting and finding food for them.

Doubtless the Bushmen were invaluable to Simon Kooper, not only because of their extraordinary knowledge of the Kalahari's terrain and food plants, but because they spoke Khoekhoegowab. Indeed, it might well be that it was a result of a long association with the Koopers that the Kruipers became fluent in this language and gradually lost the use of their native Bushman tongue. I suspect that a man as avowedly independent as Makai would not have stayed with Kooper's band indefinitely, and he and his extended family probably moved off whenever their deep urge for new horizons and herds made itself felt. But, most unfortunately for them, the Kruipers were with the Fransman clan when the German-Nama war reached its bloody conclusion.

Kooper's territory was not only in GSWA but stretched into the Cape Colony and the British Protectorate of Bechuanaland. It included sections of the Auob and Nossob rivers close to what is now the KTP. At the start of the 1904 Nama uprising, the Fransmans were based at one of their larger settlements in GSWA, Gochas, but in early 1905 they were defeated in a small battle not far away from the town and the Germans occupied Gochas as their command headquarters. Many of the Fransmans were captured, and the rest, some 800 men, women, children and livestock, fled south to Koës with the Germans hot on their heels. Kooper decided that his women and children – quite likely in the care of Makai and his fellow Bushmen – should trek ahead while his men tried to hold the Germans at bay.

Guided by the Bushmen, and moving through the Kalahari at night, the Fransman womenfolk retreated to the Bechuanaland Protectorate and settled in a safe place, deep in the desert, which they had used on and off since the 1860s – Grootkolk. There, they were later joined by their menfolk and remained at the *kolk* until at least July 1906. This site, with its precious water, had the added advantage of the high dune defending its one flank, and, because it lay east of a particularly arid part of the Kalahari, it was impenetrable to the Germans. Not only was the Schutztruppe's weaponry heavy and cumbersome, but their horses were not accustomed to traversing deep sand and had not adapted to surviving on *tsamma* melons. Generations of Nama horses had used the melons as their main source of hydration, but the European steeds had made no such adjustment in the relatively short time of the war against the Nama. And until they were habituated to the *tsamma*, they developed swollen joints, mouth sores and diarrhoea from drinking the juice.

From his hideout at Grootkolk, Kooper became something of a diminutive Scarlet Pimpernel and, as the Blue Book puts it, 'the terror of the German settlers and patrols on the eastern frontier'. His skirmishes in GSWA claimed a couple of dozen German soldiers' lives in the next few years and resulted in a number of rifles, equipment and horses being stolen. Back in Bechuanaland he conducted a brisk trade, bartering livestock for arms from local traders such as Scotty Smith, while the British authorities tried to keep tabs on his movements and report them to the Germans. He remained frustratingly elusive.

But in early March 1908, Kooper's luck ran out. He, about 35 of his horsemen and six to eight men on foot – one of them could well have been Makai (although he did not carry arms) – ambushed a German patrol near Koës, killed all six soldiers of the unit and robbed their pouches, saddles, ammunition and oxen. The guerrillas fled back to Grootkolk and then on to some new settlements that the clan now occupied. It was autumn and because of the paucity of available food, the Nama had split up into smaller groups and relocated to Polentswa's wells and some pans much deeper into the Protectorate such as Molentsan and Seatsub – or Sitachwe as it is called today – very near the northern border of the KTP in

Botswana. And the raiding party left tracks that the Germans were, for the first time, able to follow.

The game-change in German strategy that had happened during the previous year was their decision to acquire camels to pursue the Nama guerrillas. Captain Friedrich von Erckert was appointed commander in the southern region in April 1907 and charged with subduing the Fransmans. He quickly realised that his soldiers were invariably forced to abandon their pursuit of Kooper's men because they and their horses ran out of water. Camels would be able to go much further on much less water, and, if the Germans timed their expedition when the *tsamma* melons were in short supply for the Fransmans, that would help restrict their movements. Like Kooper, Von Erckert would now also use Bushman trackers, the most famous of whom was a man called Damap.

A period of intense training and preparation followed for what would later be dubbed the 'Kalahari Expedition'. Hundreds of camels were specially imported from Arabia, along with one Arab trainer per ten camels. Under their tutelage the German troops learned how to load, lead and ride the camels. The British government was informed of Germany's intention to pursue Kooper into the Protectorate, but gave no official consent for the manoeuvre in its territory. The Germans decided to go ahead with their campaign despite this, and deal with any negative consequences at a diplomatic level later.

On 4 March 1908 a massive German column set out along Kooper's trail. It comprised 23 officers (led by Captain von Erckert), 373 rifles, 120 'non-white' auxilliaries, 4 machine guns, medics, oxen, mules and a staggering 710 camels. They reached Grootkolk a week later and immediately saw its merits for an advance base. Not only was there water in the *kolk* (albeit not enough for their huge numbers; they would have to import additional water), but the dune on which we were standing with Oupa Dawid would provide a perfect vantage point for a heliograph – an apparatus designed to communicate over great distances by means of flashing the sun's rays off mirrors in a kind of Morse code. From Spioenkop they would be able to telegraph messages to Windhoek about the progress of the mission.

'You youngsters must look for the blocks of the cannon now … Makai saw a cannon here and he said it was white,' Dawid instructed Isak and Klein Dawid. The 'White Cannon' remains one of the mysteries of Grootkolk. Makai was convinced that the Germans had one in their arsenal and described it to his son and grandsons. Historians say otherwise – that local legends have confused the cannon with the machine guns that Von Erckert's forces brought to the Kalahari.

The Kruipers spread out across the dune and we soon heard an excited shout from Toppie. He had not found a block but a *n!abba*, the Kalahari's famous truffle whose delicate, musky taste easily rivals that of its expensive cousins in France. The Bushmen now hunted for *n!abbas* with enthusiasm, and the quest for the cannon blocks was quickly lost. Perhaps the blocks were incorporated into those built for the trig beacon, I thought, as our hunt gradually lost its allure in the brain-frying heat.

We headed down the hill to the truck and Richard and Karl positioned Dawid for a last, short interview before we headed back to our camp on the fence. Out of the old man's mouth came a story that stunned us all. It was the story of a battle between the Germans and Nama on the plain opposite Grootkolk, which he had never told to outsiders. I sat near him, battling to assimilate what he was telling us because his tale correlated with nothing I had previously learned about the 1904–08 German-Nama skirmishes.

Before we left on our great adventure, Dawid had asked me to get permission to walk into Botswana because he wanted to show us something about a 'big battle' from the war. I had assumed he meant the site of the last clash between Kooper and the German forces at Seatsub Pan. But Seatsub is a full 80 kilometres from Grootkolk, so this clearly was not the battle Dawid knew about.

Dawid, though, was adamant. 'It happened here, I'm sure, and tomorrow I will show you where the Germans dug their trenches.

From there they shot at us, the Bushmen and the Nama, during the big battle here.'

We hauled our tired bodies onto the Land Cruiser and my thoughts raced all the way back to our camp. Wulf Haacke and my good friend, Mike Main – both enthusiastic amateur historians – have done extensive work on the Kalahari Expedition and had told me about the German occupation of Grootkolk. So Dawid was spot on in what he had described on the dune. But a big battle? Neither of them had mentioned anything like that, and neither had the literature I had read. Eventually I stopped worrying about it and gave myself over to the expectation of what we would learn the next day. 'I'm finished,' I recorded before falling asleep. 'I don't know how Dawid keeps going!'

We returned the next day, at our customary late hour, and parked in the same spot where the *kolk* had once been. 'Near here was the Spioenboom [Spy Tree] in the old days,' Dawid said after he had climbed down off the vehicle. 'The tree burnt down in 1972 or 1973. We had a great fire in the Kalahari that wiped out so many trees, bushes and game.'

The Spy Tree was a magnificent camel thorn whose high branches provided the Bushmen and Nama – and later the Germans – with an uninterrupted view of the Nossob valley, its game and dangers. 'Konigsbaum' (King's Tree), the German troops named it, and, when they commandeered Grootkolk, they hammered stirrups into its trunk as a kind of ladder, to make climbing it easier. 'Vetpiet's son, Didi, has some of those,' Dawid told us.

'Now we need to go and find the German trenches,' he said as he pointed his crooked fingers towards a low dune on the other side of the camp's access road. I followed him to the long dune, and watched while the Kruipers spread out to scan the site for evidence of the Schutztruppe's occupation. Within ten minutes their search had borne fruit. Toppie rushed to Dawid and presented him with a couple of old bully beef tins with faint German words punched into their undersides. The 'bohne' I saw on one of them could quite likely have been a remnant of the words 'Rindfleischmit Bohnen' – beef with beans – so Wulf Haacke later told me. Willem followed with the bottom half of a broken green bottle. The glass was thick, which indicated that it was probably old. Then came Am Am with the remnants of a metal ammunition box.

Our pile of goodies grew until it looked like a mini scrapyard. I called a halt to the search. 'Archaeology rules say that we may not move – or remove – anything we find on a historical site,' I told them. 'We must stop now. At least we're sure that this is where the German trenches were.' Much debate followed as to what to do with our finds until Dawid said something to allay my concerns: 'You know, Mama, Joep knew about this place. He said we should walk around here and see if we could find ammunition and guns … and perhaps the white cannon. And we dug and dug and found tins and empty cartridges.'

That put my mind at ease – at least we had not interfered with a pristine site. We wandered around the dune for another hour, during which time Willem found what looked like a grave. He called Toppie and they cleared away the grass that was threatening to overtake the burial site. Willem made a rudimentary headstone and breastplate out of some bits of rusted trunk and placed them at the dead man's head and on his chest. The two Bushmen took a step back, bowed their heads and said a few words of forgiveness for what they presumed to be a German soldier who had breathed his last so far from home.

Later in the afternoon it was time for Dawid to resume the story he had begun on Spioenkop. It came out in a series of unsequential, disconnected and confusing anecdotes that I later pieced together.

After the German troops had occupied Grootkolk, Makai decided to return there and ask them for some tobacco. 'Like grandfather, like grandson,' I chortled to myself as Richard translated Dawid's words. The Germans promptly tied him to a tree (it may have been Spioenboom) and questioned him on the whereabouts of the Nama and their Bushman 'boys'. During a storm that night – or perhaps as much as three days later – Makai managed to free himself and he ran to the Fransmans as fast as his renowned athletic legs could manage. 'The Germans are here,' he told them. 'We must go.' And they fled to Rambuka, a pan en route to Seatsub, but not before a bloody engagement with the Germans, which Dawid then told us about.

The Nama were positioned on the other side of the Nossob River, opposite Grootkolk. Simon Kooper and the 'Germans' big boss' had a meeting at Grootkolk under the aegis of a white truce flag, and, in a very gentlemanly fashion, decided to fight the next day. Kooper returned to his men, they constructed decoys out of some dark objects and placed them at points on the dune behind which they were positioned.

During the night, the Fransmans crept across the river valley and up to the German trenches. At dawn, and the moment the black flag (or it might have been red, Dawid was unsure about this) went up, the Fransmans opened fire from below and shot several Schutztruppe before fleeing back to their camp.

The Germans followed them, shooting from the protection of one low dune after another, until they caught up with the Nama, fixed bayonets and the hand-to-hand combat followed. 'My grandfather said to me you couldn't walk after the [battle] because this man's leg is shot off, he can't move, he's lying with his weapon in his hand and anyone that walks past he'll shoot,' the old Bushman told his silent and awed listeners.

'But there's nothing about this in the history books,' I said, feeling totally confused by what Dawid was relating.

'It was a big massacre,' he replied. 'The Germans are cruel people. You see that's why Patricia said she didn't see it in a book. People don't want to hear, and a lot of German people ask me if I want revenge for the war. And I say, no, I don't want revenge, it's in the past and we must forgive each other.'

Such a loving thing to say after such a gruesome tale, I thought.

'You see,' Dawid concluded his tale, 'that is why my father, Regopstaan's, name was !Gam!Gaub in Nama. It means "shot at but shot over [his head]". My grandmother was pregnant with him when they were running from the Germans. They shot at her and missed and that's why Old Makai gave his son that name.'

And the incident at Grootkolk also gave the Kruipers a surname – something that Bushmen did not have at the time. The family was named 'Crawler' after Makai's now legendary escape from the Germans. It translates as ≠Hanasen in Khoekhoegowab – the name Dart et al. had been given on their visit to Twee Rivieren with Donald Bain in 1936.

Many questions remained, but at least some of the puzzle's pieces were beginning to fit together and I felt hugely privileged to have been witness to a story that Dawid had kept buried for so long. Quite why he had done so was yet to be revealed.

'Tomorrow we'll go and find the Nama graves,' Dawid concluded at the end of our fascinating day in the veld. I could not wait.

You Can Never Wash It Away

T hings were not good in camp the next morning. Willem was sitting next to the fire looking very grim. 'It's my heart,' he said. 'I feel really bad.'

I was alarmed by his grey colour and weak voice, and by the fact that we were now so far from the Askham clinic. Karl stepped forward and said he would welcome the opportunity to use the Molopo Lodge's Internet connection as he had work that he needed to catch up on. He would be happy to take Willem to the clinic, and also return Isak and Klein Dawid home so that we could swap them with the other two youngsters. He would return with Buks, who was feeling much better, as I had established by satellite phone. Richard would film the day's events in Karl's absence. I felt sorry that Willem, Buks and the cyber trackers would not be with us for this important day in our discoveries, but was hugely relieved by Karl's offer. 'This trip is a logistical nightmare,' I muttered to myself as we left camp.

Back we drove to Grootkolk – I was beginning to know the road well – and walked slowly across the Nossob riverbed into Botswana. After about 3 kilometres, at the start of the low dunes that formed the eastern bank of the river, Dawid stopped, sat on his haunches in the shade of a tree and rolled a cigarette. We gathered around him and he picked up his story.

'Behind these little dunes is where the Nama were stationed,' he began.

170

Suddenly the rest of the Bushmen broke into excited chatter in Khoekhoegowab. They had spotted a Cape cobra lying under a nearby bush.

'*Ag*, leave him,' Dawid told them. 'It's our forefathers. It's Makai … he's just saying that he's with us.'

He went on to talk about another mystical visit – one that had happened the night before. He and Willem had been woken by the sound of something – or someone – walking around our camp.

'What is that?' they had whispered to each other. 'I thought it was a lion,' Dawid told us, 'then I thought it was a man. But it was very big.'

Richard and Sue said that they, too, had heard the night's caller, but I had heard nothing. At dawn, the Bushmen had walked around our tents, looking for the spoor of the man-beast. But there were none.

'Now, you see,' Dawid continued, 'we greeted that German yesterday [in his grave] and his spirit came to us last night. He might want revenge because we picked up his tin and stuff. He was looking for another soul and that is why Willem is ill this morning. You don't have to believe me, but I know it works like that.'

I was struck by the fact that it was Willem who had found the grave and Willem who was ill in the morning. 'I had chicken flesh when I saw [the grave],' Toppie added. 'That man came to take the soul of a Bushman in revenge, I'm sure of it.'

The mystery drifted away on the morning's light breeze and Dawid returned to his war story.

'Okay, when the shooting started, Ou Makai had already fled. The big battle happened a bit further on from here … They [the Germans] went over that second dune and [the warring parties] stabbed each other.'

So if Makai fled *before* the fighting, how come he knew where the graves were? I thought to myself and decided to risk asking Dawid yet again about the sequence of events, which was still unclear to me.

'I can say this a hundred times,' he replied testily. 'Perhaps somebody can just rinse my brain!' And he went through the whole story of the flight from Gochas again.

I realised I had to back off and try to work out later what had happened or I would piss Dawid off. Richard agreed.

'Okay,' I said, 'let's go and find these graves.' I rose to my feet and Dawid put out his cigarette in the sand.

'Look,' he said. 'There's another question I have.' His manner was suddenly emphatic. I sat down quickly and Richard switched the camera back on.

'My oupa told me another thing, and whether it's ugly or pretty, it *was* what my oupa told me. Those [German] men had towels, you know the ones you use to dry yourself after you've washed? One Nama woman was tied up and she couldn't do anything. The Germans stood, one behind the other, like they were in a queue at the bank. Each one came and had his turn, he wiped himself and then it was the next one's turn. Some [penises] were long, some short, some thick, some thin. And the woman couldn't do anything. That's what my oupa told me. It was here, at this place, Grootkolk.' He jabbed his index finger towards the ground.

My mouth dropped open as Sue translated Dawid's ghastly story.

'Now can any woman tell me how she would feel if she'd been that Nama woman?' Dawid asked.

'Ugly and dirty,' Sue replied.

Dawid agreed, shaking his head. 'You can wash and wash but you can never wash it away.'

Deep within me, I suddenly felt that perhaps *this* was the greatest of the secrets that the Kruipers had held onto for over a hundred years. And the reason for their secrecy was clear when Dawid next spoke.

'Yes, it is the truth, but ... we must think [about what to do with the information]. It's on the tape and it must be in the book. [But] can we open this up? Can we show it? There are Germans who are still alive and then they'll see what their forebears did. If this reaches German ears, this truth, what would the Germans think of me who tells this truth? ... If you carry on [like this], a German or any other nation, you are nothing. A dog does everything in front of you but a Bushman has got pride and he won't reveal these kinds of things, not even in front of his children. It's a disgrace. It's the biggest disgrace in the world.'

Given Dawid's horror at what his grandfather had witnessed, I tried – and failed – to imagine how profound Makai's horror must have been, living, as he did, at a time of such strict Bushman sexual mores. And he would not have been alone in his outrage. The Blue Book reported in 1918: 'Evidence of violation of women and girls is overwhelming, but so full of filthy and atrocious details as to render publication undesirable.'

The deep and traumatic effect of those 'details' is branded on the Bushmen's consciousness to this day, and they might well have been the most violent aspect of colonial oppression that they en-countered – with devastating consequences that still persist. As Jan van der Westhuizen explained to me: 'That was the time when the way of living broke and bad things came out of it. It became like an illness, people got addicted to the sexual spirit and it kept on growing and growing until it got to where it is now, and we have HIV and AIDS.'

It took several hours, and several square kilometres' search be-fore we found the seven or eight graves that validated Dawid's story – and perhaps even his life. His Bushman GPS had helped him to locate something that Makai had told him about and which he had seen 50 years before, as a young man of 26, when he and Agerob were collecting wild honey on the banks of the Nossob.

The graves were low, coffin-sized mounds that were virtually denuded of grass and topped with a black crust, perhaps from the fires that occasionally tear through the Park. Driedoring, or three-thorned shrubs, were growing out of several of them. 'And there are many more graves over that dune where the Nama were camped,' Dawid added. I watched as the old man grew increasingly confident and excited with each of our finds. Standing on one of the graves he gave us a testamentary interview that was redo-lent with relief and gratitude that he had been able to pass on this knowledge to his children. 'I was scared,' he said, 'scared to speak the truth, to show the graves. But I'm not scared any more.'

In the late afternoon we started making our way back to the truck, all of us silent with emotion at what Dawid had revealed to the world. We walked across the valley in single file. In the middle of the riverbed Am Am shouted from the back of the line: '*Kyk hier!* Look here!' He had found a bullet, an old bullet that was lying exactly on our path through that huge landscape and which we had all stomped past without noticing. The Kruipers passed it to one another and chattered excitedly in Khoekhoegowab. Was it a German or Nama bullet – or even that of one of the Park's hunters or poachers? That I cannot say, but perhaps one day I will ask for it to be brought out for analysis from its hidey-hole in Oupa's museum at Verdwaalskop.

Back in 1908, after a day's rest at Grootkolk (during which time Von Erckert's troops tried unsuccessfully to have him declared insane by the medical officer because they regarded the pursuit of Kooper to be so dangerous), the Schutztruppe moved out during the night of 13 March, following Kooper and his raiding party's spoor in a north-easterly direction into Bechuanaland. The half moon provided sufficient light to follow the Nama's tracks and Von Erckert hoped that the night's cool temperature would prevent the troops and their animals from consuming too much water.

Just past Rambuka Pan they set up another heliograph, for communication with Grootkolk and thence Windhoek, and they reached Molentsan Pan the following night after travelling after dark once again. Here they found signs of the Fransmans' camp, but it was deserted. Von Erckert left his troops to do some reconnaissance and soon got lost in the dunes. He fired a flare, and his men answered with another. These were seen by Kooper who, some sources say, worked out his plan of defence, gave his guerrillas their battle orders and then left them to their own devices.

Von Erckert's scouts stayed on the Nama's spoor, and, on the night of 15 March, they found the Fransmans near Seatsub Pan. The Schutztruppe encircled Kooper's men, slowly and silently, and waited for orders to attack, which came at dawn. Wulf Haacke writes that Kooper underestimated the strength and size of his adversary because his Bushman scouts had not reported seeing any wagons. He wrongly assumed that the Germans might show their white flag and negotiate a truce. This proved to be a critical error, but, nonetheless, the Fransmans were ready and waiting in their trenches and behind their barriers when the Schutztruppe opened fire.

One of the first to be killed by the Nama's answering guns was Von Erckert, followed soon by the captain to whom command was delegated. But the German attack was still well executed. Their rifles and machine guns fired on the Nama camp for about an hour, and then the Germans fixed bayonets and charged.

About 25 Fransmans fled to a gap in the line of German troops and escaped back towards the Nossob River, possibly to Polentswa, where some of their womenfolk were camped at the wells. Those left at Seatsub soon capitulated or were killed. The battle was over in just under two hours and it proved to be the last of the German-Nama war.

Fifty-eight Nama guerrillas lay dead on the dunes, along with the two German officers and eleven of their soldiers. Nineteen Germans were wounded, some of whom died on the way back to Grootkolk. It is not recorded how many of Kooper's men were injured, but his famous white horse was shot in action, and four of his women were taken prisoner, including his wife, Helena. She was transported to Windhoek in the hope that she had become a useful bargaining tool against her husband. 'Kooper is said to be much attached to this woman,' wrote the Imperial Governor of GSWA to the British High Commissioner in Johannesburg. 'She is, however, not very charming.'

Simon Kooper and the remnants of his clan eventually fled further into Bechuanaland and settled at Kgatlwe, which is near Lokwabe in modern Botswana, where some of his descendants live to this day. The British and German governments negotiated a deal with the increasingly frail old man that, in return for a regular stipend, he would desist from mounting incursions into GSWA, an agreement to which he stuck until his death in 1913.

Exactly where the battle of Seatsub took place remains a mystery, as does the location of Von Erckert's and his men's graves. Elias le Riche saw the graves as a boy, but the posts marking them were destroyed in one of the great Kalahari fires. At least seven expeditions have been mounted to find this important historical site, but the researchers have come back empty-handed, and the gravestones that were made to mark the resting place of the German soldiers remain at Gochas.

During the three years that Simon Kooper and his men were launching their raids into GSWA, the human rights abuses in that country escalated to an extent that has only come to the attention of the general reading public in recent years, largely thanks to a remarkable book by David Olusoga and Casper Erichsen called *The Kaiser's Holocaust*. What becomes clear in this work is that Simon Kooper and those of his clan who fled to Bechuanaland were immensely fortunate. They escaped a full-scale horror in GSWA, which some historians regard as a blueprint for the ghastly genocidal techniques that were perfected in Nazi Germany 30 years later.

Those Herero who survived the battle of the Waterberg, and the pitiless Kalahari to which they fled afterwards, were encouraged to surrender by missionaries. The local German government told them that they would be pardoned by the Kaiser, would be given food and blankets and could then return home. This was an outright lie and a heartless trick. Of the 13 000 'broomstick-thin' Herero who took up the Kaiser's offer and came to the collection sites, roughly a third were given out to farmers as slaves, and the remaining 8 500 were rounded up, put onto cattle trucks or force-marched to Konzentrationslager (concentration camps). It soon became clear that some of these were, in fact, nothing more than death camps.

There were five camps, all positioned near German settlements, which could benefit from the free labour that the inmates would provide. The largest of the camps was in Windhoek. There were two in Hereroland and two near the ports of Swakopmund and Lüderitz. Lüderitz's camp was situated on a small island in the bay, and its name, Shark Island, came to embody all the suffering and terror of the camps.

From early 1905, the inmates of the camps were shackled and put to work unloading ferries and ships, building railway lines, jetties and government offices. The majority of them were women and children, and in Swakopmund they were formed into teams of eight and forced to pull wagons and railway carriages. The prisoners were given minimal food and 'housed' in tents, at best, and sacking hovels, at worst. There was no sanitation in the camps and infectious diseases such as dysentery, syphilis and scurvy were rampant, as were lung conditions such as pneumonia that were greatly exacerbated by the cold, wet, coastal climate. 'The camp[s] quickly became infested with flies and maggots, which spread infection further,' Olusoga and Erichsen write.

Herero women and young girls were routinely raped, the prisoners were made to work, regardless of their weakness or sickness, and flogged mercilessly. A Hollander in Lüderitz was appalled by what he witnessed. 'Fifty lashes were generally imposed,' he is quoted as saying in the Blue Book. 'The manner in which the flogging was carried out was the most cruel imaginable … pieces of flesh would fly from the victim's body into the air.' Not surprisingly, the victims began dying like the flies with which they shared their abominable conditions. Some committed suicide by wading into the freezing water of the south Atlantic and drowning.

From February 1906, following the suppression of the Nama rebellion in the south, the Herero in the camps were joined by what was left of their southerly neighbours, starting with the Witboois. When they were rounded up, they were completely unaware of their destination – Windhoek concentration camp. There, Governor von Lindequist addressed them, saying that they would pay for their 'crimes' by suffering the same fate as the 4 000 Herero already in the camp – forced labour. The Nama were put to work on the nearby railway and found the work extremely taxing due to their small stature. Approximately 1 400 of them, 67 per cent, died within the first eighteen months. The local settlers complained that they were unfit for work and, on top of that, were a security threat due to their warlike reputation.

Von Lindequist decided to deal with the 'problem' by sending them to Shark Island and they were joined here by the remnants of Simon Kooper's people from Gochas. The difference between this camp and the others was that, although some of its inmates were put to work, Shark Island's express purpose was the elimination of the people sent there. By mid-February 1907, 70 per cent of the Nama on Shark Island were dead, and the rest were too sick to work. Some of the prisoners had been subjected to various medical experiments, while they were still alive, in which they were injected with drugs such as arsenic and opium.

The massive deaths in the camps gave rise to a lively trade in Nama and Herero skulls, skeletons and, sometimes, whole heads, by the German troops. *The Kaiser's Holocaust* describes how, in the Swakopmund camp, 'female prisoners were forced to boil the severed heads of their own people and scrape the flesh, sinews and ligaments off the skulls with shards of broken glass. The victims may have been people they had known or even relatives.' The bones and skulls were then sold to German universities and museums, where they were used by the scientists of the day to prove specious racial theories about the inferiority of the black races.

When Germany's campaign of extermination against GSWA's indigenous peoples was finally over, and the death camps were closed in 1908, 80 per cent of the Herero population and 50 per cent of the Nama had been wiped out. What was also wiped out until very recently, it seems, is the collective memory – in both Germany and its former colony – of what was perpetrated in the concentration camps.

There is not a single official monument to the camps in modern Namibia. Shark Island is now a municipal camping site, and at the mass grave of its victims in the desert nearby, many bones have been exposed by the wind and not re-interred. Tourists ride dune buggies over the holocaust victims' graves in a huge cemetery outside Swakopmund, and Windhoek's camp, which was situated outside its fort, nowadays features rolling green lawns and a statue of a German mounted trooper.

What proportion of the local Bushman population was killed between 1904 and 1908 is unknown, but after the war, as Robert Gordon points out, there was an 'ominous distinction [made] between *eingeborenen*, indigenous inhabitants, and *Buschleute*, bush people' by the German authorities, and the 'bush people' became decidedly third-class citizens. Those who remained in GSWA either retreated to areas where they could not be found, or went into the service of the settlers. Were they to have the temerity to report their employers' cruelty to the local police they were invariably flogged and returned to their masters. Missionaries gave verbal evidence to the British inquiry of 1917 and 1918 saying that 'a great cause of trouble between the Germans and the Bushmen was that the Germans would persist in taking the Bushman women from their husbands and using them as concubines'. The area around Grootfontein, which was rich in copper deposits that the Bushmen had utilised for decades, was taken over by the settlers. What were once their traditional hunting grounds were declared game reserves and the Bushmen were evicted.

Relations between the German settlers and GSWA's Bushmen deteriorated over the years until the Bushman rebelled in 1911 and began murdering farmers in the Grootfontein area, stealing livestock and any copper found on workers travelling to and from the mines. The government's answer to these incidents was to declare what Robert Gordon calls '[an] explicit German colonial policy to wipe out Bushmen'. Patrols and commandos scoured the land looking for, killing and/or capturing Bushmen. Those who were not shot or hanged were distributed to farmers as serfs. Eventually, just like the Herero and the Nama, the Bushmen of GSWA were well and truly routed.

In 2004, at a function to commemorate the centenary of the

war, a representative from the German government read out to the Herero crowds that had gathered an acknowledgement of guilt for what her nation had perpetrated, and she asked for their forgiveness. It was a welcome apology and since then there have been talks between the two governments about compensation and reparation for the peoples of Namibia. They remain controversial because, as Ciraj Rassool maintains, the Namibian government refuses to press the German government on the matter because Germany is a major aid donor to Namibia. The return of some skulls in 2011, Rassool adds, was made possible because of the willingness of the leadership of Berlin's Charite Hospital and not because of any policy by the German government.

'My heart is full,' I recorded as Sue cooked supper after our momentous day in the field. 'I'm so relieved for Oupa and I hope he feels unburdened. He told Suzie, apparently, that he feels like he's taken a whole lot of stones out of his backpack. It seems we've really learned something extraordinary today but Dawid's recollection is often confused and meandering. I cannot seem to lock things down. Is that because he's old and his memory isn't good? Is it because information gets lost or misinterpreted in an oral tradition? I don't know, but I'm full of unanswered questions. Why would Makai and Regopstaan insist that this place be kept a secret? Why would Makai flee from the Germans one minute and then saunter up to ask them for *twak* the next? If he left before the fight, why did he know about the injured men, and why did he know about the graves? Why, why, why? Things just don't add up.'

The agony and the ecstasy of Dawid Kruiper's life. © KS

|Hanaku at the Empire Exhibition,
Johannesburg, 1936. © MA

Agerob Bladbeen. © NF

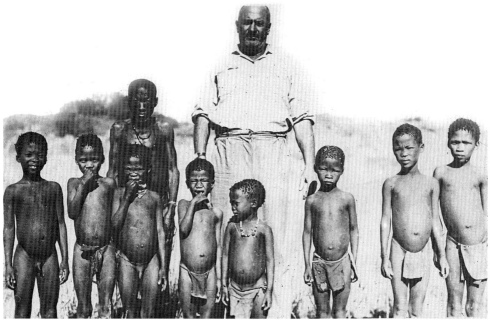

Donald Bain, Abraham Witbooi and Khomani children. © BF

Jan van der Westhuizen. © PG   Tokolos Org. © PG   Lena Malgas. © PG

Bitterpan. © KS

TOP LEFT: Lokwabe Koopers: Karel Barkaath (left) and Charles Kooper (right) at Simon Kooper's grave. © PG

TOP RIGHT: Tsabong Koopers: (front) Rebecca Kooper, Mary Kooper, Hendrik Kooper (back) © PG

LEFT: Gochas Koopers: Front row, left to right: Christina Kooper, Maria Kooper, Magriet Goliath, Lena Kooper, Piet Jaars. Back row: Isak Coetzee and Isak Klaasen. © PG

The team at work. © SO

Dawid and Toppie with the bountiful ostrich. © SO

© KS

Buks with a *gifbol*. © SO

Kabe and Mefi with *tsamma* melons. © PG

N!abbas, Kalahari truffles. © KS

Toppie and Jeffrey. © PG

Am Am, talented hunter. © KS

Galai making her delicious pot bread. © SO

Cyber trackers Klein Dawid and Isak. © SO

Priscilla's mobile clinic. © SO

Sue and Mefi in Priscilla's kitchen. © PG

Richard with our most precious resource – water. © KS

Dawid Kruiper, Oulet Kruiper and Phillipa Holden. © PH

David Grossman, Dawid Kruiper and Oeliset Org. © PH

Nanette Flemming and Lena Malgas. © PG

Am Am Kruiper, Toppie Kruiper and Richard Gordon. © RG

ABOVE: Claire Barry and |Una Rooi. © CB
RIGHT: Blits, the Bushman Boy – before … and after. © BJ

CHAPTER 13

We Are With You, You Are With Us

The morning after our visit to the graves we started a slow return trip through the Park, going back on tracks that had led us to a turning point in all of our lives. I was struck by the ignorance with which I had blundered onto the path to Grootkolk, and by the responsibility of sharing Dawid's secret with the world – a world in which rape is so tragically commonplace. Would these revelations be underestimated, or even dismissed? And would a modern country in which human rights are protected fail to appreciate the fear and vulnerability that caused the Kruipers to seal their lips? I knew that the family would not be in any danger by sharing Makai's ghastly experience. But did they truly feel that, too?

We spent a night at Nossob camp so that Dawid could visit a clearing he had noticed from the truck and which he thought might have been an old Bushman settlement. On the way there we came upon a pair of magnificent lions and sat quietly in the truck while they performed their ancient courtship ritual.

We walked 2 or 3 kilometres to the site through herds of springbok, hartebeest and gemsbok. The animals stared at us, then fled in all directions once they registered our humanness. We reached a grove of trees under which the ground was bare, but the area contained no other evidence of its previous occupants. I wondered how the Kruipers would determine who they had been.

The Bushmen spread out and started examining the tree trunks, feeling the bark and digging sand away from the trees' bases. 'Ah,' said Dawid after just a few minutes, 'it was herders who lived here – probably Nama people.'

How on earth did he deduce that? The Kruipers had found old and all-but-invisible signs that twine or wire had been strung between the trees to corral the livestock. Once again, I was astounded by their attention to detail and how the history of the Kalahari resides not in palaces or monuments but in the smallest impact of humankind on its environment.

We continued south to the most beautiful camp of our trip, once again tucked well out of sight of the Park's tourists. It was in the area around Moravet Pan (Get Fat Tomorrow Pan). According to Elias, the pan was named after a speckled cow that grazed here when the Park was farmed. Buks, though, said that its name derived from the time when the Park was not fenced and eland could migrate here and get fat on the pan's sweet grasses. The terrain was typical of the Kalahari's expansive savanna veld: gently undulating dunes with scattered trees that are generally taller than they are further south.

We set about the now familiar procedure of pitching tents and Priscilla's gazebo. The Kruipers cleared a space for the fire under two camel thorns that arched over our communal area like benevolent sentinels. Buks stalked his surroundings for hints of what it might yield in the coming days while Richard and Karl filmed yet another spectacular sunset. My pace was now as unhurried as the Bushmen's. Instead of fretting about what we should record the next day, I spent time carving out a Halloween head from a *tsamma* melon for Kabe. I placed a lighted candle inside it and handed it to the little boy. He looked mystified to be the recipient of such a grand present and gazed at the mask in wide-eyed surprise.

We huddled together around the fire with our backs to the

Kalahari's fierce winter cold, our banter easy and light. The fire warmed the copper tones of the Bushmen's skins till they looked rich and burnished. Elsewhere the night was dark and still and so appropriate for the ghost story that dominated our post-supper conversation. The spirit they described is that of Jan Kruiper, a family member who died many years ago but who still visits the family regularly at Witdraai.

'He likes the winter and leads people around,' John told us.

'*Ja,*' added Buks, 'he takes people sometimes 30 kilometres out of their way and when they come around their feet are blistered and they don't know how they got there.'

Evidently Jan looks and speaks exactly as he did when he was alive, wears his hat pulled down over his eyes and targets people who are drunk. 'Now you go home,' he says, 'you go straight home and if you don't it'll be you and me.'

'He told us he wants to get to know the entire Kruiper family, so it's not as if he's gone. He will come back to teach us a lesson,' John murmured as he gazed into the flames.

I watched Dawid chortling at the stories and cuddling his grandson on his lap. 'His face is completely different,' my audio diary remembers. 'He even seems to be lighter skinned and kind of floats above the ground. He's absolutely delighted by this whole trip and I'm amazed how my feelings for the Kruipers are beginning to change. I had a very rough introduction to these folk. I saw the worst of them and now I'm seeing the other side. And I have a feeling that I will make friends here for life and that my fate with this community has been sealed, that I will forever more be doing work with and for them.'

Our visits to Moravet Pan and Bitter Pan seemed to be superfluous to the heritage mapping, and I got the feeling that we were going there just to extend the duration of the trip. So what, I thought, they are going back to hell on earth so let's enjoy a holiday together. But the journey was now clearly taking its toll on Dawid's old legs. He was often in extreme pain, and had to lie down next to the truck after our field trip to Bitter Pan. One of the youngsters was now sharing his tent with him in case he needed help in the night, and his interviews on camera were vague and repetitive.

There was some excited chatter and finger pointing at a depression near Bitter Pan but the Bushmen's conversation was in Khoekhoegowab. Ah, maybe there is some secret to do with that place, I decided. Well, great. As long as the children know, we do not need to.

Buks was digging like a man possessed near our camp. He had discovered – no, probably remembered – an area containing *geluk-houd* (the good luck plant). 'It helps people make decisions in our favour, like when we go to court or when we are owed money,' he explained as he chopped up a few roots and shoved them into his studded handbag.

Not far from our camp was a windmill that Buks had helped build while working for the Park. Richard positioned him in front of it for a chat about his times as a ranger and general labourer for the KTP. Despite his very short stature, Buks was given the job of driving the Park's graders, sitting on an old army coat so that he could reach the pedals. And it seems he was something of a terror behind the wheel. 'Those two needles would look as if they were broken!' he told us with glee.

Sometimes Buks would chase lions off their kills so that he could steal meat for the family and on occasion the lions followed his bloody trail back to Twee Rivieren and he would be in deep trouble with Elias. Camped out next to the roads, Buks became the ears and eyes of management and reported any suspicious activity to them. Elias remembers an occasion when Buks radioed through to say that he had found the head and hooves of a gemsbok. 'By the time I got there,' said Elias, 'all the poachers' evidence was gone – Buks had eaten it all!'

When not performing the more mundane tasks required of him as a ranger, Buks worked with the many researchers who came to the KTP to study its animals and insects, and he is fondly remembered by them. He shared many hours in the field with scientist Gus Mills, who was studying the Park's carnivores. Buks remembers one incident – which Gus does not – when he was left with a sedated cheetah while Gus went off to check on something else-where. 'Next thing a pride of lions arrived,' Buks related, 'so I pulled the cheetah into a tree to prevent them eating it – and me. Then the cheetah started waking up and I didn't know what would be worse, to stay in the tree with a pissed-off cheetah or face the lions on the ground!' Fortunately, Gus arrived in time to prevent him having to make the difficult decision and the lions fled at the sound of the vehicle.

Our chat with Buks next to the windmill echoed the theme of so many others on our trip: the old days were free and peaceful, the present just a nightmare. 'I don't want an arse-keeper when I'm in the veld,' he moaned, 'someone watching my backside when I walk to that dune.'

He explained to us how bountiful the Kalahari was to those who knew how to utilise its offerings, such as how to make tradition-al Bushman beer using wild honey and a combination of yeasty plants and bird droppings.

'We had our own SA Breweries,' as Dawid put it, 'but our beer didn't make us sick.'

Buks talked about the taboos attached to hunting the Bushmen's iconic spiritual animal, the eland. 'If you kill an eland, it cries and that is very sad for us. We are proud of the eland, we don't kill it because that's as good as killing your mother.'

By the time Buks was an adult and working for Park manage-ment, life for the Khomani had changed considerably for the worse. During the decades following Donald Bain's interventions, their movements and traditions were gradually restricted to the point that, by the 1950s, their lifestyle hardly resembled that of Bushmen. Every Thursday, Joep went to Askham to collect the post and buy rations for the Khomani left in the Park. They were de-nied permission to hunt 'reserved' – or large – animals and their dogs were shot. When Jens Bjerre visited the Khomani in 1958 he found them 'living as pensioners … from time to time the Game Warden shoots a deer for them. They themselves are only permitted to catch smaller animals such as jackals, desert hares, and the like, but they have already lost so much of their skill that they cannot find enough food for themselves. Ten years ago the colony consisted of 28 Bushmen; now only half of them are left, living an artificial life on misplaced charity.'

Makai, Bjerre tells us, was deeply concerned about the rapid erosion of the Khomani's culture and continued to teach the myths and traditions that he saw disappearing so quickly. 'He also confessed that he had been twice in prison for killing a gemsbok and declared that it was the most terrible experience of his life – to be shut up in a small room. Although it was many years ago, there was still a tremor in his voice as he spoke of it. He still cannot understand why they must not shoot the animals that they used to eat for food and which the white man himself does not eat.' Bjerre gave him the reason: 'Because we like to look at the animals.'

There were several incidents of the Kruiper clan members being caught for poaching during the mid-1900s. Regopstaan, Agerob, Makai and Dawid's brother, Andries, killed a gemsbok outside the Park and were caught by the police's camel patrol. They were arrested and taken to Witdraai police station where they dug the cell-caves that are there to this day. Andries was given six lashes and the others were sent to jail in Upington. Makai and Agerob were sentenced to two months each because they were old, and Regopstaan to six months. Like all Bushmen prisoners, when they were discharged they were told to walk back to their homes in the Kalahari – a distance of some 300 kilometres.

During the time the three men were away in prison the Kruipers stayed at Welkom and came close to starving to death. Once again, Joep came to their rescue and offered Andries a job and the family a home at Twee Rivieren. How long they were there no one could tell me. It is difficult to trace the Kruipers' comings and goings from the Park during the 1950s, 60s and 70s. The older generation are illiterate and tend to remember events as happening 'after the big fire', or 'in the year that the Nossob came down in flood'. It seems that during these decades, either some or all of the Kruipers would leave the KTP after some or other contretemps with management, then return until the next one, or until some other work beckoned.

What is clear, though, is that their relationship with the Park's managers deteriorated through these years, in part due to the fact that attitudes towards 'non-white' groups hardened in apartheid South Africa and in part because of the Le Riches' belief that the Bushmen should be 'tamed'. The Bushmen told me that the Khomani who stayed in the KTP were forbidden to sleep with people outside the clan and if young girls were caught going to visit their Nama, Tswana or coloured neighbours, Elias stretched them over a barrel and beat them with a hose pipe. In Hannes Kloppers' book about Joep, it is suggested that this was in an effort to 'keep a group of full blood Bushmen so that they would not disappear from the face of the Kalahari'.

No doubt keeping them 'pure' also made them a useful tourist attraction, but the Le Riches' actions constitute social engineering of a most despicable kind. '[Joep] had the authority to do what he liked,' Jan recounted. It was like a small boy playing a game … And because old Joep did this, Elias did it a bit more when he was Park Warden … It was so bad that your eyes couldn't believe it, it was just so bad.'

Because some of the Bushmen defied Elias' orders and had children with non-Bushmen, he regarded them as having been disqualified from having the right to protection in the Park. As far as he was concerned they were now 'Basters' (bastards), and he resented the fact that on top of rations and medical attention, they wanted, as is reported in Kloppers' book: 'to keep dogs again and hunt freely. They wanted to come and go as they pleased. They wanted to receive visitors as they saw fit. And they wanted better housing, very untraditional. But they did not want to work. To summarise they wanted a small earthly paradise.' The fact that the Bushmen were now prisoners on their own land seems to have escaped him.

The reputation that Bushmen have of being averse to hard work has plagued them throughout history and in some cases has merit. As Buks puts it, 'We're like dogs, you know. If we see someone who has a bigger bone for us, we'll leave you. But don't worry, when we've finished that bone we'll come back!'

Several businesses in the Kalahari have stopped employing the Khomani on account of their drinking problems and 'unreliability'. It is certainly the case that managing Bushman employees requires creativity and compassion. !Xaus Lodge, a luxury, 24-bed, thatched camp situated inside the !Ae!Hai Kalahari Heritage Park, is co-owned and staffed by Khomani and Mier people. It opened in July 2007 and provides a small income for both communities and SANParks. The Khomani allege that their employers there are heavy-handed and racist at times. By contrast, the !Xaus management's experience is that the Khomani are essentially still hunter-gatherers at heart, they do not like to commit to long-term employment, they like to keep their options open and need to be with their families. Those who feel like making and selling crafts at the lodge are brought in from Andriesvale for a couple of weeks, then taken home and swopped with a new group.

About the work ethic of the older generation of Kruipers, however, Joep was full of praise, and is reported in Kloppers' book as saying how precious they were to the Park. This might account for the fact that Dawid, Buks and a few others continued to work in the KGNP – on and off – even after the final eviction of the Khomani took place in 1973. Elias disputes that the Khomani were evicted, saying that they left of their own accord. The Bushmen, by contrast, vehemently believe they were thrown out of the Park having been accused of, among other things, drunkenness, begging from tourists and selling biltong from 'poached' buck.

Perhaps the truth lies somewhere in between – that conditions were sometimes so intolerable for the Bushmen that they would rather cast themselves into the farming diaspora than stay in the Park.

On one occasion they left on orders from head office when some tourists asked Makai if the Bushmen were provided with meat by Park management and he had replied that when the big bosses shot meat for them some of the meat was used for biltong, some went to the police constables and all that was left were the bones, which were given to the Khomani. The final mass exodus happened after the Bushmen killed a couple of leopard cubs and were caught and beaten by Joep. Regopstaan was so angry that he gathered up his family and left. He worked on various farms before settling on Welkom's outskirts, while his relatives, and some other Khomani, continued to be employed by the Park, on and off until the mid-1990s, but still subjected to summary dismissals.

After our Moravet camp we headed back to Dawid's veld school at Bobbejaanskop to map and record some of the material that we had not had time for during the first leg of the trip. Sue and I moved camp while Richard and Karl took Buks on what sounded to me like a wild goose chase.

'About twenty years ago, when I was still working in the Park,' Buks told Richard, 'I found about ten ostrich eggs under a tree south of Nossob camp. They had been used to store water by Makai and his fellow travellers and were directly on the route they took when they were travelling to Twee Rivieren. The wind had blown the sand off the eggs and the hyenas had broken all but one of them. So I put it in the crook of the tree to prevent it from being broken like the others. Please could you give me a chance to find that egg?'

When Richard told me about this conversation I was frankly sceptical that Buks had any hope of finding the tree in the Kalahari's vast landscape, notwithstanding the location skills he had already demonstrated several times. The footage that the guys returned with, however, removed any doubt I might have had about the old man's extraordinary memory. It had been a long day for the crew, with a drive along a particularly rough sand road. Even Richard and Karl had begun to doubt the old man's claims after several hours of constant assurances that the tree was 'around the next corner, around the next corner'.

But the moment came when Buks told them to stop the car, got out and walked confidently towards a tree not far away. He bent

189

down underneath its low branches and felt inside them. Gently he removed a perfectly preserved ostrich egg, with its telltale hole in the top. He placed it in the sand and then began to sob. 'There's Old Makai's handwork,' he mumbled, as he arranged the shards of the broken eggs around his prize. 'This makes me so heart-sore. When I think of my granddad I feel so much pain. And this shows that we've been here for ever and ever. It's our Park.'

Buks slowly emptied the sand out of the egg, rose to his feet and carried it towards the car, wiping his nose and eyes. Then he stopped, turned and whispered some final words to Makai: 'We found your place, Oupa. We are with you, you are with us.'

With the light fading fast Buks walked into our *skerm* carrying the ostrich egg with all the reverence of a museum curator handling the Cullinan diamond. He gingerly gave it to Dawid, who passed it from one Kruiper to another while they talked excitedly in Khoekhoegowab.

'How does he know it was Makai's?' I asked Richard.

'Oh, he knows,' was his reply. 'He's convinced.'

Somehow I did not doubt it. Dawid asked me to look after the egg until we could find funding for a heritage museum at the Park's Twee Rivieren gate. 'It will just get broken if I take it home,' he said to me as he handed it over. I was deeply moved by his trust in my custodianship of this precious, fragile item.

The next day an even smaller artefact from the past revealed itself – this time to Dawid and at the place where he spent his toddler years – the area where the Nossob and Auob rivers meet. It was here that Joep built his house on top of a calcrete rise so as to enjoy a spectacular view of the Nossob's caramel-coloured valley and its high, grassy banks. Not far away was the Khomani's village where Dawid first crawled around the sand that would define him. The foundations of Joep's house are barely visible now, but, unlike the view, his house looked as if it had been small and humble.

Karl set up his shot while Richard and I walked around the site, and, when the camera rolled, Richard showed Dawid what he had found in the ruins of Joep's house. It was a small, funnel-shaped pipe fashioned out of an old tin and used by the Khomani ancestors when they did not have their bone equivalents. Dawid pursed his lips and lifted the pipe to them. 'Oooo my,' he said, 'the hands that held this pipe are not here any more and that is why I want to protect and preserve it.' He decided to take it to his museum at Verdwaalskop but then changed his mind and handed it back to Richard for safe keeping until it could be archived.

Knowing that we would not have many more opportunities to interview Dawid, Richard and I encouraged him to reminisce about his life and what he felt we had achieved on the trip. He described the great privilege of meeting Nelson Mandela, who asked him to remember that he was not only the leader of the Bushmen but of everyone in South Africa and had a duty to look after them. Dawid returned to his now-familiar themes: being allowed to use dogs and donkeys in the Park and the sad predicament in which the Khomani find themselves.

'I'm not a person that asserts myself. I don't toyi-toyi. Through doing that, people get a lot of things. I don't want to hurt anybody by who I am, but first it was God and then he made the Bushmen.'

Dawid sat down on the edge of the calcrete mound and looked down at the road that brings so many tourists to his land. I watched his wrinkled, peppercorned head turn from side to side as he drank in a sight that he might never see again. He looked tired but content.

'All the things that I put away here [in my heart] are now out in the open,' he said. 'It feels to me that I'm finished everything and I can rest a bit now. I want to rest. Let the children carry on now with the things I have taught them.'

But there were still a few places that Dawid wanted to show his family, one being the grave of his great-grandfather, Ou |Galakab, Agerob's father. |Galakab was one of the Bushmen whom Joep had found starving at Sewepanne in the early 1930s and brought under his care. |Galakab was a loner, evidently, and children were afraid of him, perhaps because he was one of the last of the Khomani who was allegedly able to transmogrify into animals and is reported to have taken on the guise of a lion and wander far from home to sort out problems in other clans.

We headed for Twee Rivieren's staff houses, parked and waited for Dawid to direct us. But he seemed confused. He approached a family leaning against their fence. 'I'm looking for a big white stone,' he said to them. 'Have you perhaps seen it?' They directed him to a spot a few metres away, next to the sand road between the houses. The rock was bright white and bound with wire so had clearly been used to stretch skins, like the one we had seen at Agerob's kraal, but there was no other evidence of a grave. Dawid, John and Willem surrounded the rock and looked down at it with anger in their eyes.

'See here,' Dawid pointed at the stone. 'This was once |Galak-ab's and we used it for his head stone. But when Park Management needed to use it for something else they just took it. And when they were finished they just chucked it here. Now we have no idea where my great-grandfather is buried – only that it's somewhere around here. How can people behave like this?'

The following day was our penultimate in the Park and Dawid decided to end our journey where his life had begun – the place where he had been born on the high red dune near Houmoed. He struggled to the top of a dune in sight of Regopstaan's old kraal but it was too far for his old legs to manage.

'My biggest yearning is to go to my birthplace with a vehicle, but we wouldn't be allowed to drive on the dunes,' he muttered, before saying with some frustration that at his age, Makai was still jogging. We sent off the youngsters and Am Am to GPS the kraal and settled down for one last chat with the old man.

I asked him if he thought he had made mistakes in his life.

'Many mistakes, but the mistakes I made I learned from. And the consequences of the mistakes I made [should] come to me, not to another person.'

I was about to pursue what those mistakes might have been when we were interrupted by shouting from the valley below. 'Come, come, look here!' the Kruipers yelled. Dawid took off down the dune at a pace that would have made his grandfather proud. We caught up with him when he finally stopped next to a dead ostrich. It lay with its legs outstretched, as if frozen mid-stride.

Tina and Toppie stood over the giant bird with huge smiles on their faces. They had been walking the surrounding veld when they noticed the spoor of a cheetah on the hunt and started tracking it at speed. Not long afterwards the cheetah ran away, deserting his prey for the safety of some trees in the distance. The Bushmen fell upon the bird like seasoned butchers, wielding their knives with speed and knowing exactly how to skin, dismember and joint the carcass.

Dawid sat with his legs astride the ostrich's neck, picked up its head and made funny talk to its empty eyes before setting about the task of removing its windpipe. 'This will make for a nice feather duster,' he told me, his hands red with blood. 'I'll dry the pipe till it becomes hard, then put feathers into one end.'

The rest of the menfolk started cutting into the ostrich's massive hip-bone, sawing and hacking into the sinew until they had separated one of the bird's upper thighs from its body. Toppie carried it off – his quarry easily the size of his torso. Dawid followed with one of the wings and Am Am with the stomach and the stones they had found inside it, which would make for strong talismans when the family needed protection or healing.

'What about the rest?' I asked them. 'Don't you want to take more?'

'No, no,' they said, 'we always leave 80 per cent for the one who did the hard work. The cheetah needs to eat and he'll come back once we're gone.'

The Bushmen hurried down the dune to our truck, packed the meat under the seats and we returned to camp. The ostrich's thigh was wrapped in grass and branches for transport home the next day and they put the rest on to boil for supper. I was relieved that the Kruipers had finally eaten meat from the veld.

Fifteen minutes later Richard came to me in the gazebo. 'There's trouble. They're very worried that they've done something illegal and will be in trouble with SANParks.'

I rushed to the fire and found the family consumed by doubt and fear. Buks especially was terrified of the consequences of what they had done. They had been chucked out of the Park for 'crimes' of this nature before and were convinced it would happen again. I tried to calm them down by explaining, as Phillipa and Grossie had done so often before, that this was land over which they had cultural and heritage rights and that they were permitted to take what they needed from the veld, as long as it was done responsibly and was recorded. Nothing helped to calm them so I undertook to see the Park's head, Nico van der Walt, on our way out to explain our actions. But the mood in camp remained subdued for the rest of the evening, and was so different from the happy farewell feast I had imagined us having.

I thought about how far the Khomani have to go before their understanding of the land claim agreement is matched by the confidence needed to exert – and enjoy – the rights contained within it.

We packed up our camp for the final time the next morning and did the last of our 'profile' interviews. John walked to the top of the dune and dug down to the moist layer of sand that lies about 25 centimetres from the surface. He took a small handful of soil and ate it, as a way of reconnecting with the land of his birth and to cleanse his stomach. Finally he tied a knot in a tuft of grass 'to keep the sun captive on our land', and walked back into camp.

Sue and I distributed the leftover food between the various branches of the family. I paid the Kruipers the balance of their salaries and we took photographs of our little group that had been on so much deeper a journey than I had been prepared for. Am Am came up to me and shyly presented a walking stick that he had crafted on behalf of the family. Into its shaft he had burnt the words: 'Patricia Glyn we appreciate your goodness.' I hugged him hard and told him how grateful I was for all he had done to help us around camp. Next, Buks reached up with his parting gift. It was a talisman he had made to keep Priscilla and me safe on the road. Thin roots from three of his lucky woods were twisted into a human-like form. He had placed what looked like a doll near its head. 'See, Mama,' he said gently, 'I gave it long legs like yours, but I put a little Bushman on your shoulder to remind you of us.'

As if I need a reminder, I thought as I laughed and cried with him. I think I am going to have a Bushman on my shoulder for the rest of my life!

I watched the Cruiser disappearing over the dune for the last time and drove off in Priscilla soon afterwards, using the drive to dictate my thoughts at the close of this remarkable journey.

'I think the analogy of a bull in a china shop is fitting here, you know. If you go blundering into the Bushman community you've got to look at it not as a china shop but as a Waterford crystal palace. You cannot come in here in a mindless way and bombard your way through their world view and psyches, because you'll come away with nothing but shards that will cut you deeply, just as they will them. I also have this feeling that some of what happened on this trip was magical or mystical, beyond my understanding, like it will take a long time to absorb. Or am I getting all mushy and over-imaginative now? What I'm sure of, though, is that they have great wisdom but it's coupled with what so many people have called child-like qualities. It's a strange coupling of innocence and wiliness. On this trip they were ten steps ahead of me at any time, they knew what they wanted, how they were going to get it and how they were going to get me to give it to them. But I see it now as a survival tactic and I have to applaud them for it.'

Portrayals of Bushmen as 'child-like' have often had pejorative intent, but I am now of the opinion that it is a good description when meant in a kind and admiring way. Craig Foster is certainly right when he says that 'part of their foraging technique is to appear very innocent', and the Kruipers undoubtedly use their 'innocence' to achieve what they want.

But what makes the Bushmen appear to be like children is that they seem to experience life with an uncomplicated immediacy that we have abandoned. They are emotionally accessible where we are closed and defensive. They are impulsive where we are restrained and cerebral. They are unselfconscious, they laugh a lot and they are physically demonstrative. And the effect of being with them is to have the child in us called out.

Laurens van der Post may have been wrong in a lot of what he said about the Bushmen, but he was right about this: 'The child in me had become reconciled to the man.'

Our odyssey was at an end but I still had much work to do, sifting through what Dawid had told us and finding people who could confirm or debunk his Grootkolk story. And I had so much more that I wanted to learn from this damaged, difficult, charming, knowledgeable, wise and funny family. As had happened to so many other FOKS, my feelings for the Khomani had come full circle. I had started out with a kind of naive affection and admiration for them. That had been betrayed and exploited many times on our journey and no doubt they felt the same about me. But here we were at the end of our trials and I felt a loyalty and commitment to them that almost overwhelmed me. Claire Barry was right – this was indeed like falling in love. We had gone through an intense and hurried affair in which both parties disappointed each other before emerging on the other side and finding themselves in a far more understanding kind of romance. And I had made some progress towards the state that Nan Flemming had reached after eight years with the community, a 'place beyond judgement, beyond everything'. I remembered what she had also said: 'The Kalahari first takes before it gives.'

I stopped off at Twee Rivieren to report what had happened with the ostrich to Nico. He was quite happy about the Kruipers taking a bit of it and was also glad that our expedition had been successful. I found Dawid sitting in the back of Karl's bakkie at the camp's fuel pumps and told him the good news.

'He looked tiny and utterly, utterly exhausted,' I recorded later. 'I think he held everything together as best he could but it was a very gruelling trip for him.' Time would reveal just how tired Dawid actually was.

CHAPTER 14

Dawid's Treasure Hunt

'Makai was a German spy, did you know that?'

Elias le Riche's words landed like a punch to my throat. 'He told me himself. And Stoffel Brand, who delivered water to the Germans at Grootkolk, also told me that Makai was with the Germans there. Makai said that the Germans approached him in Gochas and asked him if he would do it. He stayed at Grootkolk because he was too scared that the Namas would see him as a spy. So he stayed there; the Germans went ahead and had the battle, and when they had finished it he moved back with them to Gochas.'

I paused the recording of Richard's interview with Elias, and my eyes scanned the ceiling of my study. 'How on *earth* do you tell a community that their hero, the great Makai, was a German spy?' I agonised. 'Can this *possibly* be so?'

I pressed the play button again and Elias followed with another blow. 'And I would put my head on a block there is no way there are graves at Grootkolk. You must remember that sometimes when the sand blows into the *driedorings* and so forth, if the bush then burns down, that heap stays there and it might look like a grave [but it's not].'

And so began journeys within a journey for me, quests to save – or perhaps, sadly, otherwise – both Dawid's and his beloved grandfather's reputations within the Khomani community, and to try to corroborate the old man's account of what happened at Groot-kolk. The search took me to archives, libraries and to Simon Koo-per's descendants in Namibia, Botswana and South Africa. I hoped that at least one of these written and oral sources would be able to confirm what Dawid had told us.

First I turned my attention to the available, published material about Grootkolk. It soon emerged that sorting fact from fiction is all but impossible because the accounts are radically different and contradictory.

The famous travel writer and amateur historian, Lawrence Green, visited the area in 1936 with some University of Cape Town students and wrote up a dramatic version of the story. Unfortunately, he does not name his sources, and they are not listed in his copious notes preserved by Joan Yates-Benyon. Some have suggested that Scotty Smith was his guide, but Smith was dead by then. We can safely presume, I think, that Green's information came from local white farmers, traders and the like. He wrote that Kooper put his snipers into the camel thorn trees at Grootkolk, and, at daybreak, they opened fire on the Germans in their trenches.

'It was a hopeless situation. The surviving Germans jumped on their horses and headed west. This was exactly what Cooper [sic] knew they would do. Cooper's mounted men barred their path and captured the survivors. They were led back to Geinab ... Cooper's men stripped them of their uniforms, then told them to march back naked to their own country. The Germans marched ... As they marched, the Hottentots [sic] [Nama] shot them down. No doubt some of the Germans ran, making better sport for the Hottentots. It was a war in which no quarter was given, and the survivors of the Geinab garrison were shot in the back to the last man.'

Hannes Kloppers' book about the KGNP and the Le Riches contains a whole chapter on Grootkolk, and states that it was the site of the 'last humiliating battle between the Germans and the Hottentots [sic]'. This concurs with Dawid's belief, but not with any other written sources. Furthermore, Kloppers' statements about the 'the tyrannical leader' Simon Kooper are highly questionable.

He writes, for instance, that Kooper and his men were in the habit of murdering white boys, babies and grandfathers in GSWA while their womenfolk were forced to watch – conduct that I very much doubt as I have not seen it described elsewhere in the literature that I have consulted.

Kloppers cites three sources for his information on Grootkolk: Stoffel le Riche, Stoffel Brand (who delivered water to Captain von Erckert's men) and Simon Kooper's son, Markus. While he mentions a man called 'Damap' as being the most famous of the Germans' Bushman scouts, there is no mention of Makai. Kloppers also writes that the Fransmans fled south from Grootkolk to Polentswa. This proved to be an important new piece of information, as I found out later.

The anthropologist, H.P. Steyn, who worked with the Khomani in the 1980s, was told by none other than Regopstaan himself that 'German troops from the then German South-West Africa were involved in a skirmish with a party of Geelkams [Fransman] Nama. Afterwards, the Geelkams buried their dead in shallow graves and left the scene. A group of Bushmen, including Old Makai, used the opportunity to dig open the graves to remove the tobacco pouches from the dead. The culprits, however, were tracked down by mounted Geelkams, who tied the Bushmen to a tree and shot them. Old Makai's life was spared because one of the Geelkams knew him to be a good man. Regopstaan was born on the day of Makai's return to the camp of his people, somewhere on the Auob and Nossob rivers, and was subsequently named after Makai's narrow escape.'

But Regopstaan's account of what happened during this alleged incident was entirely different when he related it to anthropologist John Marshall. This version is contained in Sandy Gall's excellent book, *The Bushmen of Southern Africa: Slaughter of the Innocent*. Regopstaan told Marshall that about twenty Bushmen were captured by a German patrol, tied to a tree and shot. 'As the soldiers were tying up the Bushmen, the commander overheard one of them who had been educated at a mission school telling the soldiers in

German to hurry up and shoot, and get the whole gruesome business over and done with. The officer immediately ordered him to be untied and spared, since he needed an interpreter. The rest of the party, including the Bushman's wife, was shot. When the opportunity arose, the Bushman escaped, taking with him his young son who had been hiding nearby, and fled into the Kalahari far to the south-east, to the Nossob valley, on the South African border … The boy … was given the name Regopstaan.'

Makai, educated at a mission school and able to speak German? His wife shot and killed in the incident? These claims do not stack up with the Kruipers' oral history and that of other members of the Khomani community. So, did Marshall get it wrong? Did Regopstaan? And, whatever the version of the tale, were the graves that we saw the result of this incident and not a battle at Grootkolk? If Makai did indeed steel tobacco pouches from the Fransmans' dead bodies he might have been too ashamed to talk about his actions to anyone but his son and request that Regopstaan – and later Dawid – keep them a secret. Added to this, Memory Biwa, a PhD student at the University of the Western Cape, whose thesis is about the German-Nama war, told me that grave robbing was a concern during the war, and that this could have made the Kruipers keep the graves' location a secret.

Wulf Haacke is unquestionably the researcher who has done the most extensive and meticulous research on the Kalahari Expedition, which he has published in articles for the *Namibia Scientific Society* and *Botswana Notes and Records*. Haacke has also been involved in several expeditions to try to find the location of the German graves near Seatsub. His work on Von Erckert's campaign is invaluable as a means of trying to make sense of Dawid's statements.

Oupa told us, for instance, that it was Makai's tracks that the Germans followed from Gochas, and that he was running to warn the Nama at Grootkolk of the Schutztruppe's approach. What Haacke says about the events of 15 March, however, the day before the final battle, seems to put this incident, or a very similar one, at a different location: 'Early that morning Bushman tracks were found [by the Germans, near Molentsan Pan] and then shots were fired at these Nama scouts, who escaped … During the afternoon … a recently vacated camp was found, with the coals of some fireplaces still glowing, suggesting that this site had only been vacated after the Bushman scouts had brought the warning of the proximity of the German column.'

So perhaps Dawid was incorrect, and the '!Gam!Gaub incident' occurred much further into the Protectorate than Grootkolk. Or perhaps the Bushmen were fired at more than once.

It is extremely difficult to establish from the German records whether or not a battle occurred at Grootkolk because, as Haacke points out, the official campaign report, the diary of one of Von Erckert's soldiers and the second file on Simon Kooper have all disappeared from the Windhoek Archives. Under the heading 'The Geinab Debacle', Haacke analyses several popular accounts of what allegedly happened at Grootkolk, such as Lawrence Green's, and concludes: 'The supposedly quite substantial losses have so far not been traceable in the otherwise very efficient and detailed German official records of that period [meaning the death and injury registers].'

Haacke also writes about reports by the Cape Mounted Police camel patrols and the British High Commissioner in Mafeking (now Mahikeng). These suggest that German-Nama skirmishes might have occurred at Grootkolk *after* the final battle at Seatsub, as part of GSWA government's measures to monitor Simon Kooper's movements and prevent him from further incursions into that country. A German patrol, for instance, surprised about 40 Nama guerrillas at Grootkolk on 8 July 1908, but the Nama withdrew after a short exchange of fire. Subsequently, on 27 August in the same year, an engagement between the Germans and about 60 Nama took place there, and, once again, the Nama retreated. No loss of life was reported in either incident.

There were some 200 small engagements between German and Nama forces between 1904 and 1908, many of which were so small as to remain unreported, so it is possible that Dawid's 'battle' was one of these and that it took place a few years before the final battle of the war. Regopstaan consistently claimed that he was born in 1905. If that is true, then his mother and father being pursued and shot at must have happened during that year or some time in 1904.

Are the graves really graves? I very much doubt that Agerob, a Bushman with such detailed experience and knowledge of the Kalahari landscape, would have mistaken post-veld fire mounds of sand under the three-thorn bushes for graves. But the task of establishing the veracity – or otherwise – of the burial site must now fall to an authorised and professional team of archaeologists. Memory Biwa (who is Nama herself) told me that the Nama people are vehemently opposed to having their graves excavated, but by using metal detectors, it could be confirmed, perhaps, whether or not there are human remains there.

Next I turned my attention to the matter of whether Makai spied and tracked for the Germans or the Nama. First, I went to see Elias le Riche on one of his farms near Andriesvale, and Nan accompanied me as interpreter. Elias emphatically confirmed what he had told Richard.

'Is it possible that Makai was captured by the Germans and forced to do that work?' I asked him. No, was his emphatic reply, adding that Makai was proud of his work for the Germans and the fact that they had chosen him to do it because it showed him to be a master tracker.

Nan and I left our meeting with Elias in a state of sadness and shock.

'How am I going to substantiate what he told us, Nan? Or otherwise, of course?' I asked her as we made our way back to the farm cottage.

'You know,' she replied, 'I heard that there was an old Kooper guy still alive and living in Upington. Let me try and find out how to get hold of him.'

It was not long before Nan's unparalleled network of Kalahari contacts came through with a telephone number and we went to see the old man the following day.

Piet Kooper is the grandson of Simon's brother, Christian, and we found him enjoying a small square of shade outside his house in Upington's township. His version of events was that the Bushmen were fleeing from the Germans. They met up with Simon Kooper at Gochas and the two groups went on together to Grootkolk where there was a battle.

'And were the Kruipers among those Bushmen?' I asked Piet with my heart in my mouth.

'They were together and the Bushmen were there to look after the women and children ...' he responded.

'And did Simon Kooper mention Makai Kruiper?'

'Oh yes, we are like family,' Piet replied.

I needed to be sure.

'So Makai was working with Simon Kooper?'

'Yes, he worked with him.'

'So he didn't work for the Germans?'

'Uh uh, no, no, no, he worked for the Nama,' Piet said, shaking his head vigorously.

I could have hugged him. His words brought to mind a comment I had heard in the Khomani community to the effect that the Kruipers should actually be called Koopers because they were so closely allied to the Nama family and because Simon Kooper took many displaced Bushmen under his wing during and after the war.

'But you can ask the Koopers from Botswana and Namibia if you like,' Piet added. 'They're all together at the moment because they need to discuss an offer by the German government for compensation or something. Simon's grandson is there and he knows more.'

Once again that good old Bushman synchronicity had landed an unsolicited gift in my lap and I would have a chance to chat to several of the Fransman clan members in one go, and without having to travel hundreds of kilometres to Namibia. I allowed myself a superstitious whisper: 'Thank you for lining them up, Makai. We *will* get to the bottom of this.'

I had left my passport in Johannesburg, so Nan drove through to Botswana and brought the four men to meet me on the South

African side of the Bokspits border post. Daniel Kooper is Simon's last living grandson and the head of the family in Botswana. He brought with him Isak Klaasen, who lives in Gochas and has collated a small archive about the famous Fransman *kaptein*, and two other elderly men who are part of the Kooper clan in Namibia.

We sat on the grass outside the customs house and slowly I went through my core questions once again.

Did they know of a battle at Grootkolk? No, but there was some fighting between there and Polentswa. And when either side wanted a break they sent a messenger with a white flag and there would be a cessation of fighting for coffee and a meal. When the red flag was raised, the firing resumed.

Had they heard of Makai Kruiper? No, but Daniel remembers his father telling him about a Bushman tied to a tree by the Germans.

Did they think it was possible that Makai spied for the Germans? Well, the Germans sometimes got information from those who stayed behind when Kooper and his men were away fighting, so this was possible, said Isak.

The conversation was helpful but I still was not satisfied that I had tied down the facts as thoroughly as I would have liked to.

'I have lots of Simon Kooper's letters in Gochas,' Isak said, 'and there are some old people there who may be able to help you.'

'Well, it looks like I'll be going to Namibia anyway!' I said to Nan as we drove away.

Six months later, once I had finished all but this chapter of the book, I set out for Gochas. The gravel road that leads travellers through what was once Simon Kooper's territory is wide, white and well maintained, and it cuts through a landscape that is flat and depressing. The ground is stony and the plants it supports are uniformly grey and dwarfed. Every 20 or 30 kilometres a farmhouse appears. The signposts indicate that the farms belong, without exception, to Afrikaners. Perhaps some are the descendants of the trekkers who settled there in the late nineteenth century and who, Kloppers alleges, were the victims of terrible cruelty at the hands of the Nama.

When I got out of the car to change a burst tyre I gulped down mouthfuls of hot air and dust. 'How the hell do people *survive* in 50 goddam degrees day after day, let alone enjoy life?' I muttered to myself as I struggled to remove the wheel nuts. They would not budge and eventually I decided to walk to a farmhouse to ask for help, feeling a tad pathetic. But the farmer also failed to loosen the stubborn nuts, so he went back to his workshop and returned with some kind of monster bolt remover that finally did the job.

I passed Koës, the place to which the Nama and Bushmen fled from Gochas on on their way to Grootkolk. 'Must say I wouldn't have lurked here, even if I didn't have the Schutztruppe hot on my heals,' I recorded. 'What a backwater – if one can use that description in such a dry place!'

After a six-hour drive, the last section of which comprised a Big Dipper dune ride, I rounded a corner and the beautiful but dry Auob River lay before me. It was dense with waving green trees and its banks were made up of round hills topped with flat sandstone turrets. Now there was life wherever I looked: people, sheep, horses and glossy fat cows. A short time later the turn-off for Gochas appeared. My, my, Simon Kooper, I thought, you certainly knew how to pick a capital!

These days his town – perhaps 'town' is too generous a term – is situated on the eastern bank of the Auob where the river appears to curl back on itself several times, winding around the sandy citadels. On my way to a local campsite I passed a farm with the name 'Simon Kooper' on its gate and felt deeply moved that I was at last on the famous man's turf. Where I pitched my tent, as I found out later, was exactly on the site of Simon's old settlement, next to the fountain that his hunting dogs had found and which supported his clan for decades. That old Bushman synchronicity at work again, I decided. But as I also later discovered, Gochas is not as peacefully bucolic as it first appeared to be. Simon's farm remains in Afrikaner hands, and the lush trees of the area are invaders called prosopis. Their pods have become a reliable source of food for livestock during the dry months, but the trees are doing great damage to the local flora and water table.

I found Isak Klaasen in a location just outside the town centre. His neighbourhood bears all the hallmarks of South Africa's occupation of Namibia during the apartheid years: small brick houses in straight lines with minute yards and few trees. About 3 000 Fransmans live here, a marginalised, minority group that has seemingly been forgotten by the Namibian authorities. All the other Nama clans have been granted land in modern Namibia, but not so Simon Kooper's people.

Isak and I arranged to meet the next morning so that he would have time to assemble people who could help with my enquiries. He and his relative, Isak Coetzee, greeted me at his front door wearing bright shirts in the Fransman colours: orange and yellow. On a couch in his tiny lounge were four old ladies. A middle-aged man sitting on a chair next to them had a face that looked vaguely familiar. It turned out that Piet Jaars is a descendant of both the Kruipers and the Koopers. On the coffee table was Isak's collection of his august ancestor's photographs and letters.

Slowly and methodically I went through my questions, yet again. Was there a battle at Grootkolk, which might account for the graves we saw? No. The main battle was at Polentswa. 'Are you sure?' I asked. 'The historians seem to think that the battle was at Seatsub.' Yes, they were sure. Did they know about the concentration camps? Yes. Practically every family in Gochas had someone who was sent to Windhoek's camp. They were captured at Grootkolk and marched for seven days to the fort. Did Simon Kooper leave the battle at Seatsub before it started? Yes. He was sick and in need of medication. Did they know the names of the Fransmans' Bushman trackers? No. Had they heard of a Bushman called Makai Kruiper who might have spied for the Germans? No, said the old ladies.

Then from my right-hand side came a loud 'Yes!' It was Piet Jaars. Makai was spying for the Germans but not voluntarily, he said confidently. The Kruipers were definitely at Gochas. Makai was working for the Koopers; he was captured, and, probably out of fear for his life, told the Germans where the Nama were.

I felt a warm rush of delight that Makai had again been exonerated from his awful charge. Our conversation meandered through different aspects of the German-Nama conflict and I picked up several new insights into Simon Kooper's mind and character while paging through Isak's collection of papers. The letters confirm the guerrilla leader to have been far from intimidated by the powerful colonisers that surrounded him. I particularly liked his letter to the Commissioner of the Cape Mounted Police saying that he 'knows nothing of people who sit on the other side of the sea and draw lines'.

After about an hour I felt that our chat had run its course and that the old ladies wanted to leave. I asked one last question. Had anyone heard the story about the Bushmen robbing some Nama graves and being shot? Again it was Piet who responded.

'That is true,' he said emphatically. 'I heard it from my father and my grandfather but I don't remember where it took place. Both the Koopers and the Kruipers kept the graves a secret but when the Bushmen dug them up the secret was out and Simon Kooper was furious. So he shot them.'

Quite why there had been a need to keep the graves a secret Piet could not say but I was pleased that at least some aspects of Regopstaan's tale had been corroborated. I asked Isak if there might be someone in Botswana who I should talk to in a final attempt to solve the mysteries of what Dawid had told us. He directed me to a 97-year-old, blind man who lived in the village of Lokwabe where Simon Kooper had settled with some of his people after the war.

Priscilla and I took off for this small, remote town soon afterwards. The temperature nudged 50 degrees while I set up camp in the bush outside the settlement, 'donating blood to the tampans' in the process, as Toppie would have described it. The head of the Kooper family in Botswana is Charles Kooper and he was waiting for me at the *kgosi*'s (chief's) office so that we could let him know what brought me to Lokwabe and get his blessing for my mission. That done, Charles led me to Jacob Khabee, grandson of one of Simon Kooper's soldiers, Steven Coetzee. The old man was on a mattress in the corner of a room, the tiniest of men with pale, abundantly wrinkled skin and cheeks black with age and sun damage. He sat with one leg curled under him and the other hugged to his chest, resting his head on one knee while he listened to Charles explain why I had come to see him. Jacob is not only blind but virtually deaf so our conversation was loud and slow. While Charles translated his responses, Jacob would drift off to sleep and have to be roused for the next question. It soon emerged that he remembered very little about what his grandfather had told him, but he was positive that the war ended at Polentswa and not at Seatsub. I decided we should leave as soon as possible so as not to exhaust what little strength Jacob had left.

Outside Jacob's house, Charles asked if I wanted to visit Simon Kooper's grave. We set off for Kgatlwe Pan, roughly 10 kilometres away, where the Fransmans settled after the war until their wells dried up and they had to move to Lokwabe. Karel Barkaath, the grandson of Simon Kooper's secretary, joined us. The pan is broad and brilliant white and we crossed its crusty surface to get to Simon's grave. Some black horses cantered in the distance, their coats starkly contrasted with the bleached background of the pan.

The guerrilla leader's resting place is in a fenced enclosure and its marble headstone cites the important events of his life in Khoekhoegowab on the one side and in German on the other. Nearby are two other graves but they are humble and covered only with calcrete stones. They belong to Simon Kooper's horse handler and the latter's mother – testimony to how much the old leader valued his famous steed. The three of us stood in the searing sun around the grave and Karel began to talk enthusiastically about the man who lay beneath our feet. His ancestor, he told me, was the man who wrote the letter to the Germans during the battle of Seatsub. He carried it to enemy lines in a forked stick with a white flag in his other hand. The letter requested a cessation of firing so that Kooper's men could have a coffee break.

Bingo, Dawid dear, I thought. That is two accounts mentioning flags so you were right about them, if a little confused about their colours.

Karel confirmed that there was a break in the German lines through which Simon Kooper and some of his men fled from Seatsub to Polentswa and that that is where the war ended. Then Kooper's troops split up, some went back to Gochas and the rest to Kgatlwe. Neither Karel nor Charles had heard of the concentration camps, they had no information about the graves Dawid had shown us, and they had not heard of Makai.

'I heard that Isak's aunt, Rebecca Kooper, lives here, and that she might have some information,' I said to the two men.

'She's not here at the moment,' replied Charles. 'She's in Tsabong, so you'll have to go there if you want to talk to her.'

Gawd, Dawid, I thought as I headed for Tsabong the next day, you certainly are sending me on a wild treasure hunt!

The road between Lokwabe and Tsabong is among the worst I have driven and it had deteriorated since Sue and I used it during my 'Bushman walk' recces four years beforehand. Priscilla's wheels were sucked into deep ruts left in the treacherous sand by other vehicles that had braved this 250-kilometre track, her belly ploughing through the high *middel-mannetjie* (ridge between the ruts). We slipped and slid along for two hours before the sandy stretches began to alternate with patches of badly graded calcrete stone, along which we growled and rumbled in the appalling heat. Thirty kilometres from Tsabong, Priscilla resigned from her job of getting me to our destination and we came to an abrupt stop. Smoke was pouring out of the engine, there was oil everywhere and an alarming 'tucker, tucker, tucker' sound was coming from between her front wheels.

I got out my satellite phone and called Sue in Johannesburg. 'Please find someone in Tsabong who can tow me in?' I asked her, and she set about looking for the telephone numbers of garage owners in the town.

A group of South African holidaymakers stopped and tried to help me but the men knew as little about vehicle mechanics as I do. We poked our heads into Priscilla's recesses, tried this and that, but she was *not* going to move. Then one of the guys suggested I should try taking the car out of four-wheel drive, and, eureka, my old girl inched forward.

It was late afternoon by the time we limped into Tsabong and I found Rebecca Kooper. She was dressed in a brightly coloured patchwork dress and sitting under a tree outside another of Botswana's typical township houses – square, small and two-roomed. Rebecca was married to Simon Kooper's eldest son, Hendrik. She is 95 years old but her memory is fully intact. She has the kind of dainty, high cheek-boned Nama features that had become familiar to me by now, and her brown eyes twinkle with humour and intelligence. Soon afterwards her daughter, Mary, came out of the house and sat down next to us with an emphatic, sullen look on her face.

'So, you're here for information about our history,' she challenged me in broken English. 'And we give it to you, like we've given it to so many other people [from universities] – South Africans, Australians, Germans – then you leave. And what happens then? We carry on living like this [in desperate poverty] and we never see you again.' Mary lifted her chin defiantly when she had finished her challenge.

It was a complaint that I knew well, having heard it from the Khomani so often. I explained that I had a contract with the Kruipers that committed me to compensating them from the book's profits, but that I could not offer the Koopers the same deal because the book was principally about the Kruipers. But I promised her I would return with a copy of the book and would pay Rebecca, as I had all my other interviewees. I added that I was familiar with the kind of exploitation to which her family had been subjected and that I would quite understand if they did not want to talk to me.

Mary lent back in her chair and her eyes scanned my face intensely. A rapid exchange in Khoekhoegowab ensued between her, her brother, Hendrik and Rebecca. Finally she turned back to me and said: 'No, it's fine, we'll talk to you.'

I settled down and started going through my all-too-familiar questions. It was a struggle, and, unfortunately, the information I gleaned lacked fine detail due to my poor Afrikaans and Mary and Hendrik's rusty English.

I drew a rough map of Grootkolk and its environs in the sand at our feet. 'Here's the Nossob,' I said, tracing a loosely waving line, 'here's Grootkolk, Polentswa and Seatsub. And here are the graves that Dawid showed us. Do you know if there was a battle there?'

'Yes, yes,' was Rebecca's excited reply. 'The Nama were hiding in some dunes on the Botswana side of the river and there was some fighting there. But I don't know about the graves.'

I almost felt Dawid tap me on the shoulder and say I told you so! Rebecca confirmed that the war ended at Polentswa; that she knew about the concentration camps but had not heard of the Kruipers. We chatted for a while before I raised the burning question that I had put to all the Koopers I had met, in South Africa, Namibia and now Botswana, and which none could confirm. It was the question regarding the incident that the Kruipers felt most insecure about, and the question that had become the most personal and important for me as their biographer.

'Rebecca,' I said gingerly, 'have you ever heard about Germans raping Nama women?'

She watched Mary's face intently while her daughter translated my question and as soon as the Afrikaans word '*verkrag*' (rape) came out of Mary's mouth the old lady turned to me, her face filled with anger and outrage.

'Oh yes, I certainly know about those. The rapes happened at Polentswa and there were many women involved. I don't know how many. It was a terrible, terrible thing and even Simon's wife, Helena, was raped. She lost her baby and eventually her life because of those rapes. When Simon found out about what had happened to the women he was so angry that he said, "Now we fight!" And they fought and then the war ended. Helena was captured by the Germans because she refused to flee with the other women. Her little son, Petrus, hid in the bushes and then ran all the way from Polentswa to Kgatlwe to tell everyone that she had been taken.'

The passion and conviction with which Rebecca replied to my question left me in no doubt that she was telling the truth, or at least *her* truth, and what she said about the capture of the women at Polentswa was precisely what Isak Klaasen had told me during our chat at the Bokspits border post. Wulf Haacke, however, maintains that Helena was captured at Seatsub, and, to my knowledge, although she lost her baby en route to Windhoek she did not die and eventually returned to Simon in Botswana.

'So, if.there were rapes, is there German blood in the Botswana Fransmans?' I asked Rebecca after telling her how valuable her information was and how grateful I was to receive it. No, was her response. Does not make sense, I thought as we wound up our chat. I said my goodbyes to the last of the Koopers who had so generously shared their traumatic history with me. The next morning I began my journey home to Johannesburg in poor, crippled Priscilla. We made it – just – but Priscilla's mechanical problems were severe and expensive to repair.

The last word on what allegedly happened at Grootkolk and Polentswa belongs, fittingly I think, to Buks. About a year after our trip he decided that he was ready to speak about things that he had not revealed on the expedition. In two conversations with Richard, one of which took place at Polentswa, Buks went through his grandfather's experience, and the fluidity of his narrative leads me to believe that it is very largely creditable, despite containing a few inconsistencies. Buks described Makai's flight path from Gochas, via Koës (where he joined up with Simon Kooper), Grootkolk (where the Germans shot at him and his wife and where there was a 'big fight'), Rambuka and, eventually, Polentswa. And it was at Polentswa, Buks is adamant, that Makai was captured by the Germans, tied to a tree and witnessed the rape of both Nama and Bushman women. Buks repeated to Richard the ghastly details of the rape that Dawid had given us. Simon Kooper arrived, saw what was happening to the womenfolk and so raised a white flag and made peace with the Germans. After the truce, the Nama and Bushmen were allowed to go. They dug the pits that we visited on the trip and then trekked in separate directions.

Why did the Kruipers keep the story of the rapes a secret? As previously described, they suffered from a deep fear of German retribution and of offending the descendants of their former adversaries. But perhaps Makai felt that by passing the story on only to the first- and, in Buks' case, also the second-born son of succeeding generations, he could ensure that it would be kept alive in their oral tradition but would do no psychological harm to the other members of his family, particularly the women. Perhaps Makai also had in mind to protect the children of the raped women from prejudice or ostracism. Or perhaps his – their – silence is just the Bushman way. As Piet Kooper said to Nan and I: '[The Bushmen] don't talk about these things ... they keep quiet and keep it in their hearts.'

I cannot claim to have fully corroborated Dawid's take on what happened to his grandfather. Many inconsistencies in his testimony, and in my other interviewees' recollections, remain, the chronology of events is not clear and neither are their locations. I find it interesting that the oral tradition largely maintains that Polentswa was the site of the final battle of the war, and not Seatsub, which the written archives assert. Perhaps we will never find the truth. My instincts at the time of our trip led me to record in my audio diary that 'something went on that they don't want to tell us' and I still believe so. As I know all too well, one of the Kruipers' defence mechanisms against nosey outsiders is to fob them off with fabricated or embellished stories. And that is exactly as it should be. The core purpose of our trip was to assist Dawid and Buks in handing on the family's history to their children and grandchildren – not to the outside world, although we, too, have been graced by being let into at least some of it. As Grossie wrote to me after reading a draft of this book: 'There are many guesses that will remain just that for now, so speculation is pretty useless ...

With most of the elders gone, I just hope that Dawid's message to his sons and to Willem was clear to them because I think that that was the purpose of his trip. It is their truths, past and present, that were important to him.'

CHAPTER 15

Lion of the Kalahari

During the year following the expedition, Nan Flemming and I translated and transcribed the interviews we had done on the trip and I went to see Oupa several times to check things that needed further explanation and to clarify statements that were contradictory. He looked happy and he had grown the little 'boobies' he always had when he was flourishing.

'How is my book coming on?' he would ask me. 'It's going to be a thick book, isn't it? Thick. And the truth, only the truth must be in it.'

I teased him about how many new grey hairs his book had given me and how clever he was to be sitting on a sand dune, smoking dope, while I worked so hard on his project.

'When you do important things, only then are you grown up,' he replied. 'Your grey hair shows that you are doing an important thing.'

I asked the Kruipers how they would feel if I wrote about the problems we had had on the trip. 'I think what a person did is what a person did, so I don't think you should cut things out about how it was,' John said emphatically. I was amazed by his honesty and courage.

'And am I right that you were deliberately testing me? On the journey I often felt as if you were seeing how far you could push me and whether I would desert the project.'

215

Again, their reply was frank. 'You see, Mama,' said Buks, 'some-one comes here, puts a string in our noses and says, "Come with me." You know we Bushmen can be a bit false, you need to *klap* [hit] us around the head sometimes. We understand now where you are coming from and we are very glad you are here today and you will light the path for us from now on.'

I overheard Oupa telling someone that while I sometimes looked hard I had a soft heart. And Sue had been labelled 'the little angry one'. Clearly they were not used to the kind of strong and straight talk that both of us are capable of, and it had taken time for them to get the measure of us. In fact, they confessed that for the first week of the trip they did not know who was boss – Sue or me!

During those follow-up visits my relationship with the Kruipers deepened and I came to understand why Phillipa and Grossie are so committed to them. Gaining their trust is like being graced by a simple, pure acceptance of who you are and what you bring. There need be no purpose for your visit or direction to your conversa-tion. There is no awkwardness when you sit in silence and no ur-gency when you tell your tales. The unwritten contract is: 'We will love you despite yourself – and you will do likewise. That is all.'

When the time came for me to return to Johannesburg I always left Dawid with the same line: 'Don't you dare die on me, you hear? You've got to come to the launch party for your book in Johan-nesburg!'

It was Nan who later remembered that the last time we parted Dawid said to me: 'Don't take too long now because I'm going to die.' And I learned later that he had often told Grossie during that year that he felt *doodproef* (death proof), that he was sick of all the politicking, was ready to go but was worried about his children's future.

A text message came through the FOKS network to say that Dawid was injured. There had been a fight and a drunk woman had hit him with a rake. Now his neck was so swollen that he could not swallow food or water and was so weak that he could not walk. A torrent of SMSes, emails and calls ensued between Phillipa,

Grossie and myself. I organised for Dawid to be rushed to a private doctor in Upington, who did not seem to be alarmed by his condition. A few anti-inflammatories and he would be fine, the doctor said. On the way back to Andriesvale, Dawid wolfed down a burger and chips and walked with ease from the car to his hut. What's the issue here? I wondered. Have they not been feeding him properly or what?

Two weeks passed and Dawid seemed to be recovering. Then I got a panicked call from the community's office to say that he was 'talking rubbish' and was slipping in and out of consciousness. Phillipa and I organised for him to be rushed to Upington's government hospital where he was scanned, X-rayed, tested and examined. For three days I phoned and phoned for their report but was told by the rude and indifferent doctors that I was not a member of his family and they would not discuss his condition with me. Finally someone broke ranks and told me the worst: everything in his old, injured body was finally giving up. They would keep him comfortable but did not think there was more they could do for him. Oh, and he had not been given the anti-inflammatories for his neck, did I know that?

I felt a cold anger seep into my heart. Why had he not had his pills? Later that day I learned that there was a constant stream of visitors to Oupa's bed, despite my request for a private ward and a guard at the door to keep everyone but the immediate family out. 'Get him to the private hospital and I'll drive down tomorrow,' I instructed them.

Phillipa caught a lift with me early the next morning, our drive dominated by confused and concerned conversation about what was happening to Dawid. Five hours from Upington, Phillipa's phone beeped with the message we had both been dreading. Oupa was gone. Our friend and mentor, the man dubbed the 'Lion of the Kalahari' was dead. We stopped the car and walked in different directions to try to collect our emotions. Never before had I felt a death so befitting of that over-used description 'the end of an era', and I felt desperate that I had not listened closely enough to his warning that he would go soon. Could we have saved him? The doctors said no. But I was wracked with guilt for not getting this book out quicker and for not giving him at least one more night of peace in the private hospital so as to prepare for whatever lay ahead of him. Maybe he had achieved that anyway because when we got to his bed Phillipa thought he looked as if he was deep in thought. To me he was serene, and in death he was the image of Makai.

I touched his warm, wrinkled neck, and sobbed as I have not done in decades. And as I looked at his face for the last time I renewed my commitment to try to help the FOKS see justice brought to his family and community.

Two weeks later I was back in the Kalahari for Dawid's funeral. A cement cross lay on a mound of sand next to his grave. The crucifix was bright purple and matched the carpet placed around a deep hole in Witdraai's valley. It was lined with brick and cement and looked imposing next to the small burial mounds on either side of it. Brass vases filled with pink plastic lilies were placed at intervals along the edge of the carpet. I stood in mute disbelief at the incongruousness of the scene.

The South African government had undertaken to give Dawid a state funeral and to bear the costs of it. They moved their graders onto Witdraai and carved roads through it for the dignitaries' cars, utterly destroying its delicate ecology in the process. Thousands of bottles of water were imported for the mourners. Clearly the national and local government heavies were not going to drink the water they had always deemed fit for the Khomani. For the first time the farm had toilets, albeit for just a day.

Large white marquees were erected in between the Kruipers' shacks and the chairs inside them were draped with black covers and bright yellow bows. The Bushman womenfolk were busy cooking meat in huge black pots. It was more food than they had seen in a long, long time. When I summoned the courage to go to Dawid's little hut, it was not there – he had decided to move to a place halfway up the dune only days before he died, I was told.

I remembered him saying that the Bushmen are like weavers – they build a nest here, get sick of it and build another one there. Oupa's dog was lying in the shade of a nearby truck. None of his relatives could remember her name and none knew who would look after her now.

I do not doubt that the organisers of the funeral thought they were giving Dawid a send-off befitting his stature, but it was a travesty of all that is Bushman. Although the Kruipers were consulted about arrangements, they were unaware of the details and gawked at the proceedings from the sidelines, their expressions a mixture of horror and hilarity.

How Dawid would have regarded the shindig is hard to tell. I feel sure he would have chortled heartily at the fact that his instruction 'Bury me quietly, I'm a child of the dunes' was so wholeheartedly ignored. But he would have felt validated by all the fuss, and flattered that some 2 000 people pitched up for his send-off. He would definitely have been amused by the attendance of various political groupings that had sought his endorsement over the years in order to lend credibility to their claims and movements. And he would undoubtedly have gasped at the cheek of the parliament of thieves who gave the eulogies.

The event was typical of many in South Africa that are attended by brazen political opportunists who seem unperturbed to face the very people they have robbed, wronged or neglected. The province's Member of the Executive Council for Economic Development, John Block – at the time facing charges of corruption – was there, surrounded by a dozen obsequious minions. So was Petrus Vaalbooi, who had been on the Community Property Association's Management Committee when hundreds of thousands of rand were allegedly stolen from the community. He wept into the microphone and clutched his chest like a Hollywood pro, calling his old adversary 'my brother, my father, my leader'.

The Khoisan groups renamed Cape Town //Hui !Gaeb (Where Clouds Gather) in Dawid's honour and their leaders arrived from the Cape, clothed in buckskins that strained across their enormous naked stomachs and headdresses that looked like lampshades. Some wore cotton shirts featuring the animals they hunted long ago. One had been made with the material upside down, and the antelope tumbled towards its wearer's ample bottom. The police who had harassed Oupa for his use of dagga right to the last days of his life provided a guard of honour, and preachers from various denominations screamed, Baptist-style, into the microphone, exhorting the government to fulfil its promises to the Khomani. Even Willem strutted his stuff, warning pretenders to Dawid's throne, of which there are already several: 'We walked barefoot and now we want a leader who walks barefoot. We don't want people who wear shoes.'

Phillipa could not face being inside the tent and wandered around outside it, watching the crowds and their reaction to the unfolding events. Richard and Karl jostled with other cameramen while I sat in the ninth row with Sue and some SANParks staff. I dictated my impressions of the jamboree into my recorder while people 'praised the Lord' all around me. 'This is just amazing! Every agency that ever failed him is being invoked here: God, the government, the community and the modernists.'

After several hours the event moved to the gravesite where the flag of the nation that had so disappointed Dawid was presented to his weeping sister. 'The Last Post' was played as his shiny coffin was lowered into the pit, then pushed into a side chamber before being barricaded by a piece of corrugated iron. Because he had left several different instructions on where he wanted to be buried, Oupa's children had decided that lying next to his wife for eternity was the best choice.

Did you want it like this, Oupa? I thought while people jostled around me. To be buried with a whole lot of tacky European fanfare? And trapped in a crypt so that the Kalahari sand can never take you back? And what about being buried in the Park? You told us that was what you wanted. You even joked about wanting to be stuffed and put in a glass case at Twee Rivieren so that the tourists could stare at you. And when the Nossob next came down in flood it would float you down to Upington! Ah well, at least you will be close to your Gaisie, Dawid dear, I said to myself, and she can keep you in check for eternity!

Teenagers started playing loud Christian rock under a nearby tree and the mourners started to boogie. After throwing a handful of sand onto the coffin I turned and walked away, dry-eyed and dumbstruck with grief and rage.

Our Place and Purpose

I dreaded my next visit to Witdraai, knowing that Dawid would not be there. But when I pulled up at the Bushmen's shacks, I was the only one weeping. The Kruipers were composed and resolute.

'I'm heart-sore, but I'm strong,' Toppie said.

'We must go on,' John added, 'and do the work he wanted us to do.'

The monstrous roads on Dawid's farm were still there, and the flowers on his grave were now dry and messy. But the hole in my heart was not echoed in the land that he had fought so hard for. It seemed indifferent to the grief of those who had loved Oupa, and to our anxiousness about life without him.

I sat alone at his grave with my electronic therapist and tried to calm my mind: 'This place, the Kalahari, doesn't know that we even exist; it doesn't care about our passage through its dunes or our responses to its beauty. It merely is. And maybe that's why the Bushmen are so accepting of their loss. These trees and grasses have taught them that life doesn't stop for any of us. Or perhaps the Bushmen are so "together" because they've become used to death and loss? Maybe it's because of their belief that Dawid is not far away, he's just behind a thin veil?'

The community is vulnerable after Dawid's death, but unified in their belief that now is the time to put their divisions behind them and work towards healing. It may be that Oupa's passing brings some long-overdue attention to the plight of the Khomani, and, even if our government does not deliver what it promised at his funeral, we FOKS will continue to work for the restoration of the Bushmen's pride and dignity. And the fact that Dawid did not live to see his community fully restored to health and prosperity is motivation enough for us to make sure that he did not live and suffer in vain.

The Bushmen continue to teach me through their gentle, wise ways and their astounding capacity for forgiveness. I am inspired by the FOKS' ability to give without expecting anything in return, by their selflessness, their loyalty and their dogged pursuit of justice for this beleaguered group of people. It is work that brings great rewards, of course, because, as Gandhi once said: 'The best way to find yourself is to lose yourself in the service of others.'

With what little funding Phillipa and Grossie have managed to raise, they have set up a community office, training programmes, conservation projects and tourism enterprises. Erin has been re-stocked with game donated by Tswalu Kalahari Game Reserve and SANParks, and has hosted its first commercial hunts using Bushman trackers and guides. The area has been listed as a tentative World Heritage Site and there are plans for a Khomani heritage museum at the Twee Rivieren gate into the Park. The community has its own fenced camp in the Contract Park, called Imbewu, which is used by those who enjoy spending time in the Park but want some protection against lions. Phillipa's and Grossie's long-term vision includes a wholly Khomani-owned and staffed community lodge in the !Ae!Hai Kalahari Heritage Park and for their land to be entirely managed by the Khomani.

It will be a while before the community is ready to do without technical assistance and support from the FOKS and there is much work still to be done. We hope that financial backing will come that can provide the Khomani with their own school and a curriculum that embraces Bushman culture and traditions. They are in dire need of housing, basic facilities and social interventions to address the community's poor self-image, alcohol and drug abuse and domestic violence. The modernists' farms have been overstocked and overgrazed, so policies and procedures need to be put in place and enforced to correct this, and avoid it in future.

Nonetheless, fourteen years after the Land Claim, the atmosphere in Andriesvale is beginning to resemble the hope-filled time immediately after the handover. As Dawid used to say: '*Ons is nie meer op die pad die, ons is daar!*' (We are no longer on the path, we are there!) All of our dreams and projects are outlined on the website: www.khomanisan.com.

Toppie has taken over his father's veld school because he is such a gifted and enthusiastic teacher. John is tipped to be the Khomani's next traditional leader, although the community has yet to vote on this position.

My work with the community concentrates on heritage preservation. A major portion of the profits from this book will go into a trust to finance trips into the Kalahari, and enable the few elders left in the community to teach the youngsters who are interested in their culture. Our work is urgent because the thread joining the old ways with the new is increasingly fragile.

Vetpiet was killed with eight others in another of the Khomani's tragic car accidents. The last person to see him alive was his old friend, Anne Rase, who witnessed him, most uncharacteristically, come close to stepping on a Cape cobra next to the car.

'I think it was a harbinger of his death,' she told me.

Jakob Malgas died of pneumonia, and, in the year of Oupa's death, the Khomani lost three other elders who still had veld and cultural knowledge: |Una Rooi, Abraham Malgas and Buks' wife, !Nat.

And we came close to losing Buks, too. A few months before the publication of this book, he and I were in a supermarket in Upington with Nan's partner, Lize van As. I bought each of us a packet of crisps and walked to the exit, turned around but Buks had seemingly vanished into thin air. After a three-quarter-of-an-hour search I discovered that he had been 'arrested for shoplifting a packet of crisps'. And when Buks was finally brought to me he was in a very bad way indeed. As he later related, a security guard had taken him to the back of the shop, handcuffed his hands behind his back, threaded some rope through the handcuffs, hoisted Buks up and hung him from some railings. The guard then beat and kicked Buks savagely and when he came out to me he had blood on his shirt, deep wheals in his wrists and a cut over one eye. A couple of days later Buks laid an assault charge and I sat with him while he stuttered through the whole, horrifying incident. But his statement did not express the pain and terror he endured, and how the incident mimics what his ancestors and contemporaries have put up with in the 'Wild West' for centuries.

In order to reconnect the Khomani with critical aspects of their culture that were lost during the post-eviction decades – such as the hunting of big game, trance dancing and healing – we will need to take them to communities in Botswana and Namibia who still practise these ancient arts.

People in my audiences sometimes ask whether it is not futile to try to resuscitate traditions that have outgrown their usefulness. Am I not trying to take them backwards to a Utopia that is merely a memory?

Certainly I think we must accept that it is not feasible to revive the N|uu language, despite its symbolic importance. And I am not naive enough to believe that living entirely off the desert is either viable or enjoyable. One of the things I learned on our trip is that the old way of life was extremely hard for the Bushmen. But there are plants and animals in the Kalahari that will always be physically and spiritually nourishing for them, and knowing their veld craft is of economic value to the community's youngsters because they can be employed as guides and trackers, and set up their own businesses, in an area with very few economic prospects.

Above all, I believe that there are attitudes towards wilderness – and wildness – that the Bushmen once had from which we can all benefit. Indeed, they are the attitudes that we city dwellers are trying so desperately to re-learn in order to save ourselves – attitudes like non-materialism, respect and gratitude for what the earth provides, conserving our resources, taking what we need, not what we want.

Ultimately, my heritage work with the Khomani is an effort to give them that most basic of human rights: choice. The right to know where they came from, what is of use from the old ways and what has relevance to their lives today, the choice to live in a more traditional way, to embrace modern culture, or perhaps a bit of both. As Phillipa puts it, it is about facilitating an intelligent and sensitive cultural transition. We owe it to them to assist them in achieving this, given our universal culpability in their demise.

Rupert Isaacson, a writer who journeyed with Dawid about fifteen years ago, maintains that people go to the Kalahari to heal. Looking back, I understand now that some deep imperative had led me there to learn about my aboriginal psyche. Our time in the KTP had called out parts of me that had been neglected on my other odysseys. Those adventures had been physically and mentally exhausting. They had been characterised by passage *through* a landscape rather than a sinking into it, by distances and destinations rather than stillness and observation. This time my pace had been set by an old, wise man who taught me not to confront my life but to explore it, slowly and gently. I had let the wilderness, my wildness, find me, rather than chasing after it with urgent breaths and aching legs. And I had experienced the profound calm that comes from being with people for whom speed and ambition are anathema.

After we had finished Dawid's trip I returned to the Upington kennels where Blits was recouperating. On the way there Sue and I took a bet on whether he would remember me.

'It's been nearly six weeks,' I said to her. 'There's no way he will.'

'We'll see,' she replied. 'I'll put 10 rand on it.'

I looked over the wall to where he was caged and saw a dog I hardly recognised, except for his dancing eyebrows and flicking white-tipped tail.

'Blits!' I called. And he went berserk, running the short length of his pen and dancing on his back legs like a Lipizzaner.

'I think you owe me,' Sue laughed.

Since then, Blits has fully lived up to his name. Not only is he fast but extremely bright, enthusiastic and affectionate. But Johannesburg's parks are too small and too green for my Bushman Boy and sometimes I fancy I can see a yearning in his bright eyes for the hares he once hunted in the soft sand of his native land. When I go back to the Kalahari with him he starts whimpering as soon as we turn onto Witdraai. He and his brother greet each other with bridled indignation for a few minutes before seeming to remember the days when they suckled at the same teats. Then they catapult and tumble over the dunes where my old friend used to walk.

Makai !Gam!Gaub Kruiper, beloved grandfather, veld master and community hero was killed by, of all things, a candle-pod acacia. The year was 1966 and he was well over 100 years old. Makai was out collecting firewood near the Bushman settlement at Twee Rivieren when a stick flipped up and gouged his leg. The wound went septic and within a week the old man was dying. Dawid rushed to see him after his day's work was finished and found Makai naked on the sand. 'Those little red ants had already started eating him,' Dawid remembered. But Makai sat up and spoke to his grandson at length about the duties ahead of him as a future leader of the Kruiper family. Dawid was not there when Makai died, he was away trying to fulfil his grandfather's last wish – to have a cup of cocoa. On his deathbed, Makai is reported to have told his family that the old Bushman lifestyle had finally been taken from him and that he had no more will to live. Perhaps it was just as well that he was not alive for the Khomani's final eviction from the Park less than a decade later.

Makai's funeral was well attended but humble. 'In those days, people didn't waste like they do now,' Buks told us. 'Today, when you're buried they slaughter so many animals and people come just to eat and drink. That's why when I'm dying I want to be left in the veld to be taken by the hyenas.'

Makai was wrapped in skins, like his forefathers, and laid to rest at a spot that Park management had designated as the Bushmen's graveyard. It was the last place we visited on our expedition so that the youngsters could see – and GPS – where their famous ancestor lay. But the only grave we could identify was Vetpiet's because it was encircled by a decorative metal cage. There was nothing to indicate where Makai was buried, or any of the other Kruiper elders around him.

How befitting a man who walked so lightly on the earth, I thought as we stood there. No marble tombstone and no epitaph. His monument lies in the memories of his grandchildren, and its inscription is the ancient knowledge that we are trying so hard to preserve.

I looked around the site for a stone to take away with me – something I do at the end of all my journeys so as to have a memento of their great joys and teachings. There was only one in the entire area and the minute I picked it up I knew that it had known many human hands before mine. The stone was egg-shaped and smooth and it fitted perfectly into the palm of my right hand. On one side of it were four shallow grooves that cupped my fingers so comfortably that they felt custom-made.

'Look, Oupa,' I turned to my old friend, 'I think this was used for something, don't you?'

'Oooo,' he pursed his lips in his customary fashion, 'now that is from my grandmother's time. The women used those stones to grind the *tsamma* melon pips for our porridge. See how much it's been used.'

I asked him if I could take it home with me.

'Of course you can,' he replied. 'You are the right person to have it, after all you have done for us.'

The stone is beside me as I write, it sits next to Priscilla's gearstick when we are on the road and in my laptop bag when I give talks about my journey with the Kruipers. It feels to me as though the stone has absorbed all the ritual, knowledge and camaraderie of the women who used it. And it reminds me of a time when we were all Bushmen and understood our place and purpose on this fragile planet.

Select Bibliography

Adhikari, Mohamed. 2010. *The Anatomy of a South African Genocide.* Cape Town: UCT Press.

Bain, Donald. Private collection of papers in the possession of his granddaughter, Judy Orpen.

Balsan, François. 1954. *Capricorn Road.* London: Arco Publications Limited.

Bank, Andrew. 2006. *Bushmen in a Victorian World: The Remarkable Story of the Bleek-Lloyd Collection of Bushman Folklore.* Cape Town: Double Storey Books.

Bantu Studies: A Journal Devoted to the Scientific Study of Bantu, Hottentot and Bushmen. September 1937. Vol. XI, No. 3.

Barnard, Alan. 1992. *Hunters and Herders of Southern Africa: A Comparative Ehnography of the Khoisan People.* Cambridge: Cambridge University Press.

Bennun, Neil. 2004. *The Broken String: The Last Words of an Extinct People.* London: Viking.

Bjerre, Jens. 1960. *Kalahari.* New York: Hill and Wang.

Bregin, Elana and Belinda Kruiper. 2004. *Kalahari RainSong.* Pietermaritzburg: University of KwaZulu-Natal Press.

Brody, Hugh. 2000. *The Other Side of Eden: Hunters, Farmers, and the Shaping of the World.* New York: North Point Press.

——. 2002. 'In Memory of Elsie Vaalbooi'. Open Democracy, www.opendemocracy.net.

——. 2003. 'The Bushmen/San: Real, Pure, or Just Themselves?' Open Democracy, www.opendemocracy.net.

Buntman, Barbara. 1996. 'Selling with the San: Representations of Bushman People and Artefacts in South African Print Advertisements'. *Visual Anthropology*, Vol. 8: pp. 33–54.

——. 2002. 'Travels to Otherness: Whose Identity Do We Want to See?' Special issue of *Senri-Ethnological Studies.* National Museum of Ethnology, Japan.

Crawhall, Nigel. 2002. 'Reclaiming Language and Identity'. www.culturalsurvival. org.

——. 2003. 'Recovering Land and Language in the Southern Kalahari'. In *Maintaining the Links: Language, Identity and the Land: Proceedings of the Seventh Conference Presented by the Foundation for Endangered Languages, Broome, Western Australia, 22–24 September 2003*, edited by J. Blythe, M. Brown and R. Bath. UK: Foundation for Endangered Languages.

——. 2004. '!Ui-Taa Language Shift in Gordonia and Postmas Districts, South Africa'. PhD thesis, University of Cape Town.

——. 2009. *Written in the Sand: Auditing and Managing Cultural Resources with Displaced Indigenous Peoples.* Cape Town: UNESCO/SASI.

Crawhall, Nigel, interviewed by Jill Kitson. Transcript of an interview on Australian Broadcasting Corporation (ABC), 20 November 2004.

Dart, Raymond A. 1936. 'What is a Real Bushman?' *The Star*, Johannesburg.

Deacon, Janette and Craig Foster. 2005. *My Heart Stands in the Hill.* Cape Town: Struik Publishers.

'Diary of Reconnaissance of Part of the Kalahari Desert Lying Between Oup and Nosop Rivers'. Enclosure in Despatch Secret of 15th July 1908, Cape of Good Hope.

Gall, Sandy. 2001. *The Bushmen of Southern Africa: Slaughter of the Innocent.* London: Pimlico.

Gordon, Rob. 2002. 'Review of *Regopstaan's Dream*'. H-SAfrica, H-Net Reviews, March.

Gordon, Robert J. 1992. *The Bushman Myth: The Making of a Namibian Underclass.* Boulder, San Francisco, Oxford: Westview Press.

——. 1999. '"Bain's Bushmen": Scenes at the Empire Exhibition, 1936'. *Africans On Stage: Studies in Ethnological Show Business*, edited by Bernth Lindfors. Bloomington, IN: Indiana University Press and Cape Town: David Philip Publishers.

——. 2002. '"Captured on Film": Bushmen and the Claptrap of Performative Primitives'. In *Images and Empires: Visuality in Colonial and Postcolonial Africa*, edited by Paul S. Landau and Deborah D. Kaspin. Berkeley, Los Angeles, London: University of California Press.

Green, Lawrence G. Private papers and letters in the possession of Joan Yates-Benyon.

——. 1981. *To The River's End.* Cape Town: Howard Timmins Publishers.

Guenther, Mathias. 1999. *Tricksters and Trancers: Bushman Religion and Society.* Bloomington, IN: Indiana University Press.

Haacke, Wulf D. 1992. 'The Kalahari Expedition March 1908: The Forgotten Story of the Final Battle of the Nama War'. *Botswana Notes and Records*, Vol. 24.

Inquiry against Simon Kooper, Gochas, June 1908, by Imperial German
    Concillor of Martial Law Jorns as Authorised Judge in Native Matters in
    the District of Gibeon.

Isaacson, Rupert. 2001. *The Healing Land: A Kalahari Journey.* London: Fourth
    Estate.

James, Alan (compiler and commentator). 2001. *The First Bushman's Path: Stories,*
    Songs and Testimonies of the /Xam of the Northern Cape. Pietermaritzburg:
    University of Natal Press.

Johnson, Peter, Anthony Bannister and Alf Wannenburgh. 1979. *The Bushman.*
    Cape Town: C. Struik Publishers (Pty) Ltd.

Kloppers, Hannes. 2010. *Gee My 'n Man! Die Beginjare van die Kalahari*
    Gemsbokpark. Pretoria: Protea Boekhuis.

Konrad, Robert. 2008. '"Lions and Jackals": Peace Parks in Southern Africa
    and their Effects on the Local Population'. Master's thesis, University of
    Vienna.

Legassick, Martin and Ciraj Rassool. 2000. *Skeletons in the Cupboard: South African*
    Museums and the Trade in Human Remains, 1907–1917. Cape Town: South
    African Museum.

Lewis-Williams, David and David Pearce. 2004. *San Spirituality: Roots, Expressions*
    and Social Consequences. Cape Town: Double Storey Books.

Lewis-Williams, J.D. 2000. *Stories that Float from Afar: Ancestral Folklore of the San of*
    Southern Africa. Cape Town: David Philip Publishers.

Liebenberg, Louis. 1990. *The Art of Tracking: The Original Science.* Cape Town:
    David Philip Publishers.

Luard, Nicholas. 1981. *The Last Wilderness: A Unique Journey across the Kalahari*
    Desert. Middlesex, UK: Hamlyn Paperbacks.

Maclennan, Ben. 2003. *The Wind Makes Dust: Four Centuries of Travel in Southern*
    Africa. Cape Town: Tafelberg.

Main, Michael. 1987. *Kalahari: Life's Variety in Dune and Delta.* Johannesburg:
    Southern Book Publishers.

McGregor, Gordon. 2007. *German Medals, British Soldiers and the Kalahari Desert:*
    The South West Africa Commemorative Medal with the 'Kalahari' Bars Awarded to
    Imperial British Forces. Windhoek: Namibia Scientific Society.

Moffett, Helen (compiler). 2006. *Lovely Beyond Any Singing: Landscapes in*
    Southern African Writing. Cape Town: Double Storey Books.

Olusoga, David (producer and director). 2005. *Namibia: Genocide and the Second*
    Reich. BBC documentary.

Olusoga, David and Casper W. Erichsen. 2010. *The Kaiser's Holocaust: Germany's*
    Forgotten Genocide and the Colonial Roots of Nazism. London: Faber and Faber.

Perkins, Carol Morse and Marlin Perkins. 1971. *I Saw You From Afar: A Visit to the*

Bushmen of the Kalahari Desert. New York: Atheneum.

Private correspondence between Donald Bain and Professor Raymond Dart, 1937.

Rassool, Ciraj and Patricia Hayes. 2002. 'Science and the Spectacle: |Khanako's South Africa, 1936–1937'. *Deep hiStories: Gender and Colonialism in Southern Africa,* edited by Wendy Woodward, Patricia Hays and Gary Minkley. Amsterdam and New York: Rodopi.

Report on the Inquiry into Human Rights Violations in the Khomani San Community by the South African Human Rights Commission, November 2004.

Schapera, I. 1930. *The Khoisan Peoples of South Africa.* London: Routledge and Kegan Paul.

Schenck, Marcia C. 2008. 'Land, Water, Truth, and Love: Visions of Identity and Land Access: From Bain's Bushmen to Khomani San'. Undergraduate thesis, Mount Holyoke College, Massachusetts.

Silvester, Jeremy and Jan-Bart Gewald. 2003. *Words Cannot Be Found: German Colonial Rule in Namibia: An Annotated Reprint of the 1918 Blue Book.* Leiden and Boston: Brill.

Skotnes, Pippa (ed.). 1996. *Miscast: Negotiating the Presence of the Bushmen.* Cape Town: UCT Press.

——. 2007. *Claim to the Country: The Archive of Wilhelm Bleek and Lucy Lloyd.* Johannesburg and Cape Town: Jacana and Athens, OH: Ohio University Press.

Smith, Andy, Candy Malherbe, Mat Guenther and Penny Berens. 2000. *The Bushmen of Southern Africa: A Foraging Society in Transition.* Cape Town: David Philip Publishers and Athens, OH: Ohio University Press.

South African San Institute (SASI). 2002. *The Khomani-San, from Footnotes to Footprints: The Story of the Land Claim of the Khomani-San.* Upington: SASI.

Spitz, Andy. 2002. Video recordings of interviews with the Khomani.

Steyn, H.P. 1984. 'Southern Kalahari San Subsistence Ecology: A Reconstruction'. *South African Archeological Bulletin,* Vol. 39: pp. 117–24.

——. 1995. 'Report on the KaggaKamma/Southern Kalahari Bushmen'.

——. 1999. 'Southern Kalahari San Land Rights and Land Claim'. Report prepared for the Department of Land Affairs (Restitution Section).

Tomaselli, Keyan G. 2003. 'Stories to Tell, Stories to Sell: Resisting Textualization'. *Cultural Studies,* Vol. 17, No. 6: pp. 856–75.

Traill, A. 1974. *A Complete Guide to the Koon: A Research Report on Linguistic Fieldwork Undertaken in Botswana and South West Africa.* Johannesburg: African Studies Institute, University of the Witwatersrand.

Van der Post, Laurens. 1958. *The Lost World of the Kalahari.* London: Hogarth Press.

Van der Walt, Pieter and Elias le Riche. 1999. *The Kalahari and its Plants.* Self-published.

Van Rooyen, Noel, in collaboration with Hugo Bezuidenhout and Emmerentia de Kock. 2001. *Flowering Plants of the Kalahari Dunes.* Pretoria: Ekotrust.

Weinberg, Paul. 1990. *Shaken Roots.* Johannesburg: EDA Publications.

——. 1997. *In Search of the San.* Johannesburg: Porcupine Press.

Weintroub, Jill. 2011. *By Small Wagon With Full Tent: Dorothea Bleek's Journey to Kakia, June to August 1913.* Cape Town: Lucy Lloyd Archive, Resource and Exhibition Centre, University of Cape Town.

Wessels, Michael. 2010. *Bushman Letters: Interpreting |Xam Narrative.* Johannesburg: Wits University Press.

White, Hylton. 1995. *In the Tradition of the Forefathers: Bushman Traditionality at Kagga Kamma.* Cape Town: UCT Press.

Workman, James G. 2009. *Heart of Dryness: How the Last Bushmen Can Help Us Endure the Coming Age of Permanent Drought.* New York: Walker Publishing Company, Inc.

Apart from those conducted on the expedition, recorded conversations with the following people: Karel Barkaath, Claire Barry, Memory Biwa, Roger Chennells, Nigel Crawhall, Nanette Flemming, Craig Foster, Richard Gordon, David Grossman, Phillipa Holden, Jacob Khabee, Isak Klaasen, Charles Kooper, Daniel Kooper, Hendrik Kooper, Magdalena Kooper, Mary Kooper, Rebecca Kooper, Buks Kruiper, Dawid Kruiper, John Kruiper, Toppie Kruiper, Elias le Riche, Abraham Malgas, Lena Malgas, Gus Mills, Tokolos Org, Anne Rase, Phillip Tobias, Jan van der Westhuizen and Dee Worman.

Acknowledgements

I am deeply indebted to the following people for their help in making our expedition – and this account of it – possible. If I have omitted to mention anyone, I apologise unreservedly.

Mike Aldous, Gavin Anderson, Wendy Anneke, John Bain, Kevin Balkwill, Rodney Ballenden, Karel Barkaath, Claire Barry, Craig Beech, Johannes Beukes, Brendon Billings, Memory Biwa, Brenda Bladbeen, Valter Blasevic, Geoffrey Blundell, Albert Bojane, Johnny Bok, the staff at Brenthurst Library, Kathy Brooks, Barbara Buntman, Anena Burger, Tom Cartwright, Roger Chennells, Linda Chernis, Isak Coetzee, Thinus and Landa Conradie, Sue Corbett, the staff at Corporate Communications Consultants, Nigel Crawhall, Graham Crocker, Azizo da Fonseca, Michael Diaber, Lee Dormer, Christine du Plessis, Graeme Ellis, Dries Engelbrecht, Peter Faugust, Henriette Ferreira, Micho Ferreira, Nanette Flemming, Adam Ford, Colin Fortune, Craig Foster, Dick Foxton, Alan Garlick, Francis Gerard, Shirley Glyn, Magriet Goliath, Richard Gordon, Barry Gray, Sue Gregorowski, Liz Greyling, David Grossman, Louise Gubb, Wulf Haacke, Laura Hammond, Lesley Hart, Robert Hart, Moray Hathorne, Patricia Hayes, Werner Hillebrecht, Sally Hines, Lailah Hisham, Phillipa Holden, John and Barbara Hone, Grace Humphries, Piet Jaars, Rose and Michael Jordaan, Taku Kaskela, Trish Keegan, William Kemp, Jacob Khabee, Isak Klaasen, Gerald Klinghardt, Charles Kooper, Christina Kooper, Daniel Kooper, Hendrik Kooper, Jan Kooper, Lena Kooper, Maria Kooper, Mary Kooper, Piet Kooper, Rebecca Kooper, Am Am Kruiper, Buks Kruiper, Dawid Kruiper, Galai Kruiper, Isak Kruiper, Jeffrey Kruiper, John Kruiper, Kabe Kruiper, Klein Dawid Kruiper, Makai Kruiper, Mefi Kruiper, Toppie

Kruiper, Mary Lange, Roger Layton, Elias le Riche, Derek Lotter, Michael Main, Abraham Malgas, Lena Malgas, Stafford Masie, Gus Mills, Balisani Morotsi, Terry Morris, Andrea Nattrass, Ellah Ndlovu, Norman Ndlovu, William Ndlovu, Sydney Netshakuma, Peter Novellie, Isaac Nsizwane, Freddy Ogterob, Sue Olswang, Glynn O'Leary, Tokolos Org, Judy Orpen, David O'Sullivan, the staff of Outward Bound, Sven Ouzman, Sue Oxborrow, the staff at Pan Macmillan, John Parkington, Paul Perreira, Dirk Pienaar, Rita Potenza, Barbara Raats, Anthee Ramlucken, Anne Rase, Ciraj Rassool, Rosemary Renton, Ione Rudner, Ivor and Heather Sander, the Staff at SASI in Upington, Patrick Seager, Pippa Skotnes, Meryl-Joy Skuippers, Karin Slater, Himla Soodyall, Ben Smith, Andy Spitz, Luce Steenkamp, Betta Steyn, Hennie Steyn, Tina Swartz, Willem Swartz, Alexis Symonds, Karl Symons, Tina Terblanche, Jill Thomas, Phillip Tobias, Lize van As, Nico van der Walt, Jan van der Westhuizen, Vinkie van der Westhuizen, Lance van Rensburg, Ben Eric van Wyk, Mark Verseput, Diana Wall, Georg Wandrag, Ann Wanless, Roger Webster, Paul Weinberg, Jill Weintroub, Richard Wicksteed, Pam Wills, Brent Wittington, Dee Worman, Joan Yates-Benyon, the staff of Zeerust Toyota.

Abbreviations

CPA	Community Property Association
FOKS	Friends of Khomani San
GSWA	German South-West Africa
KGNP	Kalahari Gemsbok National Park
KTP	Kgalagadi Transfrontier Park
MC	Management Committee
SANParks	South African National Parks

Copyright in the photographs rests with the following photographers,
abbreviated as follows:

AP	Art Publishers
BF	Bain Family
BJ	'BB' Jay
CB	Claire Barry
KS	Karl Symons
MA	Museum Africa
NF	Nat Farbman, Gallo Images
PG	Patricia Glyn
PH	Phillipa Holden
RG	Richard Gordon
SAN	State Archives, Namibia
SO	Sue Oxborrow
WCA	Western Cape Archives